30 Great North Carolina Science Adventures

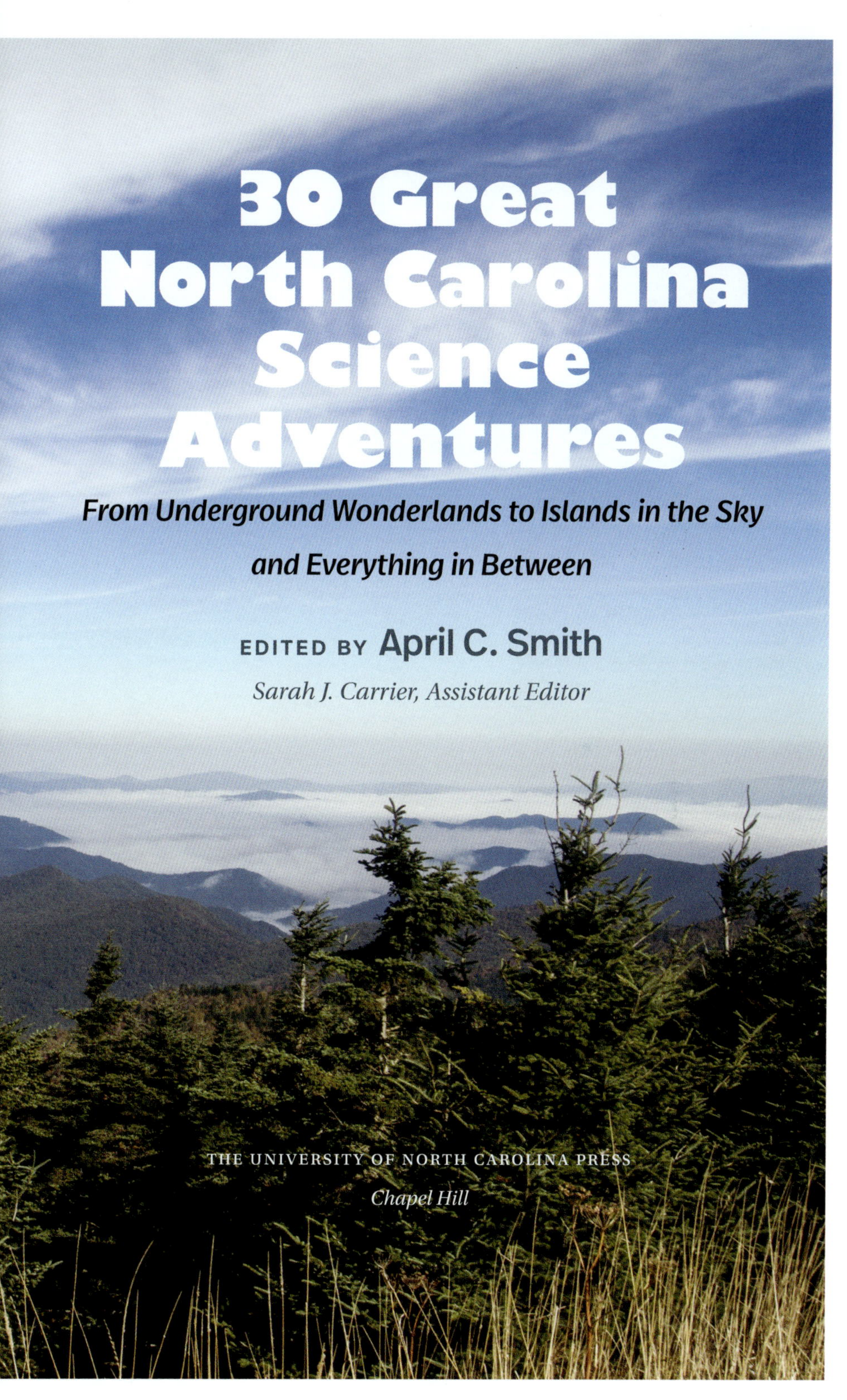

30 Great North Carolina Science Adventures

From Underground Wonderlands to Islands in the Sky and Everything in Between

EDITED BY April C. Smith

Sarah J. Carrier, Assistant Editor

THE UNIVERSITY OF NORTH CAROLINA PRESS

Chapel Hill

This book was published with the assistance of the Blythe Family Fund of the University of North Carolina Press.

Designed by Kim Bryant and set in Utopia and Real Head Pro by Rebecca Evans
Manufactured in the United States of America
The University of North Carolina Press has been a member of the Green Press Initiative since 2003.

Cover photo credits: top: Annie P. Howell; middle: Stephen B. Smith; bottom, left to right: Jesse Pope, April C. Smith, Mike Dunn

Library of Congress Cataloging-in-Publication Data
Names: Smith, April C., editor.
Title: Thirty great North Carolina science adventures : from underground wonderlands to islands in the sky and everything in between / edited by April C. Smith ; Sarah J. Carrier, assistant editor.
Other titles: Southern gateways guide.
Description: Chapel Hill : The University of North Carolina Press, [2020] | Series: Southern gateways guides | Includes index.
Identifiers: LCCN 2019041167 | ISBN 9781469658766 (cloth) | ISBN 9781469654959 (paperback ; alk. paper) | ISBN 9781469654966 (ebook)
Subjects: LCSH: Environmental sciences—North Carolina—Guidebooks. | North Carolina—Description and travel. | LCGFT: Guidebooks.
Classification: LCC F252.3 .T46 2020 | DDC 917.5604—dc23
LC record available at https://lccn.loc.gov/2019041167

This book is dedicated to every person who has stopped to observe one of North Carolina's natural wonders, from a giant mountain to a tiny ant, and said, "I wonder why . . . ." Keep exploring.

Contents

Part II Piedmont Region

Part III Coastal Plain Region

Preface

When I close my eyes, I can still smell the bite in the air rising intoxicatingly from the mixture of salt and sulfide in the marsh. I can still hear the crash of small waves and the low rumble of motors from the fishing boats leaving the inlet before dawn. And then, the first rays of golden, magical light splashed across the tall *Spartina* marsh grass on the other side of the inlet. I was six years old and it was pure love, and it was something I lived for every summer morning. I would wake to the crashing waves in sheer darkness and then quickly climb out of bed to put on my swimsuit—the only clothing needed for the entire day, or the entire summer for that matter. Quietly turning the cold silver lock on the back door, I would slip outside in the warm humid air and tiptoe down twelve dewy yellow steps. Despite the darkness, as soon as I reached the long wooden walkway, I would break into a full sprint to get settled into my spot at the end of the dock, second piling from the corner, and hang my feet over the edge. So peaceful.

After greeting the morning in my own special way, I would spend the entire day combing over oyster beds, mucking through marshy sediments, and floating quietly along with the incoming tide, up the salty, murky waters of Murrell's Inlet, South Carolina. Venturing out on my own, I could fill an entire bucket with treasures and curiosities to take back home and share. There's no doubt that I had the explorer bug early. My parents constantly encouraged me to be adventurous and try new things, but it was my grandmother who handed me my very first field guide—a field guide that I returned to repeatedly, and one that I still have on my bookshelf—and told me to identify my finds of the day. It was a winning combination: a thirst for knowledge meets a pathway to knowledge. And you know, in the very same location looking out over the inlet thirteen years later, I told my grandmother I would be pursuing a Ph.D. in marine science.

Memories of my scientific beginnings have led me to repeatedly ask the questions, "How do you inspire someone to follow their interests? How do you challenge them to take those interests a step further? What is the magic formula that creates a person who is curious about the world around them and determined to solve those mysteries?" I am now married with three children of my own, and they are my concern when I think of education on important matters, such as science. They are all wonderfully curious, creative explorers and outdoor enthusiasts. They play in the mud, they ride bikes in the rain, they climb trees, they collect insects to view under the microscope that we keep in our den, and no matter where we are in the world, they crave a good adventure. In my excitement, I'm afraid I've let the cat out of the bag early. . . . Adventure is the key. All of us need adventure to some extent, and when excitement and intrigue come together, we are engaged, and we learn, and most of the time we probably don't even know it.

Many of our favorite adventures have occurred on family vacations around North Carolina, and while I tend to focus my work these days mostly on the wee ones, this guide is for anyone who is curious about how North Carolina came to be the state we know today. It is full of trips to suit wild explorers and more cautious adventurers alike. So, jump in and enjoy the ride. You really don't have to go very far in this great state to come across an amazing adventure.

30 Great North Carolina Science Adventures

General Introduction

Thirty Great North Carolina Science Adventures: From Underground Wonderlands to Islands in the Sky and Everything in Between is a science book for the everyday explorer. If you are searching for great places to hike or canoe, seeking beautiful spots to picnic with your family, or just looking for environmental information on North Carolina that is easily understandable, this book was written for you. If you are a teen searching for your environmental passion or a mom, like me, who wants her kids to have a greater appreciation for the environment, you are in the right place. This book has been written so that the science presented is not only easily understandable and accessible but also interesting and alluring. It is our sincere hope that this book will fill many minds with wonder about the opportunities for science exploration in our state.

North Carolina has so many natural wonders, you could spend a lifetime exploring and surely never see them all. North Carolina has everything from strange plants to native creatures, from remnant volcanic island arcs to gold that washes up in streams. It is a movie-worthy place, yet so many people who live here or visit here miss the intense mysterious beauty that emanates from the hillsides and streams, and they never stop to ask why. "Why?" is an amazing question. Have you ever wondered why North Carolina is mountainous at one end and flat at the other? Why alligators don't live farther north, or why we have barrier islands off the coast? There are an infinite number of such wonderful questions—and the questions have even more wonderful answers! I want this book to help you satisfy your natural curiosity about your environment.

Sometimes science may seem difficult—but with this book in hand, whether you are out in the field or sitting in a chair, you'll have the science behind your questions answered in an easy and meaningful way. You'll come away with a compelling story and a good understanding, and you'll even be able to identify the fields of science that are most interesting to you.

In a nutshell, this is an *environmental science* book. Environmental science is a broad field. While *earth sciences* typically examine the physical aspects of the Earth, such as rocks, water, and air (geology, oceanography, and meteorology), environmental sciences include *many different fields working together* to evaluate the effects of natural processes, as well as the effects of human activity, on the rocks, water, air, plants, and animals—the entire environment that surrounds us.

Scientists use the terms "biotic" and "abiotic" to describe the different parts of an ecosystem. Biotic factors refer to the things that are living, or were once living, while abiotic factors are the nonliving parts of an ecosystem. The fields of ecology, biology, zoology, botany, forestry, chemistry, geology, and many others go into establishing the biotic and abiotic roles of an ecosystem. You will encounter all of these fields in the adventures in this book.

Living in North Carolina presents a myriad of opportunities for exploring, but if you're just visiting and looking for an adventure, we can help you too. This book has been designed to encourage and inspire explorers of all ages and abilities to get outside and learn about the world around them by presenting a scientific frame of reference. What does that mean? Well, it means that environmental science in North Carolina is exciting and we want to share that with you. Each chapter in this book has been written by a scientific researcher or a naturalist who wants to share their knowledge about North Carolina's treasures, providing the reader with a greater understanding of how this state developed the way it did, and why it is the way it is today.

Using This Guidebook

Reflecting the structure of the state of North Carolina, this book is organized into three geographical regions: Mountain, Piedmont, and Coastal Plain. Each region is then divided into chapters of adventures for you to embark upon with places to hike, rocks to find, and animals and plants to observe—explorations to get you out into nature to learn more about how North Carolina became the state it is today biologically, geologically, and ecologically. While the true purpose of these adventures is to get you out of that chair to experience some amazing things for yourself, you should have no fear; if it's an indoor day and you're just looking for a great story, you'll find that here too.

- You do not have to read the chapters in order! Skip around for places closest to you or to those that pique your interests the most. If you've found a subject that appeals to you, there are likely other chapters on your subject as well, so keep reading.
- Each chapter is written by an expert on that location.
- At the top of each chapter you will find a list of the scientific fields of study highlighted in the chapter. Perhaps there are some fields that you will find more enticing than others. The researchers, naturalists, and educators who have written these chapters know how important it is to share their passions. And while the information presented in each specific chapter highlights the importance of one or a few specific concerns, you should know it is not always possible to touch on every important factor in a scientific story. Sometimes it must be broken down into smaller pieces. With this in mind, you are again encouraged to further investigate subjects of interest.

- Words in **bold** that are found throughout the book are defined in the glossary at the back of the book so that you can reference them easily. Sometimes a word is repeated many times throughout a chapter, so only its first use in a chapter will be in bold.
- We want to spark your imagination and boost your interest in the scientific knowledge of our state, so by all means, if you are craving more information, use the references and resources provided at the end of each chapter to do research on your own. That's what they are there for.
- In many places, the scientific names of organisms are given, but for organisms that are merely listed in a chapter, "binomials," as the genus and species are called, are not provided. If you would like to find out more about a specific plant, animal, or fungus, the North Carolina State Parks Natural Inventory Database is a wonderful place to start. Try this url: https://auth1.dpr.ncparks.gov/nrid/public.php.
- Each chapter begins with a little history of the site, whether it's geologic/natural history or a more recent bit of cultural history. The middle section of each chapter is all about the scientific aspects of that location, giving you places to go, things to look for, and activities to perform, ultimately helping to provide information that completes a scientific story. The end of the chapter provides information to help you make your adventure successful.
- Some adventures provide easy opportunities for leisurely explorations or for including young explorers, such as walking along a well-defined nature path. Other adventures are more challenging, offering options for the more intrepid explorer, such as platform camping on the river, canoe/kayak trips, or longer intense hikes in the mountains. In general, these adventures can be tailored to your comfort level. Start with locations near your home. Choose a few locations to visit on your next family trip. Encourage a school or scouting group to try a new field trip or camping site.

One of North Carolina's most beloved environmental researchers, Dirk Frankenberg, wrote in his book *The Nature of North Carolina's Southern Coast*, "Nature is a movie with a plot that develops through time." This could not be truer, and it is clearly reflected in North Carolina's natural beauty and intriguing story. This book is full of exciting trips that will get you into that plot to learn directly about the science behind some of North Carolina's greatest spots. Use this book to put a little adventure and a little science in your life. You won't be disappointed.

Before You Go

Each chapter concludes with a section called "Before You Go" that provides information to help prepare you for your adventure. In some cases, you'll want to take notice of the amount of time you could or should plan to spend at a location. Many chapters make suggestions for where to drive, where to park, when to go, or other places to visit during your adventure. Paying attention to these suggestions may help to make your trip easier and more fun.

Citizen Science

Several of the chapters included in this book have associations with or make references to Citizen Science programs in which you can participate. Chapter 29, in particular, gives a detailed explanation of what Citizen Science is and how you can join in on a specific program. This is a great way to learn about various types of research and to be involved in making a difference in local scientific knowledge, and even management decisions for our state. Many of the Citizen Science programs are appropriate for kids as well (see Chapter 14, "Prairie Ridge Ecostation"), so don't hesitate to take your kids along to learn about the wonders of science and nature. Ask for information at park visitor centers or email the listed contacts for more information. Search online for other Citizen Science projects in North Carolina or nationwide: https://www.citizenscience.gov/#.

Safety and State Guidelines

Always follow basic safety guidelines for exploring natural areas, but also please remember to adhere to any state or national park regulations that are designed to protect our natural areas. Consider some of these tips when planning your trip:

1. Speak up: When I plan to explore, whether alone or in a group, I always let someone else know about my plans. Make sure you clearly communicate your intentions to a safety contact before you leave. Many of the locations in this book may not have perfect cell phone access if there is an emergency, so planning ahead for safety is crucial.
2. Have a plan: Creating a basic itinerary helps you plan your trip, and it can also help your safety contact find you in case of emergency.
3. Pack well: As a mother of three, I never leave home without wet wipes and Band-Aids, but different adventures require different gear. Make sure to research your destination thoroughly before you embark so you can pack appropriately for weather, food/water needs, and emergency supplies.

4. Drink plenty: Even a short day hike can catch an unprepared hiker in a bad position. Take plenty of water along or carry a filter so that you can refill your bottles safely. Water from rivers, lakes, and streams is often contaminated with bacteria and viruses and should not be consumed without filtration.

5. Follow the rules: Many of the locations in this book are associated with North Carolina State Parks and, as such, are governed by North Carolina State Rules and Regulations, which can be reviewed in detail online at https://www.ncparks.gov/park-rules.

   a. Hunting is allowed in some of the National Wildlife Refuges and state-established game lands. Please check the visitor information online for these sites before you visit to ensure that your location has not been temporarily closed for hunting or other events, such as weather, fire, or trail updates. If you're visiting during hunting season, wear blaze orange so that hunters can see you.

   b. Please keep in mind that the reason you are visiting these sites is to learn about how and why they are special to North Carolina. Observing the "Leave No Trace" policy outlined below will help protect these sites so that they are available for others to visit as well.

Leave No Trace

- Littering is illegal and it's ugly. Use the trash and recycling receptacles provided and/or make sure to hike out with everything you brought in so that you "Leave No Trace."
- Trees, flowers, shrubs, ferns, other plants, artifacts, rocks, and minerals should be left unharmed by your visit. There should be no collection of these items without a permit for scientific or educational purposes.
- Instead of making a physical collection of items, make notes and drawings in a notebook, or take photographs for your digital collection.

Follow these guidelines as we all work to protect our precious natural resources so that others may experience them as well. Thank you!

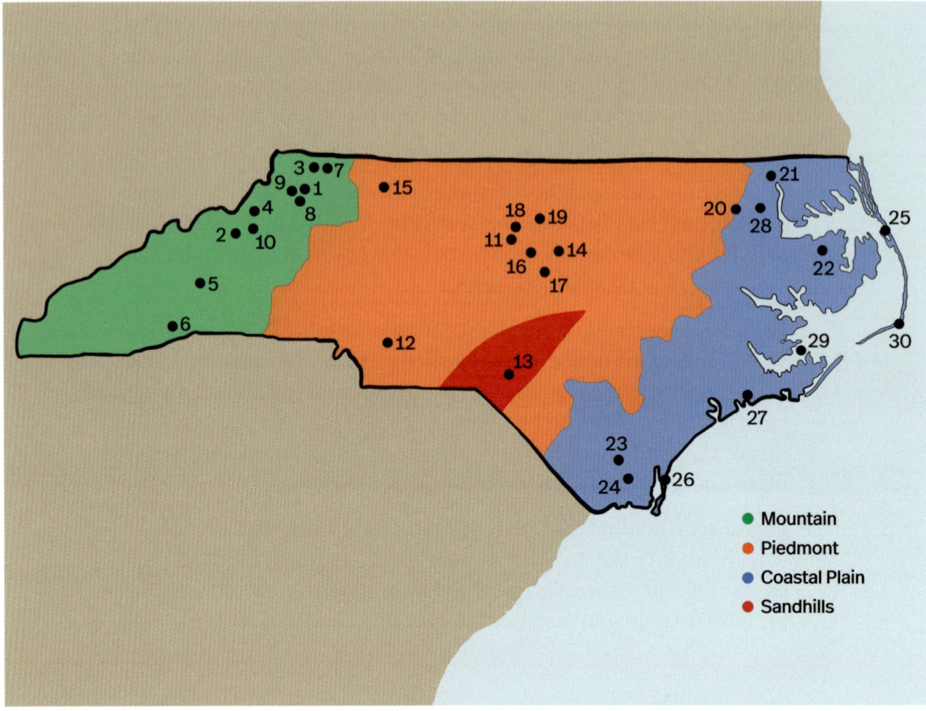

Map 1. The three geologic regions of North Carolina with thirty sites indicated for great scientific explorations throughout the state. Map by Ashleigh M. Smith.

1 Rock Garden
2 Linville Caverns
3 Bluff Mountain Preserve
4 Grandfather Mountain
5 Mount Mitchell
6 Cradle of Forestry
7 Mount Jefferson State Natural Area
8 Blowing Rock Gneiss
9 Elk Knob State Park
10 Linville Gorge
11 Haw River
12 Reed Gold Mine
13 Sandhills
14 Prairie Ridge Ecostation
15 Pilot Mountain State Park
16 North Carolina Botanical Garden
17 Hemlock Bluffs
18 Occoneechee Mountain State Natural Area
19 Eno River State Park
20 Medoc Mountain State Park
21 Merchant's Millpond State Park
22 Pocosin Lakes National Wildlife Refuge
23 Lake Waccamaw State Park
24 Carolina Beach State Park/Green Swamp
25 Jockey's Ridge State Park
26 North Carolina Aquarium at Fort Fisher
27 Hammocks Beach State Park, Bear Island
28 Roanoke River System
29 Pamlico Sound/Neuse River Estuary
30 Cape Hatteras Lighthouse

Part I
Mountain Region

Introduction

Overview

Misty Buchanan

North Carolina's mountains are famous for their beauty and **biodiversity**. The southern Appalachian Mountains dominate the counties in the western region of the state. In North Carolina, the mountains are collectively known as the Blue Ridge Mountains, which are further divided into several subranges, including the Black Mountains, the Craggy Mountains, the Amphibolite Mountains, the Balsam Mountains, and the Great Smoky Mountains.

Great variations in topography, elevation, geology, and moisture in this region give rise to tremendous diversity in the plant and animal life. Mount Mitchell is the highest mountain east of the Mississippi River (6,684 feet above sea level), while some of the valleys drop to 1,000 feet. Some of the highest waterfalls in the eastern United States are found in the Old North State, including Whitewater Falls and Hickorynut Falls. The areas of North Carolina that receive the most rainfall and the least rainfall are both within the Mountain region. Because of this incredible variation and rugged terrain, some of North Carolina's natural assets have been protected. There are more old-growth forests surviving in the mountains of North Carolina than in any other southern Appalachian state, and North Carolina's mountains are home to more species of salamanders than any other place in the world; biologists continue to discover new species regularly. These are facts that should encourage us to continue exploring and discovering, but they also provide us with an understanding of the importance of conservation and protection for North Carolina's endangered species and habitats.

The large amount of public land makes it possible for everyone to study and appreciate these wonderful places. National parks, national forests, state parks, and local preserves are abundant in the Mountain region. When you visit the mountains, be sure to use all your senses to experience and explore your surroundings. Take nothing for granted and ask plenty of questions. Whether you explore a cave, a wetland, or a rock face, if you let the outdoors be your classroom, North Carolina's mountains have an endless supply of learning opportunities.

Mountain Geology

April C. Smith

It has been said that "ecology sprang from a marriage between geology and natural history." Keeping this in mind, the high **biodiversity** found within North Carolina's Mountain ecosystems is tightly coupled with the state's geology, so a brief background of the geologic history may help you as you learn about the mountains. We refer to the mountains as the Blue Ridge Province, and the rocks found here are between ~1.2 billion and ~330 million years old, so there is a broad range in age. You can see billion-year-old rocks near the town of Blowing Rock, as discussed in Chapter 8. Most of the rocks in the Mountain region formed from cooled **magma** or lava (**igneous** rocks) or from ancient sediments (**sedimentary** rocks). All of these rocks were buried and subjected to intense heat and pressure deep inside the Earth (**metamorphic**) during continental collisions. Several large landmasses collided approximately 1.2 billion years ago and then broke apart again ~600 million years ago, leaving an ancient sea in the middle, the Iapetus Ocean. Another series of landmass collisions that began ~480 million years ago and finished ~300 million years ago helped to push up the mountains we know today as the Appalachian Mountains. Erosion is constantly at work, so the Appalachians are not as tall as they once stood, but their long geologic history has allowed for the evolution of a rich ecological domain that marks the North Carolina mountains as one of the finest mountain regions to explore in North America.

References and Resources

Levin, Simon A. "The Evolution of Ecology." *Chronicle of Higher Education*, August 8, 2010, https://www.chronicle.com/article/The-Evolution-of-Ecology/123762. Accessed December 1, 2018.

Stewart, K. G., and M. R. Roberson. *Exploring the Geology of the Carolinas: A Field Guide to Favorite Places from Chimney Rock to Charleston*. Chapel Hill: University of North Carolina Press, 2007.

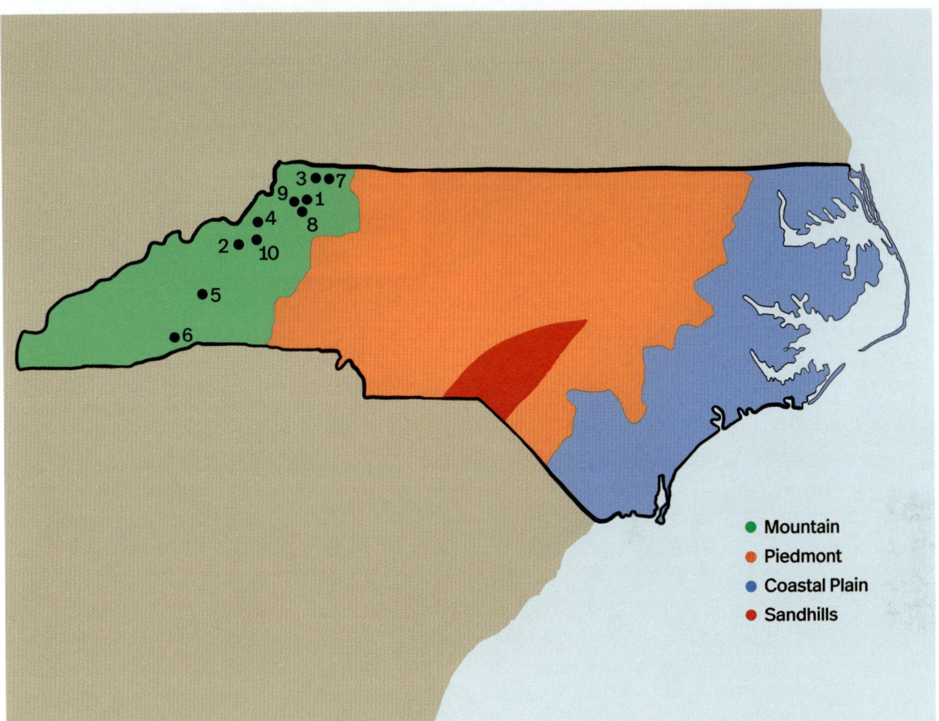

Map 2. Exploration sites in the Mountain region of North Carolina. Map by Ashleigh M. Smith.

1 Rock Garden

2 Linville Caverns

3 Bluff Mountain Preserve

4 Grandfather Mountain

5 Mount Mitchell

6 Cradle of Forestry

7 Mount Jefferson State Natural Area

8 Blowing Rock Gneiss

9 Elk Knob State Park

10 Linville Gorge

APPALACHIAN
GEOLOGY
geology.appstate.edu
5 cm

CHAPTER 1

The Rock Garden

The Fred Webb Jr. Outdoor Geology Laboratory

ANDREW B. HECKERT

SCIENTIFIC FIELD OF STUDY: *Geology*

Introduction

Geology is the study of nonliving things that make up the Earth, like rocks. Geologists are scientists who study what the Earth is made of and how it was formed. When a geologist goes into the field, he or she goes out into nature to look for rocks and then to figure out the history of those rocks by examining their features, location, and placement. Finding those rocks, however, can be difficult. Because geologists must make many inferences from their observations, it can be very challenging to assemble North Carolina's geological puzzle. Geologists must work like detectives to draw conclusions that help them tell the "story" behind rocks.

The Department of Geological and Environmental Sciences at Appalachian State University has designed a place where you can view a selection of North Carolina's rocks: the Fred Webb Jr. Outdoor Geology Laboratory, or the "Rock Garden," for short. If you have an interest in geology, this is a great place to start. In the Rock Garden, you can see all three types of rocks: (1) **igneous**, (2) **sedimentary**, and (3) **metamorphic**, represented by nearly fifty boulders, not just from North Carolina, but from surrounding states as well. A visit to the Fred Webb Jr. Outdoor Geology Laboratory can help you unravel the geologic history of North Carolina and the Appalachian Mountain region in a controlled setting before you forge out into the field to explore this amazing state. It is a place where the rocks have labels giving important information, like their locality and age, but are still "natural," meaning that each rock looks just as it did when it was part of an outcrop on the side of a mountain, along a creek, or in a quarry. Each type of rock at the lab is freely available to touch, without trees or buildings interfering. The lab was planned so that more than 1,000 students every year can experience a little Appalachian geology without ever leaving campus. We invite you to visit the Rock Garden and get a start on learning why geology is important to the history of North Carolina.

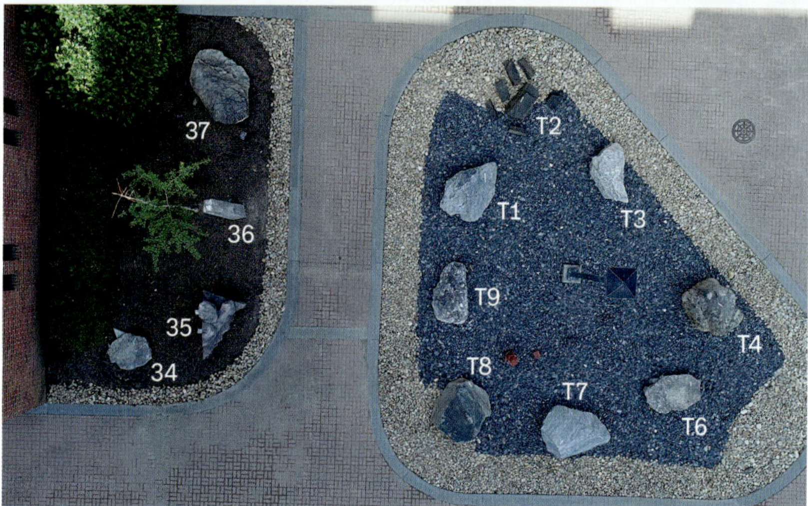

Figure 1-1. Overhead views of the Rock Garden. Each rock is labeled with a specific number for reference. Photos by Brian Zimmer.

How to Visit the Rocks

Creating the Rock Garden depends on donations of massive chunks of rocks that roughly weigh the same as a few elephants and require special machinery to move them, so we can't be too picky about where they are placed. This means that there is no real order to the rocks in the garden. Still, we have an "island" with nine rocks that represent some of the major rock types and have more signage. Each rock has a label that provides you with a geologic name, a location, a period of geologic time (like Cambrian), a numerical age estimate (how many millions, or even billions, of years old), and a geologic province, which refers to a location with similar geologic features or history. The main portion of the Rock Garden continues to grow, but it currently holds nearly fifty specimens, including two different types of stone benches and a two-part marble sculpture.

Before you begin to explore the Rock Garden, it is important to remember the difference between **minerals** and rocks. Basically, minerals are the ingredients of rocks. If you were to compare this to the ingredients in cookies, chocolate chips and nuts

Figure 1-2. The Rock Garden. Photo by A. B. Heckert.

represent the minerals that form our cookies, while the cookie itself represents the rock. A mineral is an inorganic (nonliving) chemical compound that forms crystals. In the Rock Garden, those crystals can range in size from microscopic to larger than baseballs, and they are the components that make the rocks.

There are many ways aspiring geologists can visit the Rock Garden. You could simply stroll through the garden and read the labels for the types of rocks that interest you, or you could focus your visit on the various locations of the rocks. For example, you may choose to look at sample T9 for the fantastic purple micas and rounded quartz cobbles of the Grandfather Mountain Formation near Banner Elk, the big pink feldspars and other minerals from the Lilesville Granite near Rockingham (T3), or the exquisitely crinkled surface of the **limestones** of the Beekmantown Formation from southwestern Virginia (#23). Bring along a notebook and pencil to make observations about your favorites or to document your questions.

How to "Read" the Rocks

Every rock tells a story about our past. That story unfolds according to which rock type you have: igneous, sedimentary, or metamorphic. Geologists classify, or group, rocks based on their features, and some of these features provide evidence of how the rocks were formed. The texture and composition of the rock are also important in telling this geologic story. Some of these definitions may come in handy for better understanding rocks and minerals:

- Igneous rocks are formed, usually deep inside the Earth, when **magma** or lava cools. Magma is liquid rock inside the Earth, while lava is liquid rock on the Earth's surface.
- Sedimentary rocks are formed by a buildup of sediment over time, like in the bottom of a streambed.
- Metamorphic rocks are formed by "morphing" or changing a preexisting rock to something new with heat or pressure. This occurs deep inside the Earth.

Texture refers to the size and arrangement of mineral crystals or other particles in the rock. Are the crystals large or small? Are they all the same size? Are they arranged in bands or layers, or are they randomly oriented? **Composition** refers to the kinds of minerals from which the rock is made.

Geologists make observations about the texture and composition of a rock's minerals and then decipher what these ingredients are. Let's briefly refer back to our cookie metaphor. If you make an observation that your cookie has chocolate chips, raisins, or nuts, and then you note both the size and shape of the nuts, you are making the same types of observations that geologists make when identifying rocks. To help you identify rocks in the garden, every specimen has a polished spot, which helps show the size and arrangement of minerals, or the texture.

A Guide for When You Visit

We have a triangular area with nine different rocks (T1–T9) that represent different stops along the rock cycle. The rock cycle is similar to other cycles in nature. Over time, rocks can change form from one type to another because of heat, pressure, or **weathering**, which is the breaking down of rock into smaller parts due to wind or water. Geologists study the rock cycle, or how material can shift from one rock type to another (igneous, sedimentary, and metamorphic) and all over again. For example, igneous rocks can break down when exposed to wind and rain, and these small pieces then wash down into riverbeds. Over millions of years, these small pieces build up in layers and form sedimentary rock. During a continental collision, this sedimentary rock could be changed by heat and pressure into a metamorphic rock. There are multiple rocks with similar stories in the garden, and by using this guide you can follow three examples.

The Blowing Rock Gneiss (#31), a Metamorphic Rock

Let's start our tour with a rock labeled the Blowing Rock Formation but also known as Blowing Rock Gneiss. This specimen comes from a spot just up the road from the outcrop described in Chapter 8 of this book. After you have observed the Blowing Rock Gneiss sample in the Rock Garden, take a drive over to Blowing Rock to see this formation as it exists in nature.

As part of the Blue Ridge Mountains, and like most of the rocks in the High Country near Boone, it is the product of "metamorphism." This means that intense heat and pressure deep within the Earth compressed and baked an older rock, or **protolith**. The result of the intense heat and pressure shows up in this rock as bands of crystals. The alignment of crystals, called foliation, is perpendicular to the direction that pressure was applied and is often used as a major clue for geologists when deciding if a rock is metamorphic. You can read more about this action in Chapter 8, "Blowing Rock Gneiss." This particular metamorphic rock has distinct bands of alternating light and dark minerals, so we call it a **gneiss**. The dark crystals are mostly biotite, which is a black mica, and they grew in response to the high pressure. Mixed in are lighter blobs that are crystals of quartz and feldspar—sturdier, more stable minerals that weren't affected by pressure. In this rock, you can also see speckles in between the biotite bands, so geologists like to call this particular kind of gneiss an "augen gneiss." "Augen" is the German word for "eyes." If you look closely, you

Figure 1-3. A sample from the Blowing Rock Formation (#31), which is over 1 billion years old. This is a metamorphic rock. Photo by A. B. Heckert.

Figure 1-4. A close-up of the minerals in the Blowing Rock Formation. Photo by A. B. Heckert.

may also see some brassy yellow or rusty-looking cubic crystals. These are pyrite, or "fool's gold," and are made entirely of iron sulfide (FeS). When this specimen was fresh in the Rock Garden in 2008, they were a bright brassy yellow, but many of the pyrite crystals are weathering now, oxidizing, or rusting, in our modern atmosphere.

Just like for successful detectives, the details uncovered by geologists and aspiring geologists like yourself help tell the story of an older rock exposed to intense heat and pressure to form a newer rock, perhaps as much as a billion years ago.

Figure 1-5. A sample from the Spruce Pine Formation (#29), an igneous rock. Photo by A. B. Heckert.

The Spruce Pine Pegmatite (#29), an Igneous Rock

During the formation of the Appalachian Mountains, rocks like the Blowing Rock Gneiss were repeatedly smashed and shoved deeper into the Earth's crust. Sometimes they were pushed so deep that the lighter, less dense minerals inside the rock began to melt, forming a viscous magma, or melted rock, at more than 1300°F (700°C). These magmas rose through cracks and fissures in the Earth, eventually pooling in great magma chambers. There they slowly cooled over the course of many, many years, and crystals of quartz, feldspar, and muscovite mica, or white mica, started to grow. When magma cools slowly, the crystals have more time to grow larger. So when the conditions for these growing crystals were ideal, meaning perfect temperature and combination of ingredients, gigantic crystals began to form deep inside the warm Earth. Eventually they started to grow into one another, locking together to form unpredictable arrangements of crystals that are typical of igneous rocks.

In the case of #29, the rock that formed from this action is a bright white, pink, and gray rock with large crystals called a granite pegmatite. In general, a pegmatite differs from a "regular" granite because of the presence of those large crystals. Millions of years later, this particular rock was **uplifted**, raised to the surface or near the surface, and then experienced millions of years of **erosion**, or weathering. Eventually it was exposed near Spruce Pine, North Carolina, where humans discovered it and came to consider it one of the most important rocks in the world.

That is a pretty big statement, but it is true because the three components of this pegmatite (quartz, feldspar, and muscovite mica) are all incredibly useful materials. The mining companies around Spruce Pine love the pegmatite because all the

Figure 1-6. A close-up view of the minerals in the Spruce Pine Formation. Photo by A. B. Heckert.

rock they mine eventually can be used in a variety of products. The micas are used in everything from glittery makeup to wallboard spackle and electrical insulators, while the feldspars are used mainly for porcelain. Most importantly, because the quartz inside this pegmatite contains almost nothing but silicon and oxygen, it is of such high purity that it is used to build the silicon hardware required for making microchips. The entire computer industry, which includes everything from laptops to cell phones and even the computer chips that help run your car, requires quartz from the Spruce Pine Pegmatite because of its purity. Almost every electronic device that you can think of requires computer chips, and all of those chips were built using materials from the Spruce Pine Pegmatite. You can see why it is considered the most important rock in the world.

The Pottsville Formation (T4, Bench #30), a Sedimentary Rock

The rocks that form the Earth are constantly being pushed and shoved, although slowly, in one direction or another because of movement of the Earth's crust or **tectonic** plates. Sometimes they are lifted to form mountains; sometimes they are forced underground deep into the Earth. For more than 450 million years, parts of the Appalachian Mountains have been shoved upward, eroded down by wind and water, and shoved upward again. When North America and Africa collided as part of the formation of the supercontinent **Pangea**, truly enormous mountains formed where the Appalachians are now, but at that time they lay near the equator. So rocks like the Blowing Rock Gneiss and Spruce Pine Pegmatite were pushed to the surface, bathed in oxygen-rich air, washed by heavy rains, and introduced to land plants, which were relatively new at that time in Earth's history. As a result of wind,

Figure 1-7. A sample from the Pottsville Formation, a sedimentary rock. Photo by A. B. Heckert.

water, and breaking apart from plant roots, they began to wear down incredibly fast. Some minerals, like quartz, are extremely stable at the surface. They only weather physically, which means that they are ground down to become rounded pebbles or grains of sand. Other minerals are less stable and will break down chemically, forming what you may think is a muddy mess but what geologists call "clay minerals." Heavy rains caused fast-moving streams, which then became great rivers flowing west across the continent, carrying the fine muddy clays, sand, and rounded pebbles in rushing torrents of water. As the river currents slowed, the pebbles, sand, and clay particles eventually became too heavy to be carried by the water, sank to the bottom, and became the sedimentary rock: conglomerates and sandstones we now know as the Pottsville Formation.

In the Rock Garden, the large boulder of the Pottsville Formation (T4) was formed by the deposits of one of those streams—thousands of white quartz pebbles intermingled with millions and millions of grains of quartz-rich sand that are coarse in size, meaning they are easily visible to the naked eye. Much farther downstream, or in smaller river channels with less water, the rivers moved slower and could only move sand-sized grains. Thus you do not see any pebbles in our Pottsville Formation bench, as it is composed of a much more fine-grained sand. This sand traveled hundreds of miles from the mountains and is thus very fine, with the grains rounded and well-sorted (all the same size).

Figure 1-8. A close-up view of the conglomerates in the sedimentary Pottsville Formation. Photo by A. B. Heckert.

Before You Go

Visit the Rock Garden virtually to plan your trip, to learn about opening hours, and to get an idea of how to explore the Rock Garden in person.

Website: https://earth.appstate.edu/facilities/rockgarden
Contact: email: mckinneymuseum@appstate.edu
Address: 572 Rivers Street, Boone, N.C. 28608
GPS Coordinates: N 36°12.863, W 81°40.887

CHAPTER 2

Linville Caverns

An Underground Wonderland

BRAD DANIEL

SCIENTIFIC FIELDS OF STUDY: *Geology, Ecology, and Speleology*

Imagine yourself deep in the Blue Ridge Mountains in the early 1800s. The only way to travel around is by horseback. You and your friends go fishing, and while following one particular drainage upstream, you stumble upon a place where the water appears to emerge from the mountain itself. Trout move freely into and out of the opening, and this arouses your curiosity. You find a place where you can squeeze through the opening. When you do, the light from your pine torches reveals a hidden underground wonderland. Today that space is known as Linville Caverns, and it is a site of great beauty, mystery, and folklore.

In 1858, Henry E. Colton was a talented young man of twenty-two years who traveled west from eastern North Carolina to see Linville Caverns. Once through the opening, Colton, who later became Tennessee's state geologist, discovered many beautiful geologic formations. Holler and Holler (1989) quote Colton's writings from the October 9, 1858, issue of the *NC Presbyterian*, where he wrote, "Now began the wondrous splendors of the hidden world. . . . We emerged into an immense passage, whose roof was far beyond the reach of the glare of our torches, except where the fantastic festoons of stalactites hang down within our touch. It looked like the arch of some grand old cathedral, yet it was too sublime, too perfect in all its beautiful proportions, to be anything of human, but a model which man might attempt to imitate. It was not a large, gross cavern. . . . Pendants were of a delicate lightness, and a most beautiful hue."

Colton's story is only one of many intriguing tales that comprise the rich history of Linville Caverns. Later, Civil War deserters hid out in a portion of the caverns, as evidenced by tools and a cobbler's bench found in a relatively flat, sandy area. Since the cavern temperature remains approximately 52°F (11°C) year-round, they built fires to stay warm. Unfortunately, the smoke emerging from fissures in the mountain led to their discovery and arrest. Sometime later, two boys went into the cave to explore, but one of them dropped their lantern and they were immersed in total darkness. Disoriented and suffering from hypothermia, they decided the best way to find their way out of the mountain was to follow the stream. It was a good decision, and they survived.

Geologic Processes

Learning about Linville Caverns actually begins at the parking area next to the entrance where the North Fork of the Catawba River runs beside the parking lot. Running water has played a crucial role in shaping the caverns as well as the landscape around them, and the evidence is immediately apparent. Standing on the edge of the lot, one can observe how the stream has undercut the far bank, causing large boulders and soil to fall into the stream. This downslope movement of material due to the pull of gravity is known as mass wasting. The outer edge of the curve in the stream where erosion is occurring is called the cut bank, while the inside of the curve where material is being deposited (because the water is slowing down) is known as the point bar. The stream flowing through Linville Caverns enters the North Fork of the river beside the parking lot.

To understand how Linville Caverns was formed, we must go back in time some 540 million years to when the area was covered by the Iapetus Ocean and sand. Many of the ocean organisms produced shells composed of calcium carbonate. When these organisms died, the shells accumulated over time to form a type of **sedimentary** rock known as **limestone**. Sedimentary rock is formed when sediments are compressed by weight and cemented together. This usually occurs when the water is squeezed out, but insoluble **minerals** remain around the sediment particles, causing them to stick together. The type of material determines the type of sedimentary rock formed. Shady Dolomite is the name of a geologic formation that exists throughout the southeastern United States. It is found throughout much of the caverns and is a magnesium-rich limestone. The sand from the ancient coastlines was also subjected to heat and pressure and hardened into **quartzite** (metamorphosed sand). Many of the boulders in the creek next to the parking lot are composed of quartzite.

As discussed in the Mountain Geology introduction, **tectonic** forces **uplifted** the area, forming the Appalachian Mountains. The caverns were developing below sea level at that time, and water worked to erode away the rock. About 50 million years ago, new uplift occurred in the Mountain region so that the land was raised above sea level and running water continually eroded a deeper channel until the caverns set above the actual creek bed. This caused the caverns to begin to drain as fresh water started running through cracks and crevices in the rock strata. The water eroded passageways and enlarged them, allowing more water to flow through. While water eroded the limestone over time, an additional factor was key in forming the caverns. The erosive nature of the running water was enhanced by increasing amounts of carbon dioxide dissolved in the water. The water combined chemically with the carbon dioxide to form a weak acid, called carbonic acid, which helped dissolve the soft limestone. This action is known as dissolution.

Linville Caverns is an example of karst topography—landscapes formed from the dissolution of soluble rocks, like limestone. The combination of running water and carbonic acid dissolved the limestone pockets and helped create many of the beautiful cave formations that are collectively called speleothems. A variety of speleothems can be found inside the caverns. They are often named according to their shape or appearance. Formations in the caverns include stalactites and stalagmites, cave draperies, flowstone, rimstone, and columns. Cave draperies are drops of water that trickle down a slope along an inclined ceiling, allowing a thin calcite ($CaCO_3$) sheet

Figure 2-1. The North Fork of the Catawba River flows outside Linville Caverns. Photo by Whitney Dumford.

to grow downward in folds. Flowstone is a sheet of calcite deposited on the walls by flowing water, while rimstone is a damlike calcite deposit that forms around pools of water on the cave floor. Stala*c*tites look like icicles, and the mnemonic "*c*eiling *t*ears" often helps us remember that they hang from the ceiling. They are formed when calcite-rich water drips from the ceiling, leaving behind small quantities of calcite that slowly build up on the ceiling until the long, tapered shape begins to form. The water that drips to the floor also contains traces of calcite, and this slowly builds into a conical shape pointing up toward the stalactite; this is called a stalag*m*ite. The mnemonic "*g*round *m*ountain" helps us remember that this speleothem rises up from the ground. Over a very long time, it is possible for the ends to join, forming a speleothem known as a column or pillar. One of the most interesting

Figure 2-2. A small stream from the river enters the caverns and can be followed by a footpath. Photo by Whitney Dumford.

Figure 2-3. You can see many beautiful cave formations inside Linville Caverns. Photo by Whitney Dumford.

Table 2-1. Classification of cave organisms

Cave Organism	*Description*	*Cave Use*	*Examples*
Trogloxenes	Cave visitors that have no special adaptations.	Specific part of their life cycle—nesting, giving birth, hibernation	Bats, bears, raccoons, mice
Troglophiles	Cave lovers that prefer but don't have to live in caves. They usually search for food outside the cave.	Protection, habitat	Worms, crayfish, crickets, salamanders
Troglobites	Cave organisms that are specially adapted to live there—little pigmentation, poorly developed or absent eyes, long antennae.	Entire life cycle	Cave fish, millipedes, cave crayfish, insects

Table created by Brad Daniel

features in Linville Caverns is known as the bottomless pool, a body of water with a suspended grate that allows visitors to stand over it. A weighted line dropped into the water revealed the pool to be at least 250 feet (76 meters) deep, although the weight reportedly never hit bottom.

Linville Caverns remains very active today. The delicate balance between limestone dissolution, where the limestone is dissolved, and redeposition, where those minerals are deposited in new locations, allows new rock to be formed. Flowstone, such as in the Frozen Niagara formation found inside the caverns, is formed by water flowing over the limestone surface in thin sheets. The various beautiful colors are determined by the mineral composition in the rock. Iron appears as red, yellow, or brown bands. Manganese is black. Copper is either green or blue. In some places in the caverns, you can spot milky white or clear crystals embedded in the rock. These crystals are composed of calcium carbonate or calcite. Rust-colored crystals are composed of iron sulfide, or pyrite.

Ecology, Flora, and Fauna

Because Linville Caverns had artificial light sources installed, these lights prevent the establishment of the typical zones one would find in a cave: the entrance, the twilight zone, and the zone of total darkness. In an undisturbed cave, these zones would be characterized by certain temperatures, humidity levels, and characteristic organisms.

Still, a variety of organisms comprise the ecological web of Linville Caverns. Apart from mold, fungi, and algae growing around the artificial light sources, organisms found in the cave include cave crickets, daddy longlegs (harvestmen), orb-weaver spiders, trout, salamanders, crayfish, tricolor bats, little brown bats, and one **endemic species**, which is a species that exists only in this location. It is the Linville Caverns spider (*Nesticus carolinensis*). These organisms are often classified according to how much of their life cycle they spend in the cave and whether they are specially adapted to live there.

An interesting activity is to document the organisms found in the caverns and then use them to construct a food web. Sources of **organic matter**, or things that were once living, in the caverns include guano (bat feces), decaying organisms, and material carried into the cave from outside. Bat guano is often identified as an important source of organic matter in many caves and caverns, but this source is limited if bat **populations** are low and fluctuates with changes in bat populations. Population refers to a group of organisms of the same species that are living together. Bacteria and fungi decompose the available organic matter, providing crucial nutrients for the cavern ecosystem. Bacteria and fungi are fed upon by millipedes and crustaceans, which are then consumed by organisms such as cave spiders and centipedes.

Typically, cavern organisms are distributed throughout three distinct zones usually found in caves, although these zones are disrupted in this cavern due to artificial lighting. The cave entrance varies in temperature and often has some plant life present; the animals that frequent this zone are known as trogloxenes. The second zone, the twilight zone, contains insufficient light for photosynthesis, so plants are absent. The temperature is more consistent but can still fluctuate somewhat. Trogloxenes and troglophiles often can be found in portions of the entrance and twilight zones. Finally, the dark zone is characterized by total darkness and a consistent temperature. Troglobites are cave organisms that have adapted to these conditions and, therefore, live in this zone.

White-Nose Syndrome: An Important Environmental Issue

The tricolor bat hibernates in the caverns in the late fall and winter months. The bats enter and leave through several small openings and feed on insects. If you are lucky, you will see one hanging from the ceiling. Only a few years ago, the bats numbered over 100 in these caverns. Today the number of bats in Linville Caverns has decreased, and a few bats have been identified with a common fungal disease known as **white-nose syndrome**. White-nose syndrome is caused by the fungus *Geomyces destructans* and is spread by contact with infected bats. It can also be transmitted on clothing and shoes from one cave to another, so important precautions are needed to prevent the spread of the fungus to more bat populations. As of 2018, the fungus had been reported in thirty-three states within the United States. White-nose syndrome causes bats to awaken during hibernation. Once awake, they often starve to death because their metabolism is too high and food is not plentiful. In 2017, the U.S. Fish and Wildlife Service and the North Carolina Wildlife Resources Commission confirmed that only a few bats currently hibernating in Linville Caverns were infected. Linville Caverns is working with these agencies to eradicate the disease and prevent its spread, and scientists have confirmed that this disease is not harmful to humans.

Linville Caverns opened as a privately owned tourist attraction in 1937 but closed several years later when a flood filled portions of it with rocks and mud. The business was purchased by Spencer Collins and reopened in 1941. Today the caverns are still privately owned, and they are truly an underground wonderland. This is a place where one can study cavern ecology, geologic formations, and karst processes; view the Linville Falls thrust fault; or simply enjoy the beauty of colorful features. For many people, places like Linville Caverns provide their only opportunity to explore the world underground. You never know what you might discover when you go exploring.

Before You Go

Linville Caverns is located inside Humpback Mountain just off Highway 221 in northern McDowell County. It is North Carolina's only commercial cavern and offers thirty-minute tours on an ongoing basis that highlight cavern history, resident creatures, and geologic formations. A paved walkway and lighting system help visitors move through the caverns and see much more of them. Visitors are encouraged to explore the gift shop. Bathrooms are available. Plan on 1.5 to 2 hours to experience and learn about the caverns and surrounding areas. Parking is limited, so it is best to arrive in early to mid-morning. This is especially true in October, given the number of visitors to the mountains to view the gorgeous fall colors. Photography is allowed in the caverns, but visitors are not allowed to touch the cave formations because oils from hands interfere with the mineral-forming processes. Participants might want to wear a hat to avoid the "kiss of the cave," because watery drips of Shady Dolomite, a mineral dripping from the cave's roof, can create hair tangles. All visitors must clean their shoes by stepping on a bleach pad to keep from potentially spreading the fungus that causes white-nose syndrome. Linville Falls and Linville Gorge Wilderness Area are only a short drive from the caverns. Refer to Chapter 10 for more details about Linville Gorge Wilderness Area.

References and Resources

Brown, Henry S. *Linville Caverns through the Ages: The Geological Story*. N.p., 1961.

Holler, Cato, Jr., and Susan G. Holler. *Hollow Hills of Sunnalee: The Linville Caverns Story*. N.p.: Hollow Hills Publishing, 1989.

"Learn About Caves!" National Caves Association, http://cavern.com/Learn/formations.asp. Accessed November 1, 2018.

U.S. Fish and Wildlife Service. White-Nose Syndrome Response Team, https://www.whitenosesyndrome.org. Accessed November 1, 2018.

Website: http://www.linvillecaverns.com
Contact: Linville Caverns Visitor Center, phone: (800) 419-0540; email: info@linvillecaverns.com
Address: 19929 US 221 North, Marion, N.C. 28752
GPS Coordinates: N 35°55.158, W 81°56.304

CHAPTER 3

Bluff Mountain Preserve

Appalachian Wetlands

APRIL C. SMITH

SCIENTIFIC FIELD OF STUDY: *Wetlands Ecology*

Wetlands come in all shapes and sizes, and in North Carolina they are usually associated with low-lying lands in the Piedmont or Coastal Plain regions. But have you ever seen a wetland in the mountains? They do exist, and in the past, they have been treated as most other wetlands—with very little regard. Let's talk briefly about how North Carolina's terrain, including wetlands, surprised the settlers as they arrived on the coast, and then we'll discuss the specifics of Mountain wetlands.

Sir Walter Raleigh was an explorer, soldier, and writer for the British crown, Britain's royal government. In the 1580s, he invested in several expeditions, but did not join them, to sail across the treacherous Atlantic Ocean from England to the "New World." This is a term coined by the Florentine explorer Amerigo Vespucci in approximately the sixteenth century when referring to the newly discovered landmass that would later be named for him: "America." In 1587, Sir Walter Raleigh sent a group of daring men and women—families, not soldiers—to establish a colony on Roanoke Island in the Outer Banks. By 1590, the entire group of settlers had disappeared mysteriously, and North Carolina became known as a dangerously hard place to live for explorers, primarily due to the challenging landscape. Explorers encountered land that was roughly battered by storms on the coast; swampy, low, and wet as they moved inland; but rocky and mountainous to the west. North Carolina's landforms and weather conditions provided numerous barriers to early explorers and settlers.

Yet nearly 200 years later, 2.5 million people were living in the colonies with a goal of exploring the North American continent and finding its riches. During the 1700s and 1800s, colonial settlement damaged the natural **wetlands**. Wetlands are transitional zones between aquatic habitats and terrestrial habitats where the natural level of water sits roughly at the surface of land, so sediments often remain waterlogged for most of the year. Wetlands are a critical part of natural ecosystems and are sometimes called the Earth's kidneys because they serve as natural filters of water. Benefits of wetlands include serving as habitats for threatened and endangered species, controlling flooding, filtering pollutants, serving as storm and wind buffers, and helping to decrease contributions to climate change by providing important carbon storage for hundreds of years.

We are only now beginning to recognize the important role that wetlands play in the health of our natural ecosystems. From the beginning of European settlement in the New World, people have viewed wetland areas as swampy, snaky, rodent-infested, disease-ridden barriers to overland travel. Settlers believed wetlands were an impediment to frontier survival. Pioneers primarily agreed that wetlands served no beneficial purpose for humans and therefore should be eliminated. Ultimately, most were drained by ditches that were dug to allow sediments to dry enough to be farmed. Wetland soil proved to be very fertile because of the accumulation of decomposed **organic matter**. During the past two centuries, over half of the wetlands originally found in the continental United States have been destroyed. Today, wetlands comprise only about 5 percent of the total U.S. land area in the lower forty-eight states.

While wetlands in general are notable habitats, mountain wetlands are some of the most unusual and fascinating wet and soggy sites to explore. Bogs and fens are two types of mountain wetland habitats, representing only 1 percent of all mountain landscapes. Bogs and fens have received very little attention from regulatory agencies for protection until recently because of their incredibly small size. Most of these critical habitats are less than ten acres in size, and not until we started to learn the benefits wetlands provide did we begin to take an interest in protecting them. Let's first learn what bogs and fens are, and then we will explore why they are so important, and why they need our help.

Bogs and fens are wetland habitats found at high altitudes within the central and southern Appalachian Mountain systems, and most of them are found in North Carolina. Here is your chance to experience one of the rarest habitats in the contiguous United States. Imagine hiking on a mountaintop at 4,500 feet (1,372 meters). You come through a grove of large, shady oak trees only to find a meadow of tall grasses. This is a site not often seen at this elevation, and because this meadow is so wet, you will sink up to your ankles. You have found yourself in a bog or a fen. What's the difference between the two? A bog is a wet and soggy depression in the land, receiving its water primarily from precipitation, such as rain or melted snow. As organic matter decomposes, or breaks down, in a bog, it is compressed to form a brown spongy material called **peat**. Peat has many great attributes. When wet, it is one of the Earth's best carbon stores, it serves as an important habitat for wildlife, and it can hold more than twenty times its own weight in water. However, when wetlands are drained and peat becomes dry, it is highly flammable and releases the massive amounts of carbon it has stored, becoming one of the largest sources of greenhouse gases on Earth. See Chapter 22 for a discussion of burning peat.

Bog soils are generally **saturated** by rain, meaning they are filled with water. These soils are **acidic**, having a pH of 3 to 4, compared to pure water with a pH of 7, and they are low in nutrients. While they do not support large numbers of different animals, they do provide an important habitat for certain animals that require quiet, undisturbed, remote living space. The plants that tend to grow near and around low-nutrient bogs have developed unique methods for survival. **Carnivorous plants**, such as pitcher plants, are often found here. These unique plants survive by trapping

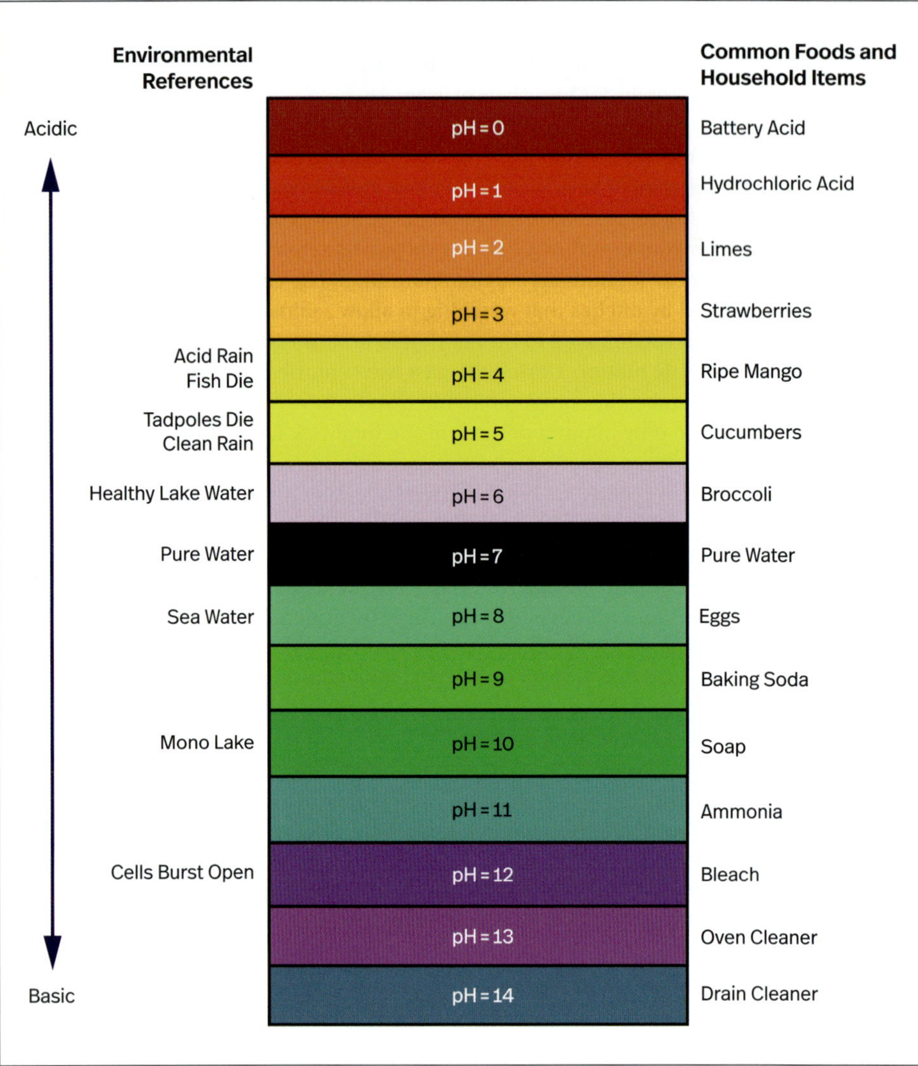

Figure 3-1. The symbol pH stands for power, or quantity, of hydrogen and is a measure of the level of acidity. These levels range from 0 to 14. Artwork by Ashleigh M. Smith.

insects inside their large pitcher-shaped leaves and using the nutrients for growth when soil nutrients are typically low.

A fen is nearly identical to a bog, with peat accumulation occurring as plants and animals die and begin to slowly decompose; however, a fen is fed by groundwater rising up from below to the soil's surface, instead of receiving water from above in the form of precipitation. As a result, the water and soils are less acidic than in bogs and higher in nutrients, allowing for the growth of more various types of grasses. The pH of fens can range from an acidic 4 to a slightly **basic** 8. In more northerly habitats, fens and bogs have formed primarily in ground depressions formed by

Figure 3-2. Mountain sweet pitcher plant. Photo by Gary Peeples/USFWS.

glacial ice that often dates back 11,000 years. In the southern United States, however, fens and bogs have formed in low areas where water can accumulate but flooding does not occur. Most often they are seen on gentle slopes, in flat valleys, or in natural depressions in the ground.

Wetlands of all types, whether found in the mountains, in the Piedmont, or on the coast, are well known for their amazing ability to manage water. If there is an excess of rain, wetlands help to hold extra water, slowly releasing it into streams and rivers and preventing flooding. When there is drought, wetlands provide water where it is needed. They also help reduce sediment runoff and improve the quality of water by filtering out silt and other contaminants. Fens and bogs are similar in these respects, so they provide the benefits of wetlands to higher altitudes.

Now we have established that wetlands are rare water-managing habitats, but why is that important ecologically? Rare species are often found in rare habitats, and **biodiversity** in these spots can be incredibly high, thus contributing to the health of the ecosystem. High biodiversity in an ecosystem means that there are many different kinds of plants and animals. A greater number of species in an area can indicate a healthy ecosystem because that area may be able to withstand disturbance better than an ecosystem of the same size having fewer species. This is most often true because a greater number of species will be composed of organisms serving an increased variety of roles in the community, thereby providing strength for survival during disturbance periods. In North Carolina's mountain bogs and fens, there are close to ninety rare, endangered, or threatened species of plants and animals. The mountain sweet pitcher plant, the water shrew, the Appalachian Mountain bog turtle, and the rock gnome lichen are a few of the special organisms that call these bogs and fens home. At one time, approximately 5,000 acres of bogs existed in North Carolina. Today, only about 500 acres remain, and many of them exist on private lands where the owners may have no idea what precious ecological resources they possess.

You can help protect mountain wetlands. If you know someone who may have wetlands on their private land, you can share your knowledge about the importance of these critical regions. Inform others that changing the **hydrology**, or the natural flow of water, of bogs and fens with ditches or culverts will destroy this unique habitat and the rare creatures that live there.

Before You Go

If you would like to experience a mountain wetland site in person, the Bluff Mountain Preserve in Ashe County is 2,880 acres of ecologically unique land, including a mountain fen that is owned and managed by The Nature Conservancy. Because of the sensitive nature of the preserve, it is not open to the public, but The Nature Conservancy schedules hikes for small groups up to ten people. There is a small fee for this hike. You can find more information on The Nature Conservancy website listed below.

This hike is a moderate 3-mile (4.8-kilometer) loop with an elevation change of ~300 feet (91.4 meters). You might consider reviewing some of the references below before you go to find names and pictures of the special plants and animals that live in these unique habitats, then challenge yourself to a game of wetland "I Spy." Consider taking a notebook to record what you see on your visit.

References and Resources

A&E Television Networks. "The 13 Colonies." *HISTORY*, http://www.history.com/topics/thirteen-colonies. Last modified June 17, 2010. Accessed November 2, 2018.

Dahl, Thomas E. *Status and Trends of Wetlands in the Conterminous United States, 2004 to 2009*. Washington, D.C.: U.S. Department of the Interior; Fish and Wildlife Service, 2011, https://www.fws.gov/wetlands/Documents/Status-and-Trends-of-Wetlands-in-the-Conterminous-United-States-2004-to-2009.pdf. Accessed November 2, 2018.

Dahl, Thomas E., and Gregory J. Allord. *Technical Aspects of Wetlands: History of Wetlands in the Conterminous United States*. 1997. USGS Water Supply Paper 2425, https://water.usgs.gov/nwsum/WSP2425/history.html. Accessed November 2, 2018.

Ellis, Amber. "Exploring Mountain Bogs." *Appalachian Voice: Naturalist's Notebook* 4 (August/September 2014), http://appvoices.org/2014/08/10/exploring-mountain-bogs/. Accessed November 2, 2018.

Lawler, Andrew. "Archaeologists Start a New Hunt for the Fabled Lost Colony of the New World." *Science News*, June 6, 2018, http://www.sciencemag.org/news/2018/06/archaeologists-start-new-hunt-fabled-lost-colony-new-world. Accessed November 2, 2018.

The Nature Conservancy. "Bluff Mountain Preserve," http://www.nature.org/ourinitiatives/regions/northamerica/unitedstates/northcarolina/placesweprotect/bluff-mountain-preserve.xml. Accessed November 2, 2018.

North Carolina Wildlife Resources Commission. *2015 North Carolina Wildlife Action Plan*. Publication no. 6718619, https://www.ncwildlife.org/ Plan#6718619-2015-document-downloads. Accessed November 3, 2018.

"What's So Special about Peat?" United Kingdom National Trust, https://www.nationaltrust.org.uk/features/whats-so-special-about-peat. Accessed November 3, 2018.

"Why Are Wetlands Important?" United States Environmental Protection Agency, https://www.epa.gov/wetlands/why-are-wetlands-important. Last modified June 13, 2018. Accessed November 2, 2018.

Website: http://www.nature.org/ourinitiatives/regions/northamerica/unitedstates/northcarolina/placesweprotect/bluff-mountain-preserve.xml

Contact: Use the website listed above for current contact information.

Address: When a reservation is made for a hike, you will be given the address.

GPS Coordinates: N 36°23.46, W 81°34.32

CHAPTER 4

Grandfather Mountain

A Mountain of Biological Abundance

JESSE POPE

SCIENTIFIC FIELDS OF STUDY: *Geology, Forest Ecology, Climatology, Lichenology*

The formation of the Appalachian Mountains from the collision of **tectonic** plates that **uplifted** the long mountain range is described briefly in the Mountain Geology section (p. 10) of this book. The Appalachian Mountains stretch from the northern portion of eastern North America from Newfoundland south to Alabama. One of the major features along the nearly 2,000-mile (3,219-kilometer) chain is the Blue Ridge Mountain range, a ridge that runs through Virginia and North Carolina. This ridge marks the eastern edge of the southern Appalachians. Along this ridge is an amazing mountain in northwestern North Carolina—a mountain unlike any other in the state. This mountain is steeped in North Carolina history, is easily recognizable from a distance, and is highly distinguishable from the surrounding landscape. The original Cherokee name for this mountain is Tanawha, meaning a fabulous hawk or eagle. Pioneers first began to call it Grandfather Mountain because it rises from the western highlands displaying the profile of an old man's face.

Many famous visitors in history have made trips to Grandfather Mountain. You could imagine how difficult a trek up this mountain would have been when your only travel options were by horseback or on foot, and it would have taken many days to reach the top. Daniel Boone hunted here in the 1760s. André Michaux, the French botanist, climbed this mountain with his companion and guide in 1794. Asa Gray, a Harvard botanist, climbed the mountain in 1841 in search of a long-missing species of plant, but instead he discovered a rare lily that is now called Gray's lily. After searching the entire world for this lily, scientists have discovered that it only lives in a few counties, where North Carolina meets Tennessee and Virginia. John Muir, founder of the Sierra Club, also climbed Grandfather Mountain in 1898, claiming to his wife that the mountain air had cured his cough.

Today we can consider the history of the mountain and use our scientific knowledge to discover why Grandfather Mountain was found to be such a unique location

Figure 4-1. Red crossbill. Photo courtesy of Grandfather Mountain Stewardship Foundation.

by early explorers. There are three things, in general, that make Grandfather Mountain particularly special and drastically different from the surrounding landscape: (1) the numerous rocky outcroppings, (2) the abundance and diversity of plant and animal life, and (3) the fact that it is both protected and accessible to the public.

First, Grandfather Mountain does not look like a typical eastern mountain peak. Years of erosion have rounded the tops of nearby peaks such as Sugar and Beech Mountains. Grandfather Mountain still has jagged peaks and looks more like a mountain from the Rocky Mountain range with its steep edges and dramatic cliffs. Several of the cliffs have vertical drops of over 400 feet (122 meters). This rugged landscape is due in part to the **minerals** in the rock that forms Grandfather Mountain. This rock contains a high degree of silica-based minerals, like quartz, which typically are more resistant to erosion, but more recent uplift and faulting also have caused this section of the mountains to remain higher and more resistant to the smoothing effects of erosion. Grandfather Mountain is bordered on the southeast side by the Linville Falls thrust fault, a **fracture** in the Earth's crust that can be seen up close at Linville Caverns. The movement of the **thrust fault** has left this ridge more rugged than surrounding peaks. The rock on Grandfather Mountain is also much younger than that of the surrounding mountains. This is because the thrust fault moved an older sheet of rock, called the Blue Ridge Thrust Plate, to cover most of the rock in the surrounding area, but at Grandfather Mountain, a section of the Blue Ridge Thrust Plate has eroded away, so the younger rock can be easily viewed and studied. As you're exploring Grandfather Mountain, make sure to look for all three different types of rocks discussed in Chapter 1: **sedimentary**, **metamorphic**, and **igneous**. Although the sedimentary rocks have been metamorphosed, you can still see the sedimentary features.

Geographically, we know that Grandfather Mountain has been an icon of the western North Carolina mountains for generations, but ecologically, far fewer

Figure 4-2. Northern saw whet owl. Photo courtesy of Grandfather Mountain Stewardship Foundation.

people are aware of the extraordinary diversity of landscapes that occur on a single mountaintop. At 5,946 feet (1,675 meters) in height, Grandfather Mountain is one of the taller in the southern Appalachians, but there's more going on here than just height, due primarily to the enormously large number of exposed rocky areas, rugged cliffs, and sheer rock faces mentioned above. These extreme habitats have dense vegetation growing in alkaline soils and are situated at high altitude, creating a cool, wet climate: the perfect recipe for the formation of its many remarkable natural communities.

The steep changes in elevation contribute to an abundance of life found on Grandfather's slopes. Many diverse natural communities can be found on the mountain, including **Northern Hardwood Forest**, **Spruce-Fir Forest**, and **Heath Bald**. These communities are each distinguished by unique plants and animals. The highest elevations are perhaps the most interesting and support unexpected life forms—the vegetation is similar to what is found in northern latitudes like Maine, New Hampshire, and parts of Canada because the cooler temperatures are a direct result of the higher altitudes. Grandfather Mountain is very different from the rest of North Carolina. Spruce and fir trees are important habitat for rare and threatened species like the red crossbill, Carolina northern flying squirrel, and Weller's salamander. There are only about 75,000 acres of this habitat in the southern Appalachians, an area smaller than the city of Raleigh. Some scientists consider the Spruce-Fir Forest to be the second most endangered habitat in the United States.

Because of the great deal of diversity and the dramatic landscape, Grandfather Mountain is cared for by multiple agencies and organizations that work together to ensure the park's protection for future generations. The North Carolina State Parks,

Figure 4-3. View from the Cliffside Overlook. Photo courtesy of Grandfather Mountain Stewardship Foundation.

Grandfather Mountain Stewardship Foundation, Nature Conservancy, National Park Service, and U.S. Forest Service protect different parts of the mountain and research the park's plants and animals to make informed decisions on managing the land. With differing management, the access is different as well. Visitors interested in having an auto touring experience can drive below the peaks of Grandfather Mountain on the Blue Ridge Parkway. Hikers and backpackers may choose to explore the miles of trails in Grandfather Mountain State Park. The Stewardship Foundation offers a unique experience with access to a variety of overlooks, park exhibits, educational programming, and more.

The nonprofit Grandfather Mountain Stewardship Foundation interprets the many wonders of Grandfather. Visitors can witness and learn about the annual hawk migration in September. The greatest number of nesting birds come to Grandfather Mountain in April and May and are a special treat to experience. Grandfather also hosts more than seventy rare and endangered species for visitors to learn about, and the impressive windswept landscape at the top of the mountain is a site not to be missed. **Citizen Science** projects, including a nestbox survey of nesting birds, salamander surveys, and a study on the timing of wildflowers, all provide opportunities for students to explore the communities of life on Grandfather Mountain firsthand. From the top of Linville Peak within the park, visitors can gaze out across the Appalachians as they lead to the Piedmont to the east and view the high wall of Roan Mountain to the west. After a cold front has passed in the winter, the views are incredible. Some days offer a visibility of over ninety miles to the east, including views of Charlotte's skyline. These incredible vistas make up one of the wonders of Grandfather, but for years the views and the park's ecology often have been disrupted with air pollution and **acidic** precipitation, also known as acid rain. Though the park is in a rural area, winds move pollution from northern cities to the park's upper elevations. In western North Carolina, the problem is made worse by the disruption of air movement by tall peaks and deep valleys. The Clean Air Act, which restricts the amount of pollution from coal-fired power plants and other sources, finally may be allowing for the restoration of both the ecology of the land and the views for explorers to enjoy.

Park naturalists monitor weather conditions as part of a long-term Citizen Science project aimed at understanding trends in the mountain's climate. One piece of equipment measures aerosols, a suspension of fine particles in the air, to help explain other aspects of the mountain's health. Some scientists monitor pollution by observing **lichens** found growing on trees, rocks, and any other hard surfaces. The species of lichens found in forests can indicate the health of the forest. Foliose and fruticose lichens, which are typically frilly, leafy, or hairy, often are more sensitive to pollutants than other species. Crustose lichens that are flat and form a crust over a surface generally are more tolerant of air pollution. See Chapter 5, "Mount Mitchell," for a more detailed discussion of lichens. Observational studies such as these can be used alongside other data to ensure the protection of this great mountain.

Before You Go

Several trails on Grandfather Mountain provide opportunities to become acquainted with this mountain of abundance. The Profile Trail within Grandfather Mountain State Park is 3.6 miles (5.8 kilometers) long and allows visitors to travel through several natural communities, including **Rich Cove Forest**, **Acidic Cove Forest**, Northern Hardwood Forest, and **Boulderfield Forests**. The trail ends on the crest of Grandfather in the Spruce-Fir Forest. Please refer to the glossary or Chapters 5 and 9 for detailed descriptions of these forest communities.

The Black Rock Trail starts from the Stewardship Foundation park and enters the state park. This trail is moderately challenging and is a good option for family groups. The forested walk is 1.0 mile (1.6 kilometers) long and passes through rhododendron and Spruce-Fir Forests to an amazing view overlooking the eastern ridges that descend below Grandfather's high peaks.

The Tanawha Trail is 13.5 miles (21.7 kilometers) long in its entirety, but most people hike shorter sections of it, as there are multiple access points along the trail. It parallels the Blue Ridge Parkway, passes over a Heath Bald, through a Northern Hardwood Forest, and then underneath the Linn Cove Viaduct—the final segment that completed the Blue Ridge Parkway.

Most of the access points to the different parks on Grandfather Mountain are within a 35-minute drive south of Boone. Visitors can learn more about the parks by visiting one of the visitor centers on the mountain. Check the website for ticket prices, ticket sales hours, and park hours during each season. The entrance to the Grandfather Mountain Stewardship Foundation's park is located on US 221, 2 miles north of Linville, North Carolina, and 1 mile south of the Blue Ridge Parkway at milepost 305.

Please refer to the "Driving Directions" section of the website for tips and further information to travel successfully to Grandfather Mountain.

References and Resources

Banks, S. "Forest Response to the US 1990 Clean Air Act: The Southern Spruce-Fir Ecosystem," *American Journal of Plant Sciences* 5, no. 3 (2014): 372–86.

Citizen Science Association, http://www.citizenscience.org. Accessed November 3, 2018.

North Carolina Division of Parks and Recreation. "Grandfather Mountain State Park." N.C. State Parks, http://www.ncparks.gov/grandfather-mountain-state-park. Accessed November 3, 2018.

Noss, R. F., E. T. LaRoe, and J. M. Scott. *Endangered Ecosystems of the United States: A Preliminary Assessment of Loss and Degradation*. U.S. Department of the Interior. Biological Report 28. Washington, D.C.: National Biological Service, 1995.

U.S. Department of the Interior. "Blue Ridge Parkway." National Park Service, www.nps.gov/blri. Accessed November 3, 2018.

Website: www.grandfather.com
Contact: email: nature@grandfather.com
Address: 2050 Blowing Rock Highway, Linville, N.C. 28646.
GPS Coordinates: N 36°5.101, W 81°50.76

CHAPTER 5

Mount Mitchell

An Ecological Island in the Sky

BRAD DANIEL

SCIENTIFIC FIELDS OF STUDY: *Geology, Forest Ecology, Island Biogeography, Climatology, Meteorology*

It is not unusual to camp on the slopes of Mount Mitchell, the highest peak east of the Mississippi River, and find yourself awakening to a remarkable scene. A sea of white fog billows below you, surrounding the peak. The fog creates the illusion that Mount Mitchell is an island in a sea of clouds, as if someone packed white cotton candy into the valleys during the night. This phenomenon is actually the result of a **thermal inversion**, and these are common occurrences on Mount Mitchell. Thermal inversions occur when cooler, denser, and therefore heavier air flows downslope at night and collects in the valleys and drainages below. Because the air temperature is cool, the water vapor in the air condenses to form fog.

Although this early morning island scene is only an illusion, Mount Mitchell, along with other peaks in the Black Mountain range, are indeed ecological islands in the sky, with ecosystems more similar to what one would find in the northern latitudes of Canada rather than North Carolina. In Chapter 4, "Grandfather Mountain," we already have approached the idea that the tallest peaks in the state are cooler because of their higher elevations, which makes them ideal habitats for plant and animal species that normally would not exist at North Carolina's southerly latitude. In the world of ecology this has many important implications, and although we are exploring Mount Mitchell as a Mountain habitat, we call this concept **island biogeography**. Island biogeography is the study of **species richness**, or the number of different species, and **community composition**, which refers to the percentages of the different species within the community. Island biogeography has a goal of trying to establish causal relationships between groups of organisms, where one event is the cause of another event. It is also the study of **biodiversity**, the variety and variability of life within a small, isolated ecosystem, like a mountaintop.

Your next question is probably, "How can a mountaintop be like an island?" Think about what separates the living organisms on a mountaintop from the organisms at the bottom of the mountain: (1) altitude, (2) temperature, (3) winds, (4) food sources, and (5) suitable habitat. If you are a bird that requires a specific tree for sur-

Figure 5-1. Thermal inversion causes a thick layer of clouds to form, leaving only mountain peaks peeking through. Photo by Mike Dunn.

vival and that tree only exists on top of a mountain, you are living on an island. Keep these ideas in mind as we discuss the unique "island" habitat of Mount Mitchell.

History

Viewed from the valleys below, Mount Mitchell is not particularly impressive. It has no sharply defined peak. It lacks the abrupt relief, or slope steepness, of Grandfather Mountain and the open exposure of Roan Mountain's balds, which have no trees. In fact, Native Americans called Mount Mitchell "black dome" because of the dark spruce-fir vegetation that dominates the peak along with the fact that it is rounded on top. And yet the high elevation creates a place of environmental extremes and contributes to supporting unique communities of flora and fauna.

Much of the Black Mountain range was logged in the first decade of the twentieth century; trees were removed, and the natural ecosystem of the mountain was heavily impacted. In response, Locke Craig, fifty-third governor of North Carolina, lobbied the North Carolina legislature to protect the area because he was concerned about the environmental degradation of the High Country. Mount Craig, the second highest peak in the Black Mountains, was named after him in appreciation for his efforts.

Mount Mitchell was the first state park in North Carolina. It was established in 1915 and named after Elisha Mitchell, a professor at the University of North Carolina at Chapel Hill, who died in 1857 while exploring the mountain. Both Mitchell and his former student Thomas Clingman were trying to determine the highest mountain in the eastern United States. This resulted in a storied rivalry that lasted for many years. Numerous mountains were measured by painstaking methods and lots of difficult climbing. After Mitchell went missing, legendary mountain man Big Tom Wilson, for whom another Black Mountain peak was named, led the search party that found Mitchell's body at the base of a 40-foot (12-meter) waterfall, now named Mitchell Falls.

Geology

The geology of Mount Mitchell is complex. The rocks that make up the Black Mountains, part of the Blue Ridge Province of the southern Appalachian Mountains, are considered very old, at approximately 500–800 million years. These rocks originally formed on the seafloor of the Iapetus Ocean and were metamorphosed as they were pushed up during the formation of **Pangea**. At one time they were much higher but have eroded down to their present heights. Along with the adjacent Craggy Mountain range, the Black Mountains are part of a geological formation known as the **Ashe Metamorphic Suite** that we also discuss in the Elk Knob chapter of this book. This entire "package" is composed of rocks that have been metamorphosed by heat and pressure to varying degrees.

Many of the rocks commonly found on Mount Mitchell were formed from layers of sand, gravel, and silt, along with **basalt** and other volcanic rocks that were subjected to different temperatures and pressures as they were metamorphosed over time. These rock types and their composing **minerals** include **gneiss**, **schist**, **metagraywacke**, and **metaconglomerate**, all of which are defined in more detail in the glossary of this book. You can see these rock types along Mount Mitchell's trails.

One important mineral found here is kyanite, which appears as bluish-gray crystals and can be found along the length of the Black Mountain chain. Since kyanite and quartz are both very resistant to **weathering**, their presence helps explain why the Black Mountains did not erode as quickly as many of the surrounding mountains and, consequently, why they remain so tall. This also helps explain why Mount Mitchell is the highest peak east of the Mississippi River.

One theme that we continually visit throughout this book is the concept of change over time. Geologically that is most often regulated by weathering and erosion. In the field of ecology, we also must consider the biological forces at hand. All of these changes have an effect on community structure over time, so we call this **ecological succession**.

The state of the rocks on Mount Mitchell is evidence of the ecological succession occurring on the mountain, and the biological driver is usually the lichens. **Lichens** are often the primary organisms, or the **pioneer species**, that establish growth on rocks, and they are fascinating organisms. They appear to be a single organism, but scientists have known for many years that lichens are, in fact, a symbiotic relationship composed of different organisms. Until recently, it was believed this relationship was composed only of fungi and algae living together and benefiting one another, but in 2016, a young researcher discovered that another organism, a yeast, has secretly been part of this relationship all along. In this relationship, the alga photosynthesizes to make food, while the fungus takes in water from the atmosphere. The presence of the yeast appears to be associated with the production of chemicals that protect the lichen from **predators** and diseases.

As ecological succession continues, lichens release carbon dioxide, CO_2, which mixes with water to make a weak acid, carbonic acid, that slowly begins to eat away sections of the rock. Next, mosses grow in the small depressions made by the acid, where tiny bits of broken-down rock are accumulating as soil. Eventually, small ferns, flowers, and seedlings begin to take hold, breaking up the rocks further. **Organic matter** mixes with rock debris to form a nutrient-rich soil that supports the forest and encourages the growth of larger trees.

Topography and Elevation

Standing at 6,684 feet (2,037 meters), Mount Mitchell is the highest peak in the eastern United States. In fact, it is the highest peak east of Harney Peak in South Dakota. Mitchell is part of the 15-mile-long Black Mountain range that contains six of the ten highest peaks east of the Mississippi River. Prominent peaks include Clingman's Peak (6,571 feet [2,002 meters]); Mount Gibbes (6,571 feet [2,003 meters]); Mount Craig (6,648 feet [2,026 meter]); Big Tom (6,581 feet [2,006 meters]); Balsam Cone (6,596 feet [2,010 meters]); and Cattail Peak (6,584 feet [2,007 meters]).

Viewed from above, the range is shaped like the letter J with Mount Mitchell sitting at the beginning of the curve. The stem of the J is oriented north-south, forming a high range over which wind and moisture must pass. Air temperature drops 3 to 5°F (–16°C to –15°C) for every 1,000-foot (305-meter) elevation gain; a ratio known as the **adiabatic lapse rate**. As the air is forced up and over the Black Mountains, it cools and the moisture within it condenses, causing rain or snow primarily on the windward slope, which is the side from which the wind is coming. This is called the **orographic effect**, and it makes Mount Mitchell a cool place to be even on a hot day. It also helps explain why Mount Mitchell is enveloped in fog eight of every ten days. More importantly, the orographic effect is the primary reason for the large amount of precipitation Mount Mitchell receives annually.

Weather and Climate

Mount Mitchell often experiences extreme weather. High winds and ice storms are frequent, winters are long and cold, and the summer is brief with less than a three-month growing season. The record low temperature was recorded at –34°F (–37°C), while the record high was a balmy 81°F (27°C). The seasonal average is only 44°F (7°C), and snow flurries have been recorded in every month of the year. While Mount Mitchell averages close to 100 inches (254 centimeters) of snowfall per year, the total has exceeded that on many occasions. The greatest seasonal snowfall recorded was 172.5 inches (438 centimeters) in the winter of 1997–98, while the greatest single snowfall was 50 inches (127 centimeters) on March 12–14, 1993. It is not uncommon for snow to still be on the ground in May.

The highest wind speed ever recorded on Mitchell was 176 miles per hour (283 kilometers per hour). Most of the wind comes from the west/southwest/northwest. High winds carry ice crystals in the wintertime that sculpt trees as they grow. This

Figure 5-2. Welcome to Mount Mitchell. Photo by Mike Dunn.

results in the formation of flag trees, which have limbs growing predominantly on one side and pointing away from the dominant wind direction. Some trees grow low to the ground and spread out in a pattern known as krumholz formation. Growing low and spreading out allows the plant to create its own windbreak, and this helps protect the plants. Bacteria and other decomposing organisms thrive in warm, moist conditions. Since the temperature on Mount Mitchell tends to be so much cooler, decomposition, or the breakdown of organic matter, occurs rather slowly. Downed trees can remain on the ground not yet decomposed for over twenty-five years.

Ecological Communities

Elevation and slope orientation (north, south, east, west) combine to create conditions for different types of plant communities, as we discuss in other Mountain chapters. Mount Mitchell contains five distinctive ecological communities:

1. **Oak-Hickory Forests** are prevalent in drier areas below 3,500 feet (1,067 meters), with white oak (*Quercus alba*), red oak (*Quercus rubra*), white pine (*Pinus strobus*), and a variety of maples (*Acer* sp.).
2. **Cove Hardwood Forests** are found in moist areas such as valleys and drainages and below 4,500 feet (1,372 meters). Common species include American beech (*Fagus grandifolia*), sugar maple (*Acer saccharum*), tulip tree (*Liriodendron tulipifera*), red oak (*Quercus rubra*), and an abundance of rhododendron (*Rhododendron* sp.).

Figure 5-3. Spruce-Fir Forest at sunset. This scene shows mostly fir trees that have been affected by either the balsam wooly adelgid or acid deposition. Photo by Melissa Dowland.

3. **Northern Hardwood Forests** are found between 3,500 feet (1,067 meters) and 5,400 feet (1,646 meters) in North Carolina. Common species include yellow birch (*Betula alleghaniensis*), American beech (*Fagus grandifolia*), eastern hemlock (*Tsuga canadensis*), sugar maple (*Acer saccharum*), and Catawba rhododendron (*Rhododendron catawbiense*).
4. Two types of **Mountain Bald Communities** are found in the park between 4,600 feet (1,402 meters) and 6,200 feet (1,890 meters):
   a. **Grassy Balds**, composed of several grass species, sedges, mosses, and flowers, and
   b. **Heath Balds**, characterized by shrubs, such as Catawba rhododendron (*Rhododendron catawbiense*) and mountain laurel (*Kalmia latifolia*).
5. **Spruce-Fir Forests** consist of red spruce (*Picea reubens*) and Fraser fir (*Abies fraseri*) and tend to dominate at the top of Mount Mitchell between 5,200 and 5,500 feet (1,585–1,676 meters). These trees can be identified by comparing their characteristics. Firs tend to be softer with flat needles that have white lines on the bottom, and their cones are erect. Spruce needles are four-sided and spikey. The cones of red spruce tend to hang down.

Spruce-Fir Forests are among the most endangered communities in the southern Appalachians, as we discussed in Chapter 4, "Grandfather Mountain." Many fir trees have been killed by the **balsam woolly adelgid** (*Adelges piceae*), a small insect introduced from Europe in the early 1900s. When fir trees are infected, small cottonlike tufts develop on the trunks, branches, and twigs.

Acid Deposition

The woolly adelgid only attacks the fir trees, but in the 1970s and 1980s, the red spruce trees were also observed dying in large numbers, leading scientists to consider other explanations. This contributed to the theory of acid rain, a term later changed to acid deposition. New growth on trees appears to be particularly susceptible to the effects of acid deposition, where rain, fog, and snow carry the acids and then deposit them on the surrounding landscape. Typically, rainfall is slightly **acidic** due to the presence of carbonic acid formed from atmospheric carbon dioxide and water; however, precipitation in the form of rain, snow, and fog on Mount Mitchell tends to be much more acidic than usual. Human-produced pollutants from factories, power plants, and cars release sulfur dioxide and nitrogen oxides into the air that combine with water to form two acids: *nitric acid* and *sulfuric acid*.

Being bathed in acidic fog eight of ten days each year has a detrimental impact on anything living. Organisms tend to exist within a range of tolerance for a variety of abiotic, or nonliving, factors, including temperature, moisture, and acidity. They have trouble surviving when those factors are particularly high or particularly low, meaning they are outside the range of what they can tolerate. This limits the type of organisms that can live in the area. Organisms that are sensitive to higher acidity levels, such as snails, crayfish, and bullfrogs, have difficulty living and reproducing in such extreme environments. Mount Mitchell has been the subject of much research on acid deposition due to its extreme environment, and there is some evidence that the Clean Air Act is making a difference.

A Very Special Resident: The Spruce-Fir Moss Spider

Even though it is in the same family as tarantulas, the spruce-fir moss spider (*Microhexura montivaga*) appears far less intimidating, since it is only 0.12–0.16 inches (3–4 millimeters) long. Listed as an endangered species, these spiders live in moss-covered rocks in humid, high-elevation forest ecosystems. They have been found on Mount Mitchell, Grandfather Mountain, and Roan Mountain. They are rare on Mount Mitchell today, and there is debate as to whether they have been extirpated there, meaning no longer surviving locally. These spiders construct small cylindrical webs among the rocks, but arachnologists, scientists who study spiders, have not determined if they use their webs to catch food, since that action has never been observed.

The spiders depend on the forest mosses for habitat and food. Springtails live in these mosses and are an abundant and preferred food source for the spruce-fir moss spider. Springtails look like tiny insects but are no longer classified by scientists as insects; true insects have external mouthparts, but springtails have internal mouthparts. Today, they are classified instead as hexapods, meaning six legs, because this is the classification for all arthropods with six legs, despite the orientation of their mouthparts. Since many mature spruce and fir trees have been killed by the balsam woolly adelgid, acid deposition, and other factors, the forest **canopy**, or the top layer of a forest, has fewer trees present to block the harsh sun. In turn, this has allowed increased sunlight to dry out the mossy patches on rocks, thereby destroying the spiders' natural habitat.

Bringing us back briefly to the concept of island biogeography, this is one of the issues that organisms face when living on an "island." A limited amount of ideal environment can be rapidly affected by any outside factor, such as acid deposition or invasive species. Island biogeography states that both the size of the island and its degree of isolation affect the rate of immigration of species, where new individuals might come in to repopulate an area. If current residents begin to disappear from the island but immigration rates onto the island are too low, species numbers dwindle rapidly, leading to direct and often devastating impacts on the local food web. Many organisms live in a delicate balance with their environment, where disturbance can lead to extirpation, which is local disappearance, or even **extinction**, meaning global disappearance.

Before You Go

Mount Mitchell is located 30 miles (48 kilometers) northeast of Asheville on the Blue Ridge Parkway at mile marker 355. The park road branches off the parkway and ascends to the parking lot at the top, passing the ranger station (at Steppes Gap), the Mount Mitchell restaurant, and the Mount Mitchell campground along the way. The Mount Mitchell museum, concession stand, picnic area, and bathrooms are located next to the parking lot. A paved trail leads to the observation deck on top of the mountain and the Balsam Nature Trail, a short interpretive trail, loops back to the parking lot. Visitors should bring extra layers of clothes, rainwear, water, snacks, and a warm hat, even when it is warm at the base of the mountain, as conditions can change rapidly and unexpectedly at the top of the mountain.

The Craggy Gardens Picnic Area and Visitor Center are a short drive from Mount Mitchell and make for a nice stop on your adventure.

References and Resources

Banks, S. "Forest Response to the US 1990 Clean Air Act: The Southern Spruce-Fir Ecosystem," *American Journal of Plant Sciences* 5, no. 3 (2014): 372–86.

Schwarzkopf, S. Kent. *The History of Mt. Mitchell and the Black Mountains: Exploration, Development, and Preservation*. Raleigh: Division of Archives and History, North Carolina Department of Cultural Resources, 1985.

Silver, Timothy. *Mount Mitchell and the Black Mountains: An Environmental History of the Highest Peaks in Eastern America*. Chapel Hill: University of North Carolina Press, 2003.

Skeate, Stewart. *A Nature Guide to Northwest North Carolina*. Boone, N.C.: Parkway Publishers, 2004.

Spribille, T., V. Tuovinen, P. Resl, D. Vanderpool, H. Wolinski, M. C. Aime, K. Schneider, E. Stabentheiner, M. Toome-Heller, G. Thor, H. Mayrhofer, H. Johannesson, and J. P. McCutcheon. "Basidiomycete Yeasts in the Cortex of Ascomycete Macrolichens." *Science* 353 (2016): 488–92.

Website: http://www.ncparks.gov/mount-mitchell-state-park
Contact: phone: (828) 675-4611
Address: 2388 State Highway 128, Burnsville, N.C. 28714
GPS Coordinates: N 35°46.14, W 82°16.44

CHAPTER 6

The Cradle of Forestry in America

A Legacy of Conservation Education

CINDY CARPENTER

SCIENTIFIC FIELDS OF STUDY: *Forest Management, Forest Ecology*

Sweeping 'round old Pisgah's crown thick with woods and meadows
Lies a sunlit land on which stretch the long-drawn shadows
'Tis a land that's fair to see, 'tis a woodland that will be,
Dear to us eternally, 'tis our Alma Mater.

These lyrics to a song from America's first forestry school paint a picture of an area in Transylvania County known today as the Cradle of Forestry in America. The historic Biltmore Forest School, operating here from 1898 to 1909 when the land was part of George W. Vanderbilt's Biltmore Estate, used these forests and fields as its outdoor classroom. Today, education is still valued here, with many opportunities for people of all ages to enjoy learning in a forest setting.

The Cradle of Forestry in America is a place of people and nature, history and the future. In 1968 Congress set aside this 6,500-acre tract of the Pisgah National Forest nestled below Mount Pisgah and the Blue Ridge Parkway to commemorate the beginning of forestry and forest education in America and to stimulate interest in and understanding of forests, forest management, and forest conservation. A large part of the established Cradle of Forestry acreage lies in the scenic 3,200-foot (975-meter) elevation of the Pink Beds Valley. The site's history gives North Carolina the honor of being "First in Forestry." Today it is managed by the U.S. Forest Service and the Cradle of Forestry in America Interpretive Association.

Since its beginning, forestry has been a profession that requires the integration of two important factors over time: (1) understanding the conditions of the land

Figure 6-1. The School of Forestry. Photo by Gustave A. Schulze (BFS 1909); National Forests of North Carolina Historic Photographs, courtesy of the D. H. Ramsey Library, Special Collections, University of North Carolina at Asheville.

and (2) understanding the demands of society. In order to explain this approach to the science of forestry, let's first discuss the history of the land now called the Cradle of Forestry; then we'll explore today's opportunities, and finally we'll complete this chapter with some thoughts about the future possibilities for forestry in North Carolina.

Before the Biltmore Forest School opened and America's first scientific forestry efforts began in the area, the mountains surrounding the Pink Beds Valley provided a natural corral for stock growers, or cattle farmers, who used the valley as summer range for their cattle. Many families raised children and tended to small farms and livestock here, working hard in this remote valley with the romantic name. Mystery

Figure 6-2. Biltmore forestry students on horses outside Pink Beds school building, 1906. Photo by Carl Alwin Schenck; National Forests of North Carolina Historic Photographs, U.S. Forest Service Photo, courtesy of the D. H. Ramsey Library, Special Collections, University of North Carolina at Asheville.

surrounds the origins of the Pink Beds name, but most stories trace it to flowers. Some records credit the pink flowering shrub mountain laurel (*Kalmia latifolia*) with providing the name for this beautiful part of North Carolina. Another record, a column in the July 22, 1966, *Asheville Citizen* newspaper written by renowned western North Carolina author and historian John Parris, cites memories of old-timers describing pink flowers of downy phlox (*Phlox amoena*) that once carpeted the entire floor of the valley, giving it the name Pink Beds. Parris's sources told him that cattle grazing in the valley since before the Civil War had destroyed the phlox's pink carpet by the year 1900.

In 1891, George Vanderbilt did something no large landowner in America had ever done: he hired a forester to care for his land and to use it for growing trees as a business enterprise. Gifford Pinchot, the first American to study forestry, used his knowledge gained in Europe to guide Biltmore's forestry efforts from 1892 to 1895. In 1905, he became the first chief of the new United States Forest Service. With Pinchot's encouragement, Vanderbilt purchased land far beyond his Biltmore Forest, naming the area Pisgah Forest after the dominant peak he could see from the Biltmore House, Mount Pisgah. This land included the Pink Beds Valley and enlarged the

Biltmore Estate to some 120,000 acres. Gifford Pinchot and Dr. Carl Alwin Schenck, who succeeded Pinchot as George Vanderbilt's head forester in 1895, saw a forest different from the one we see today. Back then a quarter of the trees were American chestnut trees (*Castanea dentata*). With so many chestnut trees in the forests at that time, Schenck's favorite tree, the tulip tree (*Liriodendron tulipifera*), was not as common as it is today.

Schenck was born, raised, and educated in Germany, studying the principles of forestry. The Alps in Germany are oriented west to east on the southern border, rather than north to south like our Appalachian Mountains, so the Alps have served as a barrier for millions of years, blocking the movement of many species between southern and northern Europe. For this reason, fewer tree species grow in the European forests studied by Schenck. Imagine his amazement at the forests of Pisgah, where so many species grow together. One of Schenck's challenges in North Carolina involved harvesting and selling trees from some areas of Pisgah and planting them in other areas for the purposes of controlling erosion and improving forest health. Recognizing the need for a forestry school, Schenck founded the Biltmore Forest School in 1898. The Pink Beds became the school's summer campus. His students, basking in his knowledge, energy, and passion for the land, became an able and essential workforce. They tended seedling nurseries, measured trees, surveyed forest stands, calculated timber values, and planned roads in Pisgah Forest so wood could be transported to sawmills and markets.

Early in the 1900s, before the United States had passed laws requiring imported plants to be quarantined, disaster struck our nation's eastern forests. A virulent fungus called chestnut blight (*Cryphonectria parasitica*) was accidentally introduced from Asia around 1904, producing oozing cankers on American chestnut trees and killing them before they reached maturity. Fungal spores were spread rapidly by tree-dwelling animals and insects, so by 1950 the American chestnut no longer existed as a forest tree. Today some chestnut sprouts survive from root systems of trees that died from the blight, but those sprouts will never reach maturity because of the persistent fungal infection. Many forest scientists, concerned citizens, and organizations have been looking for healthy chestnuts in the wild to use for genetic experiments that might allow for the breeding of blight-resistant chestnut trees. The Cradle of Forestry is proud to be one of the test sites for planting these genetically enhanced chestnut trees, in hopes that they can survive to full maturity. The Cradle of Forestry is also a conservation area for Carolina and eastern hemlocks (*Tsuga caroliniana* and *T. canadensis*, respectively), trees Schenck knew well. In the past decade, many of North Carolina's hemlocks have succumbed to another accidental infestation from Asia, the **hemlock woolly adelgid** (*Adelges tsugae*), one of several insects that are threatening the health of North Carolina's forests today. See Chapter 17 for more discussion on the hemlock woolly adelgid and Chapter 5 for a related insect infestation, the **balsam woolly adelgid** (*Adelges piceae*).

So how did Pisgah Forest become the Pisgah National Forest public land we can all enjoy today? In 1909, Schenck resigned as Vanderbilt's forester. The land no longer had a forester to tend to it. In 1911 Congress passed the Weeks Law, enabling the federal government to purchase private land. After Vanderbilt's death in 1914, his widow, Edith, offered Pisgah Forest for sale. After a team examined the land, 87,600 acres became America's first national forest east of the Mississippi. It was renamed the Pisgah National Forest, and Schenck was thrilled. Back in Germany, he wrote

Figure 6-3. The Case family at Jenny Lodge, built by Schenck. It has been restored and is now on the Biltmore Trail at the Cradle of Forestry. Photo by Gustave A. Schulze (BFS 1909); National Forests of North Carolina Historic Photographs, courtesy of the D. H. Ramsey Library, Special Collections, University of North Carolina at Asheville.

in his 1955 memoir, "Thus was my beloved Pisgah Forest saved from dissection and destruction."

Verne Rhoades, a 1906 Biltmore Forest School graduate and one of the forest examiners, became the first forest supervisor for the Pisgah and oversaw it until 1925. His devotion to Schenck and the Biltmore Forest School's legacy led him to inspire the creation of the Cradle of Forestry in America as a place where forest visitors of all ages can learn about the land's history, the importance of forestry, and the ever-growing science that supports the care and use of forests.

Today the Cradle of Forestry in America continues Schenck's legacy of conservation education. Visitors are welcomed in the Forest Discovery Center off US 276, about 14 miles (22 kilometers) from Brevard and 4 miles (6 kilometers) south of the Blue Ridge Parkway. Native plants and their pollinators thrive in the lawn-to-meadow conversion areas surrounding the parking lots. Indoor hands-on exhibits interpret the many benefits of forests, the wonders of a forest ecosystem, and complexities of managing ever-changing forests for a diverse and increasingly urbanized society. For example, the exhibit *Changing Climate, Changing Forests* interprets scientists' efforts to understand a changing climate's effects on forests and describes

Figure 6-4. Biltmore forestry students and Schenck measuring logs. Photo by Verne Rhoades (BFS 1906); National Forests of North Carolina Historic Photographs, courtesy of the D. H. Ramsey Library, Special Collections, University of North Carolina at Asheville.

everyday actions people can take to make a difference. A terrarium depicts a forest wetland with live amphibians. The *Fire in the Forest* exhibit traces the use of fire as a tool from Native Americans to today's land managers. Visitors can experience a firefighting helicopter "ride" and pick up "Scientist Cards" and other information related to forest research. Friendly hosts are available to answer questions or to help you find answers yourself.

More than sixty species of trees and shrubs, including the lovely mountain laurel, grow along the Cradle's nearly 4.0 miles (6.4 kilometers) of paved, wheelchair-accessible trails. Even more species thrive on surrounding mountain slopes and in beaver **wetlands** along the nearby 5-mile (8-kilometer) Pink Beds Trail that starts at the Pink Beds Picnic Area outside the developed part of the Cradle of Forestry. This diversity results from the southern Appalachians being the southern-most edge of where conditions are favorable for many northern species to grow and the northern-most edge for many southern species. Some are found only in the southern Appalachian region. What an exciting and amazing forest to study.

Observe the many different patterns and shapes of plants along the trails. Compare what grows in shade with what you find in open, sunny areas. Listen and look for birds, arthropods (like insects, spiders, and crustaceans), and evidence of other animals that find suitable habitats to forage and raise young. Enjoy the sights and sounds of streams along the way. Think about how the forest may change over time when you see young trees growing next to standing dead or dying trees and even fallen logs. Check the availability of guided trail tours to enrich your understanding of what you experience at the Cradle.

The Cradle of Forestry in America is part of North Carolina's Birding Trail. Trail-side plant diversity, open areas, rhododendron and laurel thickets, and forest layers provide habitat for shrub-loving **understory** birds and **canopy** dwellers as well. Nature-oriented events during the year include guided bird walks, pond explorations, and programs designed for fun as well as for increasing awareness of our forests and environmental issues.

Along the 1.3-mile (2.1-kilometer) Forest Festival Trail you can learn about Schenck's experiments, successes, failures, and goals for Vanderbilt's vast Pisgah Forest. A small seedling nursery and tree plantations represent the forester's efforts to control erosion and learn which tree species would be best suited to plant so abandoned farms could be restored to healthy, growing forests. These growing exhibits sometimes change. In 2015, hundreds of shortleaf pine seedlings were planted in a plot along the trail to assist Forest Service scientists' research on restoring this species to North Carolina's forests.

Also along this trail, an antique portable sawmill exhibit and horse-drawn road graders illustrate Schenck's methods of transporting timber to markets in nearby towns. You will see a 1914 Climax logging locomotive exhibit, complete with railroad track, a log loader, and log cars. Climb aboard the little train, ring the bell, and imagine the days in the early 1900s when the sounds of steam engines winding through the mountains were commonplace as people found employment with logging companies. Forest conservation took a backseat to providing a growing nation with wood and local citizens with jobs. Now environmental laws, forest policies, and continued understanding of forest ecosystems through research protect water quality, soil, and sensitive and rare species while providing forest products and services, including recreation, for today's and future generations.

Imagine living in the Pink Beds Valley as a farmer or a forestry student while you explore cabins, a one-room schoolhouse, a blacksmith shop, and a commissary along the Cradle of Forestry's 1.0-mile (1.6-kilometer) Biltmore Campus Trail. Think about how people lived close to the land's natural resources in those bygone days, resources we still depend on today. In the early part of the twentieth century, folks knew where their food and water came from, carried water from streams, lived without today's modern conveniences, and traveled on foot, on horseback, or by wagon. Woodcutting was a constant chore as trees provided heat for homes and cooking, light, shelter, barns, fences, and more. People had skill to work with the technology of their day and knew through experience which tree species should be used for specific purposes. The forest around them gave them life and livelihood.

Foresters think about the future, as do all conservation-minded people. The Cradle of Forestry in America offers a look at society's relationship with forests and natural resources through time. Like the people who lived long ago in the Pink Beds, your generation needs clean water, clean air, healthy forests, and the products and enjoyment they offer, just as will generations in the future. Schenck understood this as he devoted himself to forestry education in America. Though some of his students chose to pursue other careers, he knew learning about forests grounded his graduates, making them better-informed citizens. As an elderly man in his annual letter to his "Biltmore Boys," he directed them to "send the kids to the woods! They are better for them than classrooms built of bricks!" The Cradle of Forestry in America invites you to enjoy its "classroom" in your Pisgah National Forest.

Before You Go

Create your own forest stories along the Forest Discovery Trail, where a different forest view waits around every curve. You will get good exercise as you explore and observe and can rest on benches along the way as you take in the forest scenery. Consider taking along a notebook, to draw or write about your explorations.

The Cradle of Forestry in America is open daily from early April to early November and is wheelchair accessible. A small fee is charged that supports visitor services at the site. The Giving Tree Gift Shop offers forest-related books, trail maps, clothing, and local crafts. A café is often open for lunch. Check the website below or call for information on daily activities, planned programs, events, and details. Even driving the highway to and from this serene location is enjoyable. US 276 is the Forest Heritage National Scenic Byway that was created to help us view the often-unseen forest, thereby allowing us to make connections between forests and our everyday lives.

References and Resources

Forest History Society, https://foresthistory.org. Accessed November 3, 2018.

Our Forest Tells Stories, Come Listen: The Cradle of Forestry in America, Pisgah National Forest. U.S. Forest Service, n.d., https://www.fs.usda.gov/Internet/FSE_DOCUMENTS/fseprd522170.pdf. Accessed November 3, 2018.

Schenck, Carl A. "The Dawn of Private Forestry in America: Recollections of a Forester Covering the Years 1895 to 1914." Manuscript, Library, and Archives. Forest History Society, Durham, N.C.

U.S. Department of Agriculture. U.S. Forest Service, https://www.fs.fed.us. Accessed November 3, 2018.

Website: https://cradleofforestry.com

CONTACT:

April through November: Cradle of Forestry Heritage Site—phone: (828) 877-3130; email: cradleprograms@cfaia.org.

December through March: Pisgah Ranger Station—phone: (828) 877-3265.

Address: 11250 Pisgah Highway, Pisgah Forest, N.C. 28768

GPS Coordinates: N 35°21.033, W 82°46.717

CHAPTER 7

Mount Jefferson State Natural Area

APRIL C. SMITH

SCIENTIFIC FIELDS OF STUDY: *Geology, Forest Ecology, Ornithology*

In northwestern North Carolina, near the Tennessee border, an unusual mountaintop rises 1,600 feet (488 meters) from between two forks of the New River, reaching an altitude of 4,684 feet (1,428 meters) above sea level. Early Native Americans cherished this mountain and surrounding land as bountiful hunting grounds. In the early part of the eighteenth century, the mountain was called Panther Mountain because of a legend that told of a man-eating panther roaming the hillsides. In 1749, Thomas Jefferson and his father, Peter Jefferson, owned land nearby and surveyed the area near the North Carolina–Virginia border. Legend has it that during the Civil War (1861–65), the caves under this mountain served as a hideout for escaped slaves who were traveling on the Underground Railroad. Cut off from much of civilization by the surrounding landscape, this area was once called "The Lost Province," where a culture of gatherers, including Daniel Boone, would search forested areas for botanical treasures to sell, such as ginseng, sassafras, snakeroot, and catnip. The history surrounding this peak makes it a unique site in western North Carolina.

In the 1930s, a short road of less than 2.0 miles (3.2 kilometers) was built to the mountain summit, revealing its recreation potential. In 1939, a donation of 26 acres of land by local landowners made the mountain a public park, and the state began maintaining the road. Many locals wanted the local park to become a state park, owned and maintained by the state of North Carolina, but at the time the state required land to be at least 400 acres before it could be considered for state park status. Local citizens worked endlessly for more than sixteen years to acquire a 300-acre donation and raise the money to purchase another 164 acres, making the park eligible for state park status. In October 1956, the park was named Mount Jefferson State Park after the legendary landowners and surveyors, Thomas Jefferson and his father, Peter.

Mount Jefferson is part of the Amphibolite range, the tremendous rocky peaks that once dominated western North Carolina. Joining Mount Jefferson in this range are Three Top Mountain, Elk Knob, and Bluff Mountain. You may recognize sev-

Figure 7-1. View from Mount Jefferson. Photo by Vicki Randolph.

eral of these names from other chapters in this book. The massive peaks that once formed the Amphibolite Mountains were estimated to have loomed 15,000 feet (4,572 meters) above sea level at one time but were eroded away by wind, rain, and rivers over millions of years. The rocks that remain now are the ones that were more resistant to **weathering** and erosion, and the main type of rock found here is **amphibolite gneiss**. In Chapters 1 and 5, we discussed that gneiss is a **metamorphic** rock composed of distinct bands of alternating light and dark **minerals** after exposure to intense heat and pressure. Amphibolite gneiss, which contains the mineral amphibole, is usually coarse-grained so that you can see the minerals with your eye and has a dark coloring.

The tops of the Amphibolite range no longer appear as pointy, jagged peaks; now from a distance they look to be soft and mostly rounded and covered in forests that are dark green in the summer and various shades of red and gold in the fall. But each of these mountains in the Amphibolite range has something unique to teach us about how scientific research can and should be interdisciplinary, working across many different fields of science. The natural world is a beautiful blend of plants, animals, rocks, soils, and water, so research in one field of science will not always give you the entire story; however, research performed by many scientists, such as biologists, botanists, geologists, hydrologists, entomologists, and others, can be combined to help us learn about different facets of the Earth and the environment. This collection of scientific knowledge helps us piece together a puzzle that

Figure 7-2. Ranger Tom Randolph giving a presentation from the cloud-surrounded peak, another example of thermal inversion. Photo by Vicki Randolph.

began millions, or even billions, of years ago. For our investigation of Mount Jefferson, we're going to start with one simple question: "What is the connection, or the **correlation**, between amphibolite gneiss rock and songbirds who winter in South America?" It just so happens that Mount Jefferson State Natural Area has the answer. Let's begin with a discussion about the rock, and then we'll focus on the birds.

We've already mentioned that Mount Jefferson was once part of a very tall range of mountains that eroded away over millions of years leaving behind amphibolite gneiss rock; however, what we are most concerned with on Mount Jefferson is the soil. Where does the soil come from? As rocks are broken into smaller and smaller pieces, mostly by plant roots and by water freezing in cracks and expanding, pieces of rock break off and mix with decaying **organic matter**, like grass, flowers, bits of trees, and dead animals that fall to the ground. Most mountain soils are rather **acidic** (pH<7). The special thing about the soil on Mount Jefferson is that the weathered bits of amphibolite rock are rich in nutrients, especially iron and magnesium, and the pH is circumneutral, meaning closer to neutral and, therefore, slightly more **basic** than the typical acidic soils of the southern Appalachians. This makes the soil ideal for growing certain types of trees. Please see Chapter 3 and Figure 3-1 (p. 32) for more detailed information on pH.

Above 4,000 feet (1,219 meters), oak trees mixed with immature chestnuts dominate the south, east, and west slopes. Growing on the north slopes of Mount Jefferson

Figure 7-3. Amphibolite: the rocks that make Mount Jefferson an important ecological haven. Photo by Vicki Randolph.

is a healthy **Rich Cove Forest**. A Rich Cove Forest is an incredibly beautiful example of a southern Appalachian forest, found at high altitude and rich in large tree species. The Rich Cove Forest is often called the most diverse type of forest community in North America with up to twenty-five different types of **canopy** trees and numerous **understory** flowering trees. Mount Jefferson's cove forest consists of yellow birch, red maple, basswood, and tulip trees in the canopy and mountain ash, prairie willow, and black huckleberry in the understory. The herb gatherers of Daniel Boone's time wandered this forest gathering herbs from the forest floor. The trees that live on the north-facing slope of Mount Jefferson are gnarled and dwarfed because of the cold winds and icy winter conditions that exist above 4,000 feet (1,219 meters) on the mountain. Even the tall canopy trees that would be larger in warm weather conditions only reach heights of about 20 feet (6 meters) at the top of the mountain.

Mount Jefferson once had an abundance of mature chestnut trees (*Castanea dentata*). The wood of the chestnut tree is rot-resistant, so it was a highly prized resource for early settlers who wanted to build homes, stables, and fences. The chestnut tree also produces meaty, delicious nuts that were used for food by both humans and other animals. Surely most of you have heard the holiday song lyric "Chestnuts roasting on an open fire." Well, it's not as easy to find those naturally growing chestnuts these days. In the early twentieth century, a disease known as chestnut blight was accidentally introduced to America from Asia. Chestnut blight is caused by a fungus that enters wounds in a tree's bark, causing cankers, or infected areas where the bark splits. Cankers were first spotted on chestnuts in New York City in 1904 after a shipment of trees arrived from an infected nursery overseas. More than 100 years later, most of the chestnut trees in the natural growing range, which extends along the east coast of the United States from Maine to Alabama, are infected with the blight and will never reach maturity. This is a good example of what happens when a **nonnative** disease, or one that has not originated locally, is introduced and there are no natural ways to control it, such as with local **predators** or with natural chemical resistances. Today, the chestnuts growing on the mountain peak are smaller and more bushlike. They will not reach maturity, but instead their roots will continue to propagate the disease in future sprouts. See Chapter 6, "The Cradle of Forestry in America," for more information on chestnut blight.

Now let's turn our attention to the birds. Mount Jefferson provides superb habitat for many bird species that are threatened or endangered, including the scarlet tanager, yellow-bellied sapsucker, Canada warbler, black-throated blue warbler, and ruffed grouse, among others, but particularly the golden-winged warbler (*Vermivora chrysoptera*). Most of these birds are species that spend their summers primarily in northern states or in Canada and their winters in South America. However, a very small section of the higher elevations of the Appalachians provides the perfect habitat for them as well, allowing them to thrive in the lower latitudes of North Carolina. Since the 1960s, the Appalachians have lost 98 percent of their golden-winged warbler **population**. The reasons are not entirely understood, but scientists believe that a loss of habitat combined with competition and hybridization with another species, the blue-winged warbler, may be to blame.

Now let's revisit our question from earlier in this chapter: "What is the correlation between amphibolite gneiss rock and songbirds who winter in South America?" Think about this population of songbirds living in a forest, flitting from tree to tree, and think about how and where the trees are growing. Here's your answer:

> Mount Jefferson has recently been named a Globally Significant Important Bird Area for golden-winged warblers because the mountainside is composed of amphibolite rock that, when broken down, creates nutrient-rich circumneutral soil that allows a Rich Cove Forest to grow at an ideal altitude, thus providing the perfect habitat for this rapidly declining bird species.

In general, golden-winged warblers prefer young forests with a high degree of deciduous forest cover at high elevation; in North Carolina, that elevation is greater than 2,000 feet (609 meters). There also are indications that this preference may be associated with specific botanical species, such as orchardgrass (*Dactylis glomerata*), green ash (*Fraxinus pennsylvanica*) seedlings and saplings, and black locust (*Robinia pseudoacacia*) saplings. This type of habitat is not plentiful in the Appalachians, but Mount Jefferson provides that perfect combination of "home" for the golden-winged warbler.

It is because of these types of species-specific dependencies on natural environments, where species depend on specific circumstances for survival, that ecological studies become complicated. By combining knowledge from the geology of the mountain with ecological principles, bird studies, and plant studies, researchers were able to discover this fascinating relationship between the birds and the rocks.

Before You Go

Mount Jefferson State Natural Area is in Ashe County, North Carolina, north of Boone on US 221. Any time of year is a great time to visit the mountain, but the fall colors are always a treat to see. If you're visiting to look for the golden-winged warbler, they are away in South America for the winter. However, you can join in for the Christmas Bird Count in mid-December if you're interested in other bird populations such as cardinals, nuthatches, pileated woodpeckers, turkeys, and red-headed woodpeckers. Contact the park office for more information (see below).

The rangers at Mount Jefferson are known for their community involvement, and they love to lead interesting and informative hikes. Visit the North Carolina State Parks website to find more information.

References and Resources

Anagnostakis, Sandra. "Revitalization of the Majestic Chestnut: Chestnut Blight Disease." *APSnet Features*, https://doi: 10.1094/APSnetFeature-2000-1200. Accessed November 3, 2018.

Bakermans M., J. Larkin, and S. B. Swarthout. *Best Management Practices for Golden-winged Warbler Habitat in Deciduous Forests of the Appalachians*. The Golden-winged Warbler working group, http://www.gwwa.org/resources/GWWA-Habitat-Appalachian-forest-130808_lo-res.pdf. Accessed November 3, 2018.

"Important Bird Area: Amphibolite Mountains IBA." North Carolina Audubon Society, http://nc.audubon.org/conservation/amphibolite-mountains-iba. Accessed November 3, 2018.

"Mount Jefferson State Park." State Parks Website, http://www.stateparks.com/mount_jefferson.html. Accessed November 4, 2018.

Neufeld, Rob. "Visiting Our Past: People in Lost Provinces Were Herb-Gatherers." *USA Today*, September 13, 2015, Citizen Times, http://www.citizen-times.com/story/life/2015/09/13/visiting-past-people-lost-provinces-herb-gatherers/72205468/. Accessed November 3, 2018.

Patton, L. L., D. S. Maehr, J. E. Duchamp, S. Fei, J. W. Gassett, and J. L. Larkin. "Do the Golden-winged Warbler and Blue-winged Warbler Exhibit Species-Specific Differences in Their Breeding Habitat Use?" *Avian Conservation and Ecology—Écologie et conservation des oiseaux* 5, no. 2 (2010), http://dx.doi.org/10.5751/ACE-00392-050202. Accessed November 4, 2018.

Roth, A. M., R. W. Rohrbaugh, T. Will, and D. A. Buehler, eds. *Golden-winged Warbler Status Review and Conservation Plan*. 2012, http://www.gwwa.org. Accessed November 4, 2018.

Website: https://www.ncparks.gov/mount-jefferson-state-natural-area
Contact: phone: (336) 246-9653; email: mount.jefferson@ncparks.gov
Address: 1481 Mt. Jefferson State Park Road, West Jefferson, N.C. 28694
GPS Coordinates: N 36°24.12, W 81°28.2

CHAPTER 8

Blowing Rock Gneiss

Interpreting the Geologic History of a Rock Outcrop

STEVEN J. HAGEMAN

SCIENTIFIC FIELDS OF STUDY: *Geology, Tectonics*

Approximately 1.2 billion years ago, in the Middle Proterozoic Era, the rock under which Blowing Rock, North Carolina, now sits was undergoing a drastic transformation. The preexisting rock, also called the parent rock or the **protolith**, was being deeply buried beneath the Earth, where it was exposed to intense heat and pressure from the overlying rocks, causing a dramatic physical and chemical change to become a new type of rock. The new **metamorphic** rocks remained buried deep underground for hundreds of millions of years, while aboveground, the Earth's crust was very active geologically. In the Mountain Geology section (p. 10), we discuss the repeated continental collisions and the formation of the Appalachian Mountain System as it was **uplifted** gradually when North Africa slowly crashed into North America, forming the supercontinent **Pangea**.

Since then, the Appalachian region has been impacted by **weathering** and **erosion**, where wind and water gradually wore down rock surfaces to expose rock underneath. As the surface rocks were eroded away over the past 250 million years, deeply buried rocks moved up to partially take their place, and this was the first time these rocks near Blowing Rock had seen the light of day since they were formed 1.2 billion years ago.

This rock is named Blowing Rock Gneiss because it was originally described in the town of Blowing Rock, a few miles up US 321. As discussed previously in Chapter 1, "The Rock Garden," a **gneiss** (pronounced "nice") is a metamorphic rock composed of different **mineral** layers that were created or formed during exposure to intense heat and pressure. This process usually causes two main things to happen: (1) First, a rotation occurs of individual grains and crystals in the rock to align perpendicular, or at a right angle, to the direction of pressure. (2) Second, nearby minerals with the same composition come together to form larger crystals, in some

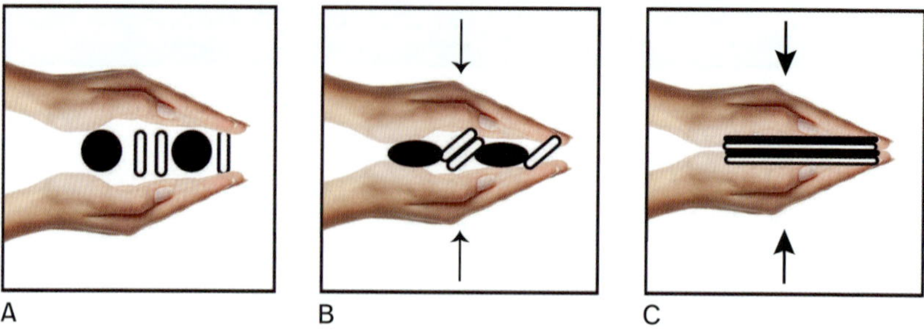

Figure 8-1. Rock A is your protolith, or parent rock (A). During metamorphism, pressure rotates and aligns the grains (B). Pressure combined with heat flattens the grains, and the results are a layered metamorphic texture (C). Illustrations by Steven Hageman.

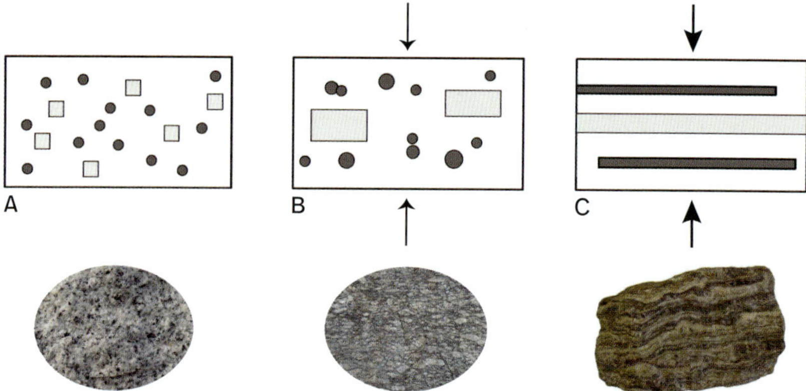

Figure 8-2. (A) Granite protolith: This is the original rock with the three minerals. (B) Augen gneiss: During metamorphism, crystals grow larger and start to group. (C) Gneiss: After intense metamorphism, minerals segregate into layers. Illustrations by Steven Hageman.

cases forming layers or bands. In Figure 8-1, see a model of the effects of pressure and heat.

Now, compare A, B, and C in Figure 8-2 to A, B, and C in Figure 8-1. In Figure 8-2, white represents very small mineral crystals, small black dots and larger light squares represent slightly larger mineral crystals, and arrows represent direction of pressure.

When these metamorphic processes occur at a large scale where you can see the alignment and banding at arm's length, geologists call the rock a gneiss (Figure 8-2C). The Blowing Rock Gneiss is a special kind of gneiss, called an augen gneiss (Figure 8-2B). Augen is German for "eyes." Up close these may look like white eyes looking at you, or from a distance the augens may look like large snowflakes on the rock.

You are almost ready to investigate the rocks up close. As you are examining the Blowing Rock Gneiss and its minerals, you will likely wonder how to tell the different minerals apart. Geologists use six characteristics to define a mineral: color, hard-

Figure 8-3. Exposure of the Blowing Rock Gneiss on US 321. Examples of major rock types are labeled C for the felsic rock and B for the mafic rock. The rest of the rock, black with white spots labeled A, is the augen gneiss. Labels 1 and 2 are locations for cross-cutting observations that help determine the relative ages of rocks. Photo by Steven Hageman.

ness, streak, luster, cleavage, and **fracture**. (1) Color is the first and most obvious; (2) hardness is a mineral's resistance to scratching. The scale to measure hardness, the Mohs scale, ranges from 1 to 10, with talc being a 1 and diamond being a 10. Glass has a hardness of approximately 6–7. (3) Streak refers to the color of powder left when the mineral is rubbed across a porcelain plate. (4) Luster is the way a mineral reflects light. Some descriptions of luster include dull, metallic, silky, oily, or brilliant. (5) Both cleavage and fracture refer to how a mineral breaks. Cleavage is the tendency for a mineral to break along smooth, flat surfaces, while fracture refers to any other kind of break in the mineral.

Now that you know a little about basic geology and the Blowing Rock Gneiss, you are ready to get up close and personal. See directions at the end of the chapter in the "Before you Go" section. Welcome to Blowing Rock, North Carolina. As you read through the information below, following the detailed instructions for finding rocks and identifying minerals will help you better understand the geology of the region, as well as how geologists work to solve similar scientific mysteries. This adventure is not physically challenging. You will merely be finding rocks and making observations, but the content presents advanced geologic concepts and theories. While these instructions have been designed for individuals who are interested in "digging a little deeper" into North Carolina's geology, they can be tailored to beginner geologists as well. Beginners should read through the steps below ahead of time and end their adventure with Step 5.

A note before exploring: Geologists are always careful to check the stability of exposed rock faces before approaching them. Look for loose rock and debris above you, and look for signs of recent rock falls at your feet. When in doubt, do not approach a rock face!

Step 1. Standing in the parking area shown in Figure 8-3, face the rock outcrop, and from a distance observe the following:

A Most of the rock is black with white spots.
B To the right side there are large bands that form black-green belts.
C There are smaller, irregular bands that are light colored or white.

These are going to be the three major rock types you will investigate during your geology exploration. Notice that they are all within the Blowing Rock Gneiss.

Step 2. Move closer to the rocks, and on the ground you will find parts of these rocks scattered about. Collect three rock samples from the ground between the parking area and the rock wall. Select one sample to represent each rock type above. They should be large enough to see details but small enough to fit in your hand. The white rocks will be smaller and less common, but you can find them when you look carefully.

Rock A black with white spots
Rock B black-green rock
Rock C white/gray rock

As you make observations for each of these rocks, remember that rocks are made of a combination of minerals, whereas minerals are made of a specific composition of chemical elements, with a specific arrangement of atoms, or a crystal structure.

Step 3. Rock A, the augen gneiss background rock, is your black rock with white spots. This is a metamorphic rock with minerals that have separated into layers. There are three minerals for you to identify in this rock:

1. Potassium feldspar: A light-colored mineral; it scratches glass.
2. Biotite: A black mineral that is fairly "soft" and breaks across flat surfaces in one direction (cleavage). Biotite is a type of mica.
3. Quartz: A grayish mineral that is very hard. It does not have good cleavage, but fractures.

Step 4. Rock B is the black-green rock. When minerals form from molten rock that cools relatively quickly at or near the Earth's surface, there is not enough time for the crystals to grow large, so the resulting rock has small crystals, as seen in Rock B. Minerals that contain iron, magnesium, and silica are called mafic minerals, and they are commonly dark in color, as this rock is. Because the crystals are so small, it's tough to determine exactly which minerals are in this rock, but we can make an educated guess as to what the main three are.

1. Biotite: A black mineral that is fairly "soft" and has good cleavage, same as in Rock A; black mica.
2. Amphibole: A dark-colored silicate mineral, meaning it has silicone and oxygen; forms prism or needlelike crystals.

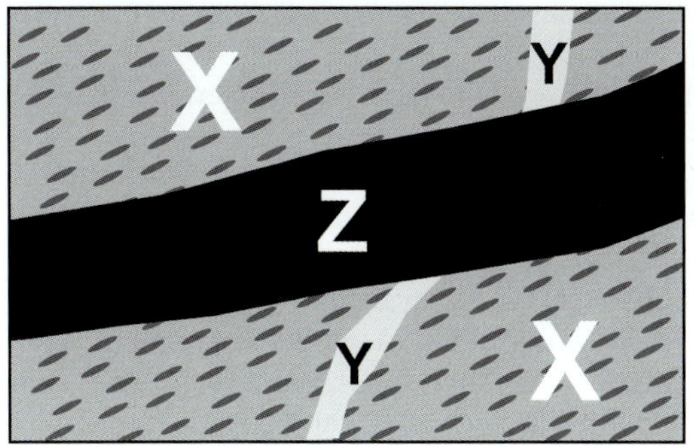

Figure 8-4. The Principle of Cross-Cutting Relationships. The X rock is behind both Y and Z, so it is the oldest. The Y rock has cut across X, so it is the second oldest. The Z rock has cut across both X and Y, so it is the youngest rock in this example. Illustration by Steven Hageman.

3. Pyroxene: Another silicate mineral; generally contains calcium, magnesium, and iron; often occurs as prismatic crystals.

Amphibole and pyroxene may be difficult to distinguish in your rock sample. Needlelike crystals will indicate amphibole.

Your sample MIGHT also contain two other trace minerals:

4. Chlorite: Provides the green color.
5. Pyrite: An accessory mineral that forms cubic, or square-shaped, crystals and is metallic (brassy); "fool's gold." An accessory mineral is a mineral that is present in small quantities and is not considered when identifying a rock.

Step 5. Rock C is the white and gray rock. There are three minerals in this rock for you to discover. These are **felsic** minerals, which contain aluminum and silica that formed from cooling **magma**. Geologists refer to large, coarse crystalline rock with felsic minerals as **granite**. Very slow-cooling magma deep under the Earth will form very large crystals. The resulting rock, which you are now holding, is pegmatitic granite. The minerals in this rock are

1. Potassium feldspar: Light-colored, has good cleavage, scratches glass;
2. Quartz: Clear to grayish in color, fractures (no cleavage), scratches glass; and
3. Rare purple fluorite: Rare, purple crystals, has good cleavage, does not scratch glass.

Step 6. If you would like to proceed further to determine the age of the rock, use Figure 8-4 and the Principle of Cross-Cutting Relationships to learn how to establish a sequence of events for the formation of rocks.

Figure 8-4 shows an example of a cliff face with a background Rock X, similar to our augen gneiss. Because it is the predominant rock here, it was formed first. Rock Y was a magma flow, or an intrusion, that cut across Rock X. The Principle of Cross-Cutting Relationships tells us that a rock that cuts across another rock in this manner is more newly formed. Rock Y is younger than Rock X. Similarly, because

Rock Z cuts across both Rock X and Rock Y, we know that Rock Z is the youngest of all three rocks.

Now let's look at the Blowing Rock Gneiss the same way to determine in which order the rocks were formed. Locate the boundary between the white/gray felsic Rock C and the background augen Rock A. You can see that the white/gray felsic rock cuts across the alignment of augens in the gneiss, indicating that Rock C is younger than the augen gneiss (Figure 8-3, location 1). The mafic rock also cuts across the augen gneiss at location 2, telling us that the augen gneiss formation is the oldest of our three rocks. Let's make one last observation. We can see in several locations across the rock face that the white and gray rock, which is the coarse crystalline felsic rock (Rock C), is older than the black-green rock, which is the fine crystalline mafic rock (Rock B), because the mafic rock cuts across it (Figure 8-3, location 2). Now we can produce a relative timeline for the creation of our rocks, from the oldest to the youngest.

1. Augen gneiss (Rock A)
2. Felsic rock (Rock C)
3. Mafic rock (Rock B)

Remember, crystal formations created at heated depth are larger because they are formed slowly over time, while crystals that are created rapidly in a cooler, shallower environment are smaller because they do not have as long to form. If an igneous rock has coarse crystals and another has fine crystals in the same place, that means they were formed at different depths. The felsic rock (C) has very large crystals, evidence that it must have formed deeply and slowly within the Earth. The mafic rock (B) has very tiny crystals, providing evidence that it formed rapidly near the surface. In between the formation of the felsic rock and the mafic rock, we can infer that there must have been an uplift event due to **tectonic** force, or movements in the Earth's crust, in this case movement upward, bringing these two together.

The long, parallel, vertical lines on the face of the rock are drill holes, into which explosives were inserted to blast away the rock to build the road. At the upper surface of the rock outcrop you can see a thin soil layer where the rocks have been broken down by water, ice, and plant roots and mixed with organic matter to form soil.

Step 7. If you would like to take this one step further, you can now construct a geologic history for this site from what you have observed and deduced, from first (oldest) to last (youngest).

- Protolith rock is pushed deep into the Earth.
- Metamorphism of the protolith creates augen gneiss (A).
- Intrusion of magma forms felsic rock with large crystals at depth (C).
- Regional uplift occurs, but rocks are still buried.
- Shallow intrusion of magma forms mafic rock with small crystals (B).
- Uplift and/or erosion occurs, but not exposure.
- Road is cut and rock is exposed for you to explore!

Before You Go

This site is located on a large exposure of rock on the right side of US 321, Blowing Rock Road, as you approach the town of Blowing Rock from the town of Lenoir. It is across the road from Greene's Trading Post and slightly north on the right. Park in the open gravel area on the right side of US 321 at the north end of the rock exposure. This is approximately 2.4 miles (3.8 kilometers) south of the Blowing Rock town limits and ~10 miles (16 kilometers) north of junction 268 at Happy Valley on US 321. This lot is the property of the North Carolina Department of Transportation. Be safe and be respectful.

The Blowing Rock Gneiss continues almost to Boone along US 321 and contacts the Grandfather Mountain Formation (greenish-black rock). The lower contact is with the Wilson Creek Gneiss (grayish layered rock without augens) just south of this stop across from Greene's Trading Post. GPS coordinates are given below.

Other Activities

If you're interested in exploring other rock formations, try these exercises:

1. Go to the GeoLex website listed below and enter the names of other formations in the region (e.g., Grandfather Mountain Formation, Wilson Creek Gneiss, Cranberry Gneiss, and Chilhowee Group). You can also use the interactive options at GeoLex to search for formations in North Carolina or in other states, or to explore where rocks of a certain geologic time interval (e.g., Triassic Period) are located in your state.

2. Check out the public websites below that have more information on relative age dating with exercises, including the Open Education Resources (OER) from Pennsylvania State University.

References and Resources

"Mohs Scale of Mineral Hardness." American Federation of Mineralogical Societies, http://www.amfed.org/t_mohs.htm. Accessed November 11, 2018.

Formations and Regional Stratigraphy Resources

National Geologic Map Database. "Geolex Search," http://ngmdb.usgs.gov/Geolex/search. Accessed October 27, 2018.

Introduction to Rock-Forming Minerals and Their Properties

"Geology of Gems, Lab Exercise 1: Mineral Identification." Geology Café, http://geologycafe.com/gems/labs/lab1.html. Accessed October 27, 2018.

Relative Age-Dating Exercises

Alley, Richard, and Sridhar Anandakrishnan. "Geology of the National Parks. Exercise 5: Puzzling Out Relative Time." Pennsylvania State University OER Initiative, https://www.e-education.psu.edu/geosc10/Exercise5. Accessed October 27, 2018

"Introduction to Geology." Geology Café, http://geologycafe.com/class/chapter2.html. Accessed October 27, 2018.

Website: While this location does not have a website, the Appalachian State Department of Geological and Environmental Sciences discusses this site and Blowing Rock Gneiss here: https://earth.appstate.edu/academics/field-trips/blowing-rock-gneiss-multiple-stops

Contact: Appalachian State also provides an "Ask a Geologist" email contact for public questions about local geology: askageologist@appstate.edu

Address: US 321 near Blowing Rock, N.C. Follow the directions above in "Before You Go."

GPS Coordinates: N 36°5.948, W 81°21.480

CHAPTER 9

Elk Knob State Park

CRYSTAL WILSON & ANDREW JENKINS

SCIENTIFIC FIELDS OF STUDY: *Geology, Tectonics, Botany*

Elk Knob State Park is located atop the second highest peak in Watauga County and is a must-see for anyone visiting the Boone–West Jefferson area in northwestern North Carolina. Because of the diversity seen here, visitors to the park will notice the forests of Elk Knob look and feel very different from other rhododendron-laden slopes and mountaintops in the area. Indeed, the forested meadows and rocky slopes of the park host such an exceptional community of plants and animals that the Nature Conservancy ranks Elk Knob and surrounding peaks as one of the most critically important ecologic hotspots in the southern Appalachians.

A key factor contributing to the diversity, and in some cases rarity, of plants in this area of the Blue Ridge Mountains is the presence of nutrient-rich soils that are more **basic** than other soils in the Appalachians. See Chapter 7 for a discussion of soil pH and Chapter 3 for a general discussion of pH. Plants sink their roots into this rich soil to soak up moisture and sequester, or take up, necessary nutrients. Millions of years of **physical** and **chemical weathering** by wind, water, and ice have broken down the unique bedrock, or the solid rock beneath the soil, which is called **amphibolite**. Weathering of the amphibolite has produced the rich, fertile soils that characterize this region of northwestern North Carolina. Elk Knob State Park is a prime location to spend an afternoon learning about the connections between geology and botany and linking the past to the present, all while enjoying a pleasant hike and breathtaking views.

Origin of the Amphibolite

So what's the big deal about this amphibolite besides the way it weathers? What does its presence at the top of this high peak mean to geologists? What can the amphibolite, and perhaps other rocks, tell us about mountain building and how the Earth may have been different in the past? Amphibolite is a **metamorphic** rock,

Figure 9-1. North/northwest view of Elk Knob State Park.
Photo courtesy of North Carolina Department of Parks and Recreation.

transformed from an older, parent rock, or **protolith**, by heat and pressure into its new classification as it was buried deeply in the Earth's crust. In the case of the amphibolite at Elk Knob, it originally formed as iron- and magnesium-rich lava flows on an ancient seafloor.

These lava flows hardened to a black **igneous** rock, called **basalt**, and formed the crust of the seafloor approximately 550–450 million years ago just as basalt forms the crust of the seafloor today. These seafloor basalts were buried very deeply in the Earth and metamorphosed by heat and pressure. The mountain-building activities that are described in the Mountain Geology section (p. 10) ultimately pushed these rocks up to become the amphibolite we see at Elk Knob today. Amphibolite is a rock that we see throughout the Amphibolite Mountain range in this part of the North Carolina Mountain region where we find important areas of biological diversity. See Chapters 3 and 7 for further discussion of the ecological impacts of amphibolite rock.

Mountain building is characterized not only by metamorphism but also by deformation due to the high strain that builds in the crust during collisions. This deformation is recorded in the rocks as evidenced by folds that formed when the rocks were very hot (see Figure 9-2). In fact, the broad, open folds that formed during mountain building have influenced the rounded shape of Elk Knob. The rounded peak of Elk Knob contrasts with surrounding linear, or straight, ridges, such as Snake Mountain, that follow ancient fault lines.

Observing Amphibolite in the Field

Amphibolite can be found at the base and the top of Elk Knob along the Summit Trail. In fact, many boulders of the black amphibolite line the beginning of the trail as it winds through a forested boulder field of loose blocks of rock that have detached

Figure 9-2. Folded amphibolite is the dominant rock type at Elk Knob and surrounding peaks in northwestern North Carolina. Weathering of this Ca-Mg-Fe-rich rock produces a nutrient-rich, basic (pH>7) soil that supports the unique and diverse forest and plant communities as well as animals. Photo by Crystal Wilson.

from outcrops above. Boulder fields such as these are the remains of ancient landslides that likely formed since the last Ice Age and blanket many mountain slopes in the region.

As you know, rocks are made of **minerals**. Elk Knob is the perfect place to practice your geology skills, as the minerals that make up the rocks at Elk Knob are large enough to see with a naked eye. For an even closer experience, we suggest you take a 10x magnifying glass to examine mineral shapes, cleavage surfaces, colors, and luster. Refer to Chapter 8, "Blowing Rock Gneiss," for a guide to distinguishing mineral properties used by geologists. It is important to be able to identify the minerals in a rock, which then determine the rock's name. For a complete introductory field guide for mineral identification, we recommend Frederick Pough's *Field Guide to Rocks and Minerals.*

The amphibolite bedrock at Elk Knob is composed predominantly of black amphiboles and white sodium-rich plagioclase feldspars. Trace amounts of red garnets can be found. So, let's take a closer look.

You will notice the amphibolite has mostly black and white crystals (see Figure 9-2). The elongated black minerals you see are amphiboles, hence the rock's name (Figure 9-3). The solid, milky white minerals you see are mostly sodium-rich plagioclase feldspars (Figure 9-4). Garnets occur as small (>1 millimeter) red crystals in the amphibolite near the summit of Elk Knob (Figure 9-5). Quartz is also present in small amounts, and it appears as smaller, glassy gray crystals when viewed with

Figure 9-3. Black amphiboles. Photo by Crystal Wilson.

Figure 9-4. White sodium-rich plagioclase feldspars. Photo by Crystal Wilson.

Figure 9-5. Trace amounts of red garnets can be found. Photo by Crystal Wilson.

Figure 9-6. Muscovite-rich mica schist. Mica schist was metamorphosed from aluminum-rich sediments that blanketed the ancient seafloor. Easily distinguished from amphibolite by its lighter color, mica schist can be found along the Summit Trail near the Peak Overlook. Photo by Crystal Wilson.

Figure 9-7. Muscovite [$KAl_2AlSi_3O_{10}(OH)_2$] and biotite [$K(Fe,Mg)_3AlSi_3O_{10}(OH)_2$]. The mica schist is "shiny" as sunlight reflects off the flaky mica minerals, muscovite (white) and biotite (black), which make up a majority of the rock. Photo by Crystal Wilson.

a magnifying glass (see Figure 9-8). Figures 9-7, 9-8, and 9-9 also show the chemical formulas, or the elemental composition, for each of these minerals, which are particularly enriched in iron (Fe), magnesium (Mg), calcium (Ca), aluminum (Al), and sodium (Na). Based on the variety of elements in the amphibolite, it is easy to understand how weathering of this rock at the Earth's surface helps to form nutrient-rich soils.

Observing Mica Schist in the Field

Amphibolite is not the only metamorphic rock type at Elk Knob State Park. Another rock, called **mica schist**, can be found alongside the Summit Trail near the Peak Overlook (see Figures 9-6 and 9-9). In fact, mica schist commonly occurs interlayered in the amphibolite throughout the region, and geologists refer to this "package" of rocks in northwestern North Carolina as the **Ashe Metamorphic Suite**, named

Figure 9-8. Quartz (SiO_2). The granular minerals interlayered with the mica are composed of significant amounts of glassy, gray quartz and lesser amounts of milky white feldspar. Photo by Crystal Wilson.

Figure 9-9. Kyanite (Al_2SiO_5) in the mica schist. The mica schist you find may have "knobby blades" from the mineral kyanite, which is very hard, measuring 7 to 9 on a hardness scale from 1 to 10. Although kyanite is usually recognized by its blue color, the kyanite at Elk Knob is white. Photo by Crystal Wilson.

after Ashe County. The mica schist formed from very fine-particled, aluminum-rich silts and clays that settled on the ancient seafloor and then were buried and metamorphosed during mountain building.

Mica schist is easily distinguished from dark amphibolite by its light color and shiny appearance (Figure 9-6). A prominent, flaky mineral called mica gives the schist its shiny appearance as sunlight reflects off the flat mica cleavage surfaces. White mica, muscovite, is the most common mica present in the schist at Elk Knob, although minor occurrences of black mica, biotite, can be found (Figure 9-7). The granular minerals you will observe interspersed with the mica are composed of significant amounts of glassy, gray quartz and lesser amounts of milky white feldspar (Figure 9-8).

Although geology students accurately associate the term "metamorphism" with "change," it is worth reiterating that the change a rock undergoes during metamorphism is the formation of *new* minerals from *old* minerals in the original rock. All the mineral, or chemical, reactions that occur while the rock is buried deep in the

Earth's crust and "cooked" happen in the *solid state*, so in other words, *nothing melts* (that would make the rock igneous). Some of the new minerals that form in metamorphic rocks are called index minerals because they crystallize and grow at *specific temperature and pressure* conditions that geologists have described. As such, index minerals are useful to geologists because they tell us how deep a metamorphic rock was buried. At Elk Knob, the mica schists contain index minerals of both garnet and kyanite (see Figure 9-5 and Figure 9-9), which indicate the rocks experienced temperatures as high as 1,300°F (~700°C) and lithostatic pressures >7 kilobars. Lithostatic pressure is a measure of the pressure exerted on a body of rock due to the weight of the overlying rocks within the Earth. So amazingly enough, not only did rocks at the top of Elk Knob originate on the seafloor, but the temperature and pressure conditions recorded by minerals in the schist indicate that these rocks were buried as deep as 15 to 18 miles (25 to 30 kilometers) below the surface of the Earth during mountain building. The rocks are exposed at the surface today because the mountains were pushed up and have been eroded down by wind, water, and ice for hundreds of millions of years. Isn't it fascinating to imagine how old these rocks are and all the places they have been?

Geology Meets Botany

The vegetation found at Elk Knob is unique in its composition because of several features, including its natural history, the peak elevation at 5,520 feet (1,682 meters), and the mountain's geology—the minerals that have helped to form the soil. These many factors have shaped both the **species richness** and the **community composition** of plants found on the mountain. Species richness refers to the number of different plant species present, while community composition describes the percentages of different plant species within a community. Many plants at Elk Knob are found in more northern latitude habitats outside the mountains, so the high elevation contributes cooler climate conditions that support these plants. In addition, several of these species would not thrive in the more **acidic** soils found in the numerous **Acidic Cove Forests** elsewhere in the southern Appalachian Mountains. The general layers of these forest communities include a forest **canopy**, an **understory**, a **shrub layer**, and a **herbaceous** layer.

The purpose of this part of the Elk Knob chapter is to follow the Summit Trail so you can immerse yourself as a botanist would, identifying both common and rare plant life that you would encounter as you explore the mountain. Below we'll discuss the different plant communities found along Elk Knob's trails. If you are fascinated by plants, this is your working introduction to western North Carolina's botanical realm. You can refer to the figures in this chapter to identify plants on the trails, but you should also consider taking along Timothy Spira's *Wildflowers and Plant Communities* as an additional resource. Make sure to carry a notebook to record your observations, and feel free to photograph your finds as well.

From the Summit trailhead (Figure 9-10) at the parking lot of Elk Knob State Park, you'll begin your exploration in a **Northern Hardwood Forest**, which is typically composed of mixed hardwoods above 3,500 feet (1,069 meters). In this forest you'll see that a very diverse forest canopy dominates, and the primary species present are sugar maple (*Acer saccharum*) (Figure 9-11); yellow buckeye (*Aesculus flava*);

Figure 9-10. The trailhead for the Elk Knob Summit Trail, which is 1.9 miles (3.1 kilometers) long. Photo by Andrew Jenkins.

yellow birch (*Betula alleghaniensis*) (Figure 9-16); American beech (*Fagus grandifolia*); and American basswood (*Tilia americana*) (Figure 9-12). A rich understory of striped maple (*Acer pensylvanicum*) (Figure 9-13), common elderberry (*Sambucus canadensis*), and mountain maple (*Acer spicatum*) (Figure 9-14) also can be seen here. Moving closer to the ground, the shrub layer in this forest includes hobblebush (*Viburnum lantanoides*) and flame azalea (*Rhododendron calendulaceum*). The herbaceous layer is very rich, meaning it is composed of many species, due primarily to the underlying geology. Some example species found in this layer include giant cohosh (*Caulophyllum gigantea*), Dutchman's breeches (*Dicentra cucullaria*),

Figure 9-11. Sugar maple (*Acer saccharum*), a common tree found along the Summit Trail, is the main source for maple syrup. The highest concentration of sugar maples in the state occurs within the Amphibolite Mountains macrosite in Ashe and Watauga Counties. Photos by Brandy Belville.

Figure 9-12. American basswood (*Tilia americana*), showing its distinctive asymmetrical leaves and bracteate (leafy) fruit. Photos by Brandy Belville.

Figure 9-13. Striped maple (*Acer pensylvanicum*), with its distinctive leaves, fruit, and bark. As the tree ages, the bark becomes striped in appearance, giving credence to its common name. Photos by Brandy Belville.

Figure 9-14. Mountain maple (*Acer spicatum*) can be seen along the Summit Trail in the understory of the forest. This tree is usually seen above 4,500 feet (1,372 meters) in elevation. Photo by Brandy Belville.

Figure 9-15. Mayapple (*Podophyllum peltatum*) blooms in late May at Elk Knob State Park. Because of many factors, including elevation, the phenology, or leafing out and/or flowering time of the vegetation, is later than that of the same species growing in the Piedmont or Coastal Plain of North Carolina. Photo by Crystal Wilson.

squirrel corn (*Dicentra canadensis*), doll's eyes (*Actea pachypoda*), New York fern (*Thelypteris novaborescense*), maidenhair fern (*Adiantium pedatum*), and mayapple (*Podophyllum peltatum*) (Figure 9-15). Along the trail, you will see that the community composition of the Northern Hardwood Forest changes into different subtypes, or different groupings of plant species.

Ascending the summit, the community composition of the forest changes as the trail passes a Birch **Boulderfield Forest** subtype. This community subtype of the Northern Hardwood Forest can be identified by the large boulders spread throughout the forest, with a sparse growth of herbaceous and woody species adhering to the rocks. Rock ferns (*Polypodium virginiana, P. appalachiana*), hairy alumroot (*Heuchera villosa*), and skunk currant (*Ribes glandulosum*) can be found here among the various moss and lichen species. Take your time to examine the rocks throughout this forest subtype to see how many species you can identify. The trees found in the canopy are mostly yellow birch (*Betula alleghaniensis*) (Figure 9-16), as well as some American beech (*Fagus grandifolia*). Along the trail you will see red elderberry (*Sambucus racemosa*) (Figure 9-17) blooming in the spring and fruiting by early summer. This is always a treat for the local birds.

The Summit Trail passes through a **Beech Gap Forest** subtype community of Northern Hardwood Forest just before reaching the summit. This incredibly rare community subtype, often found near the summit of peaks throughout the southern Appalachians, displays a canopy dominated by American beech trees. These trees often appear aged and stunted due to wind exposure, temperature extremes, and

Figure 9-16. Yellow birch (*Betula alleghaniensis*) can be seen growing throughout Elk Knob State Park. Along the Summit Trail, elements of this inconspicuous plant community, the Birch Boulderfield Forest, can be seen. Photos by Brandy Belville.

Figure 9-17. Red elderberry (*Sambucus racemosa*) is found throughout the understory along the Summit Trail. It is common at high elevation, above 4,000 feet (1,219 meters). Photo by Andrew Jenkins.

Figure 9-18. Before you reach the summit, the trail passes through a Beech Gap Forest with a distinctive look and canopy of beech trees. The herbaceous layer is composed primarily of Pennsylvania sedge (*Carex pensylvanicum*), shown here in bloom during early spring. Photo by Andrew Jenkins.

Figure 9-19. Parasitic beech drops (*Epifagus virginiana*) can be found blooming along the Summit Trail in late summer. Photo by Kelly Safley.

varying moisture regimens. The understory is composed primarily of either Pennsylvania sedge (*Carex pensylvanicum*) (Figure 9-18) or white snakeroot (*Aegeratina altissima* var. *roanensis*). Mountain wood aster (*Eurybia chlorolepis*) and parasitic beech drops (*Epifagus virginiana*) (Figure 9-19) are found commonly as well. Beech drops grow and subsist on the roots of the American beech tree. They completely lack chlorophyll, so they must collect nutrients from their host tree.

The open peak of Elk Knob sits at 5,520 feet (1,682 meters) above sea level (Figure 9-20) and houses a unique array of plants. The extreme variation in weather conditions on mountaintops causes stunted growth of the woody vegetation, as mentioned above. American beech, mountain ash (*Sorbus americana*), northern bush honeysuckle (*Diervilla lonicera*), vasevine (*Clematis virona*), and flame azalea (*Rhododendron calendulaceum*) are just some of the species that can be found at the summit (Figures 9-21 and 9-22) in this **High-Elevation Rocky Summit Community**. North Carolina's endangered Gray's lily (*Lilium grayi*) (Figure 9-20) is also found in this habitat. For more information about Gray's lily and its discovery by Harvard botanist Asa Gray, please refer to Chapter 4, "Grandfather Mountain."

Figure 9-20. The summit of Elk Knob State Park (*top*) hosts a unique and interesting collection of plant species. The rare Gray's lily (*Lilium grayi*) (*bottom*) can be found in this habitat. Photos by Brandy Belville.

Figure 9-21. Mountain ash (*Sorbus americana*) (*top*) is seen here in winter with its bright red berries. Photo by Brandy Belville. Northern bush honeysuckle (*Diervilla lonicera*) (*bottom*) is seen here blooming in midsummer. Photo by Andrew Jenkins.

Figure 9-22. Vasevine (*Clematis virona*) (*top*) and flame azalea (*Rhododendron calendulaceum*) (*bottom*) can be found throughout the park but are encountered right at the end of the Summit Trail. Photos by Andrew Jenkins.

Along the north face of Elk Knob, the Backcountry Trail takes you down to the middle elevation slopes. Many species found in the Northern Hardwood Forest along the Summit Trail also can be found down in the Backcountry's **Rich Cove Forest**. Several streams drain the mountain forming the tributaries of the North Fork of the New River. These waterways help to create rare mountain **wetlands** called **Montane Woodland Seeps**, where soils are **saturated** and plants adapt to the waterlogged habitat. Montane seeps often occur on steep gravelly or bouldered slopes at groundwater discharge sites. Water lettuce (*Micranthes micranthidifolia*);

Figure 9-23. Purple fringed orchid (*Platanthera psycodes*) (*top*) and trailing wolfsbane (*Aconitum reclinatum*) (*bottom*) are some of the indicator species you can find in Montane Seep communities. Photos by Crystal Wilson.

Figure 9-24. Umbrella leaf (*Diphyllea cymosa*). Photo by Brandy Belville.

purple fringed orchid (*Platanthera psycodes*) (Figure 9-23); umbrella leaf (*Diphyllea cymosa*) (Figure 9-24); spotted jewelweed (*Impatiens capensis*); pale jewelweed (*Impatiens pallida*); and the rare late-summer-blooming trailing wolfsbane (*Aconitum reclinatum*) (Figure 9-23) can be found throughout this area.

Before You Go

Park visitors can hike the Summit Trail, which is one of the finest trails in the North Carolina Parks system. The single- to double-file footpath follows a gentle grade and several switchbacks for a 1.9-mile (3.0-kilometer) hike up an approximately 2,000-foot (609-meter) climb to the top of the mountain (note: this is *one-way*). As one of the tallest mountains in Watauga County, the summit offers spectacular, panoramic views of the surrounding landscape, including many other prominent peaks, such as Grandfather Mountain to the south and Mount Rogers in Virginia to the north.

Make sure to bring plenty of water and a snack and plan for at least a three-hour hike, round-trip. Dress for changing weather, as storms move in as fast as they move out.

References and Resources

Abbott, R. N., and L. A. Raymond. "The Ashe Metamorphic Suite, Northwest North Carolina: Metamorphism and Observations on Geologic History." *American Journal of Science* 284 (2007): 350–75.

Aleinikoff, J. N., R. E. Zartman, M. Walter, D. W. Rankin, P. T. Lyttle, and W. C. Burton. "U-Pb Ages of Metarhyolites of the Catoctin and Mount Rogers Formation, Central and Southern Appalachians: Evidence for Two Pulses of Iapetan Rifting." *American Journal of Science* 295 (1995): 428–54.

Clark, S. H. B."Geology of the Southern Appalachian Mountains." *U.S. Geological Survey Scientific Investigations Map 2830*. 2008, http://pubs.usgs.gov/sim/2830/. Accessed November 4, 2018.

The Geology of Elk Knob State Park: An Interactive Guide, http://www.ncgeology.com/Elk_Knob_geology/pages/home.html. Accessed November 4, 2018.

Kintsch, J. A. *Amphibolite Mountains Site Conservation Plan*. Durham: A Report to the North Carolina Nature Conservancy, 2000.

Oakley, S. C. *An Inventory of the Significant Natural Areas of Watauga County, North Carolina*. Raleigh: North Carolina Natural Heritage Program, 2000.

Peet, R. K., J. D. Fridley, and J. D. Gramling. "Variation in Species Richness and Species Pool Size across a pH Gradient in Forests of the Southern Blue Ridge Mountains." *Folia Geobot* 38 (2003): 391–401.

Pough, Frederick. *A Field Guide to Rocks and Minerals*. 5th ed. Peterson Field Guide Series. Boston: Houghton Mifflin Harcourt, 1997.

Schafale, M. P. *Classification of the Natural Communities of North Carolina: Fourth Approximation*. Raleigh: North Carolina Natural Heritage Program, 2012.

Southworth, S., J. N. Aleinikoff, C. M. Bailey, W. C. Burton, E. A. Crider, P. C. Hackley, J. P. Smoot, and R. P. Tollo. *Geologic Map of the Shenandoah National Park Region, Virginia*. U.S. Geological Survey, Open-File Report 2009-1153, 2009.

Spira, Timothy P. *Wildflowers and Plant Communities of the Southern Appalachian Mountains and Piedmont*. Chapel Hill: University of North Carolina Press, 2011.

Stewart, K. G., and M. R. Roberson. *Exploring the Geology of the Carolinas: A Field Guide to Favorite Places from Chimney Rock to Charleston*. Chapel Hill: University of North Carolina Press, 2007.

Weakley, A. S. "Flora of the Southern and Mid-Atlantic States." University of North Carolina Herbarium, N.C. Botanical Garden, Chapel Hill, N.C., 2015.

Website: https://www.ncparks.gov/elk-knob-state-park
Contact: phone: (828) 297-7261; email: elk.knob@ncparks.gov
Address: 5564 Meat Camp Road, Todd, N.C. 28684
GPS Coordinates: N 33°19.98, W 81°41.472

CHAPTER 10

Linville Gorge Wilderness Area

North Carolina's Grand Canyon

BRAD DANIEL

SCIENTIFIC FIELDS OF STUDY: *Geology, Ecology, Meteorology*

Introduction

The Linville Gorge Wilderness Area is situated in the Pisgah National Forest. It could easily be called Linville "Gorgeous" because it is the closest thing North Carolina has to a Grand Canyon—a ravine more than 12 miles (19 kilometers) long with steep rocky cliffs, beautiful waterfalls, and breathtaking views. It is an area rich in natural and cultural history, not to mention an abundance of recreational opportunities. The many exposed rocky crags and cliffs make the gorge one of the best climbing areas in the southeastern United States. It is also a popular destination for backpacking, fishing, hunting, and hiking. From high vantage points in the gorge, such as Table Rock or Hawksbill, one can see many popular surrounding landforms, including Lake James in the south, Mount Mitchell and the Black Mountain range in the west, Roan Mountain in the northwest, Grandfather Mountain in the northeast, and Brown Mountain in the east. The gorge and surrounding areas have also been featured in films such as *Last of the Mohicans*.

History

The gorge was named in honor of two early explorers, father and son William and John Linville, who were friends of Daniel Boone and died in the gorge in 1766. Relations between Native Americans and settlers were not always peaceful during this time. William and John were out hunting in the gorge with a young boy whom they had employed to help cook and keep camp. Their party set up camp 10 miles downriver from the falls, but an altercation with a local Cherokee tribe, possibly over hunting territories, left the two Linville men dead and the young boy wounded. The Cherokees believed the gorge area to be a sacred and mystic place.

Various **Indigenous** tribes visited or inhabited the area for hundreds of years, and many of the natural formations found there have Cherokee names. For example, the Cherokee called Linville River *Ee-see-oh*, or "river of many cliffs." They referred to Table Rock as *Attacoa*, and it was used for important ceremonies. Other places were named after settlers. "Wiseman's View" was named after LaFayette Wiseman because he camped there frequently near the turn of the century when taking salt licks for cattle grazing on the mountain. It is not difficult to understand why he loved being there. Today Wiseman's View continues to provide outstanding views of both ends of the gorge, the east ridge—known as Jonas Ridge—and the Linville River. Wiseman's View is also one of several locations in the gorge where one might be lucky enough to see the famous and mysterious Brown Mountain Lights, which sometimes appear on a mountain located to the east of Linville Gorge. It is interesting that similar phenomena also have been reported on Jonas Ridge itself inside the gorge. Those interested in the lights can find information in Speer's scientific investigation of the phenomenon or online at the www.brownmountainlights.org website discussing current research and potential theories for the lights by Appalachian State faculty and students.

John D. Rockefeller donated money to purchase this land. Although it was first designated as a wild area in 1951 by the chief of the Forest Service and its protection started in 1952, the Wilderness Act of 1964 formally established it as part of the National Wilderness System. The 1964 act describes wilderness as "an area where the Earth and its community of life are untrammeled by man" and "which generally appears to have been affected primarily by the forces of nature, with the imprint of man's work substantially unnoticeable." Wilderness areas are established to be protected and preserved. While hunting and fishing with permits are allowed, roads, timber harvesting, and motorized equipment are prohibited. Natural items, such as rocks and plants, cannot be collected or removed.

In 1984, the North Carolina Wilderness Act increased the original 7,575 acres, and currently the Linville Gorge Wilderness area contains close to 12,000 acres. Additional acreage continues to be purchased and added to the total. It is managed by the U.S. Forest Service Grandfather Ranger District.

Geology and Physical Geography

Linville Gorge was formed through a combination of **uplift**, **faulting**, and water **erosion**. Unlike U-shaped, glacier-carved valleys, Linville Gorge is characterized by distinctive V-shaped valleys that are carved by running water. The Linville River, which has its headwaters on Grandfather Mountain, has sculpted one of the most beautiful and rugged gorges in the eastern United States. The river descends approximately 2,000 feet (610 meters) over 12 miles (19 kilometers) before flowing south into Lake James.

The gorge is oriented predominantly north to south and is found on the eastern edge of the Blue Ridge Escarpment, a geologic formation that drops off some 4,000 feet (1,219 meters) to the east, giving way to foothills, isolated mountains, and coastal plain. On the east side, Jonas Ridge contains some of the most popular geomorphic landforms within the gorge. Geomorphic refers to landforms created by geologic processes. These include Table Rock Mountain, Hawksbill Mountain,

Figure 10-1. Linville Falls, upper and lower falls. Photo by Whitney Dumford.

Figure 10-2. Wiseman's View. Photo by Whitney Dumford.

Shortoff Mountain, and the Chimney Rock formation. On the west side, Linville Mountain and Laurel Knob are prominent features. Wiseman's View, described earlier, is also on the west side, providing unparalleled views of the gorge. Elevations throughout the gorge range from a low of 1,300 feet (396 meters) on the Linville River to 4,120 feet (1,256 meters) on Gingercake Mountain (east side). The north end of the gorge features very rugged cliffs, an exposed fault line, and two prominent waterfalls known as the upper and lower falls.

The topography, or arrangement of land features, changes abruptly at Linville Falls. Above the falls, the river flows through an area with a **floodplain** and gently sloping walls. A floodplain is the flat area next to a river that floods when water levels are high. The Linville fault, a **thrust fault**, is exposed at the upper falls. Usually, younger rock is found in upper strata layers and older rock is below, but this is reversed when a thrust fault occurs—older rock is forced up and over younger rock. The Linville Falls fault has pushed older metamorphosed **granite**, including some **gneiss**, over the younger **quartzite**. Both were metamorphosed due to heat and pressure. Evidence of the thrust fault can be seen when you visit the upper falls. The upper falls is composed of the metamorphosed granite, whereas the lower falls is made of quartzite. This quartzite forms the rock floor of the upper falls viewing area. Make sure to observe the different types of rocks in these locations.

The physical geography of the Linville Gorge Wilderness Area plays a key role in the ecology of the area. Air masses and surface winds coming from the west have significant amounts of moisture strained out of them before reaching Linville Gorge. They pass over multiple mountain ranges, including the Black Mountain range, which contains six of the ten highest peaks east of the Mississippi River. Air forced up

Figure 10-3. View of Linville River from Wiseman's View in the early fall. Photo by Whitney Dumford.

and over these mountains and mountain ranges is cooled at an approximate rate of 5.5°F (3°C) for every 1,000 feet (305 meters) of elevation gained (the **adiabatic lapse rate**). As the temperature drops, moisture condenses to form clouds and causes precipitation, most often on the windward slopes of the mountains. This process is known as the **orographic effect**. You will note that because of Mount Mitchell's height, it tends to serve as a barrier, stopping the clouds as they drop moisture on the westward, or windward, side of the mountain, creating a community of plants and animals there that require moisture for survival. At Linville Gorge, the opposite is true. The tall mountains to the west have already strained excess moisture out of the air several times before it ever reaches the gorge. This, combined with the fact that the peaks of the gorge are not high enough to create cool moist environments, means that the higher altitude regions within the gorge are characterized by dry plant communities. Please refer to Chapter 5, "Mount Mitchell," for more discussion of the orographic effect.

Mountain topography can also aid in thunderstorm development. Forcing air up over topographic barriers can help create updrafts that form cumulonimbus clouds. This occurs when cumulus clouds, which appear as white cotton balls, begin to mass and build vertically into "stacks" or "towers" called cumulus congestus clouds. Over time, the tops of these clouds spread out to form the classic cauliflower/anvil shapes that characterize cumulonimbus clouds, or thunderstorms. Since the developing thunderstorm is usually moving east/northeast as it is forming, storms that dump rain on the gorge likely were formed by air that was forced upward by mountains many miles to the west/southwest.

Ecology, Flora, and Fauna

The physical geography and geology greatly affect the ecology of Linville Gorge. Variations in elevation, slope orientation, topography, and microclimate create conditions that allow many different types of communities to exist. Some factors are more important than others. In their 1998 paper, Newell and Peet noted, "Vegetation composition is most strongly associated with soil nutrients, soil **texture**, and topographic position. The combination of rugged topography, infertile soils, relatively low annual rainfall levels, and lack of anthropogenic disturbance is responsible for the unusual combination of southern Appalachian vegetation communities that characterize Linville Gorge Wilderness." In a nutshell, all of this means that the land within Linville Gorge is so rugged, with such little rainfall, with little disturbance from humans, and with soils that seem like they should not be able to grow anything, some of the resulting plant communities that do grow can be quite unusual.

The elevational gradient from the river to the top of Hawksbill reveals several types of plant communities, including **Cove Hardwood Forest**, **Dry Ridge Forest**, **Rocky Outcrop**, **Heath Bald,** and **Crevice Communities**, all described below. At the bottom of the gorge near the river, Cove Forest Communities can be found with old-growth trees. The lower elevation, proximity to the river, and shelter from the westerly winds create favorable microclimates. Old growth exists here because it was not cost effective or desirable to log the area due to the extremely rugged terrain, and as a result, the wilderness area continues to hold significant pockets of old-growth vegetation. In the southeast portion of Linville Gorge, the Mountains-to-Sea Trail borders a newly proposed extension to the national forest, called the Chimneys extension, which lies east of Shortoff Mountain and just west of Chimney Gap. Old-growth forest extends into this area and can be viewed by hiking this portion of the Mountains-to-Sea Trail. Recent reports have indicated that some of the old-growth hemlock forest nearest the falls on Erwin's View Trail have been devastated by the **hemlock woolly adelgid**. See Chapters 6 and 17 for more information on this invasive insect.

Since both ridges descend toward the south, the southern exposure helps create Dry Ridge plant communities characterized by species such as chestnut oak (*Quercus prinus*), white oak (*Quercus alba*), sassafras (*Sassafras* sp.), sourwood (*Oxydendrum arboretum*), mountain laurel (*Kalmia latifolia*), and blueberry (*Vaccinium* sp.). Conifers found in these drier conditions include eastern hemlock (*Tsuga canadensis*), Carolina hemlock (*Tsuga caroliniana*), Table Mountain pine (*Pinus pungens*), white pine (*Pinus strobus*), and pitch pine (*Pinus rigida*).

Closer to the top of Hawksbill, Rocky Outcrop, Heath, and Crevice Communities occur. Rocky Outcrop Communities contain a variety of crustose, foliose, and umbilicate **lichens**, which are similar to foliose but connect to the rock with only a single attachment point. We briefly touched on the different forms and functions of lichens in both Chapter 4, "Grandfather Mountain," and Chapter 5, "Mount Mitchell." You can refer to these chapters for more lichen details.

A subcommunity of Rocky Outcrops, Crevice Communities, are plant communities that grow in the harsh conditions of crevices within a rocky outcrop. These communities often are seen growing here, where water may be scarce for long periods and winds are generally strong. Plant types such as sand myrtle (*Leiophyllum buxifolium*) and Michaux saxifrage (*Micranthes petiolaris*) are common. Heath communities, or shrubland habitats, can be found in pockets and include blueberry (*Vaccinium*), rhododendron (*Rhododendron* sp.), and azaleas (*Rhododendron* sp.). A few other species found in Linville Gorge include huckleberry, maples, silverbell, turkey beard, ninebark, red chokeberry, orchids, and ground pine.

Common animals found in this wilderness area include black bear, raccoon, bobcat, fox, deer, turkey, grouse, owls, vultures, and squirrels. Brown trout (*Slamo truta*) and rainbow trout (*Onchorhynchus mykiss*) populate the Linville River. Two species of venomous snakes, copperheads (*Agkistrodon contortrix*) and timber rattlesnakes (*Crotalus horridus*), are common, so keep your eyes open, particularly when stepping over logs or climbing around rocky crags. Copperheads are usually found in lower elevations, whereas timber rattlers generally inhabit rocky outcrops and surrounding areas at higher elevations. Copperheads are often confused with banded water snakes, so be sure you know how to tell them apart. Copperheads have pronounced triangular heads with pits on the face and "cats-eye" pupils that are vertical slits, not round.

In October, one can observe groups of broad-winged hawks (*Buteo platypterus*) spiraling upward (in formations called kettles) as they ride the thermal wind currents. The peregrine falcon (*Falco peregrinus*), often classified as the world's fastest bird, nests in the cliffs and is commonly seen flying through the gorge. Some climbing routes are closed for periods of time due to nesting.

Before You Go

Linville Gorge can be accessed in several ways, depending on which portion of the gorge you want to visit. There are many shorter, easy day hikes from each of these locations. But trails that descend into the gorge are notoriously difficult and strenuous. Water is not plentiful in every location. Please plan accordingly.

East Linville Gorge

To get to the eastern section, including Jonas Ridge, take US 221 north from Marion to the intersection of NC 183 at Linville Falls. Turn right on 183 and continue to NC 181. Turn right (south) on NC 181 and go 3.0 miles (4.8 kilometers) to FS Road 210 (Gingercake Road). Turn right onto FS Road 210. At the first fork, turn left and continue through the Gingercake Acres housing development. The paved road becomes gravel at the end of the housing development (N 35°54.06, W 81°49.14). As you travel along this gravel road, you will see pull-offs and small parking lots for several popular trails, including Devil's Hole (Sitting Bear), Hawksbill, and Spence Ridge, which is one of the easier trails for hiking down to the river. Continue to the first intersection and turn right to access the Table Rock Picnic Area, where you will find the trailhead for the Table Rock Trail. The views along this trail are spectacular, but some sections may not be appropriate for small children. On the drive up to the picnic area, you will pass the Linville Gorge Base Camp for the N.C. Outward Bound School. Several of the rock formations along Jonas Ridge are appropriate for experienced rock climbers.

West Linville Gorge

Take US 221 north from Marion to the intersection of NC 183 at Linville Falls. Turn right on NC 183 and continue 1.0 mile (1.6 kilometers) to Old NC 105, Kistler Memorial Highway. Trailheads and parking lots accessing the western section of the gorge begin just off Kistler Memorial Highway. One of the most beautiful views of the canyon, Wiseman's View, can be accessed from here (N 35°54.234, W 81°54.3). It is a very rough gravel road in places, and four-wheel-drive vehicles are recommended. Kistler Memorial Highway also can be accessed from the south. From Marion, take US 70 east to Nebo. Then take NC 126 across Lake James and continue approximately 8 miles (13 kilometers) until turning left on Old NC 105, Kistler Memorial Highway.

Backpacking Suggestions

The Linville Gorge Loop Trail is 22 miles (35.4 kilometers) long and is a must for avid hikers with experience, allowing for exposure to much of what Linville Gorge has to offer. Plan for three very full difficult days or four slightly more leisurely days. The most popular trailhead to begin this journey is the Wolf Pit Road Trailhead. Please note that dehydration is a very real problem in the gorge. Take plenty of water, and plan to refill all containers to capacity from the piped spring on top of Shortoff Mountain. Campsites are plentiful along the trail, and the views are spectacular.

Linville Falls

A trip to the upper and lower Linville Falls is a must. The falls can be accessed from either the Blue Ridge Parkway or NC 105, Kistler Memorial Highway, on the northern end of the gorge. There is a gravel parking area for the falls at the beginning of the northern end of Kistler Memorial Highway (see driving directions above). It fills up quickly and getting in and out can be a problem, so get there early. Ample paved parking can be found at the Linville Falls Visitor Center (N 35°57.3, W 81°55.68), located just off the Blue Ridge Parkway. It is open April 15 to November 1 from 9:00 A.M. to 5:00 P.M. and has restrooms, maps, and other information. To get there, follow US 221 north until it intersects the Blue Ridge Parkway. Turn left on the parkway and travel about a mile before turning onto the paved road to the visitor center. It is marked clearly with signs.

Permits

Permits are required for hunting and fishing. Camping permits are required from May 1 through October 31. Permits are not required from November 1 through April 30. Permits are not required for visitors who do not stay overnight. Free permits may be obtained at the Grandfather Ranger District Office in Marion, North Carolina, Monday through Friday, 8:00 A.M. to 4:30 P.M. Walk-in permits, for the current week only, are available at the Linville Gorge Information Cabin, located on Kistler Memorial Highway (516 Old NC 105, Marion, N.C.). The cabin is open April–October, seven days a week, 9:00 A.M.–5:00 P.M. Advance reservations are taken on a first-come, first-serve basis beginning the first working day of each previous month. For example, reservations for wilderness camping permits for the month of July will be accepted beginning the first working day of June. Permits fill up quickly, so call early using the contact information below.

References and Resources

The Brown Mountain Lights, http://www.brownmountainlights.org/. Accessed November 4, 2018.

Newell, C. L. and R. K. Peet. "Vegetation of Linville Gorge Wilderness, North Carolina." *Castanea* 63 (1998): 275–322.

Speer, W. E. *The Brown Mountain Lights: History, Science and Human Nature Explain an Appalachian Mystery*. Jefferson, N.C.: McFarland, 2017.

Wilderness Act of 1964. Doc. No. 88-577 (16 U.S.C.1131-1136). 2d sess. September 3, 1964, https://www.wilderness.net/nwps/legisact.

Website: https://www.fs.usda.gov/recarea/nfsnc/recreation/hiking/recarea/?recid=48974&actid=51

Contact: For general contact information, call or visit the Grandfather Ranger District Station—phone: (828) 652-2144; address: 109 Lawing Drive, Nebo, N.C. 28761

Address: Follow the driving directions above for access to various parts of the wilderness area.

GPS Coordinates: Included in directions above.

Part II
Piedmont Region

Introduction

Overview

Misty Buchanan

To the untrained eye, the Piedmont of North Carolina doesn't seem to offer as much plant, animal, or geological diversity as other regions within the state. After all, compared with the beautiful Appalachian Mountains and the vast Coastal Plain, it's hard to see how the Piedmont could "stack up." North Carolina's biggest cities and highways are in the Piedmont, and about two-thirds of North Carolina's human **population** live in the middle third of the state, which roughly corresponds to the Piedmont region. This area has been settled, explored, and exploited intensively for 300 years. Can there really be much nature left there? The answer may surprise you. In North Carolina's Piedmont, biologists continue to discover species that are entirely new to science and rediscover some species that once were thought to be extinct.

The rolling hills of the Piedmont lie between the Blue Ridge Mountains in the west and the Coastal Plain in the east. The low hills that characterize the Piedmont are the remnants of ancient mountains that were formed during several large-scale geologic events as the continents were shifting. Over hundreds of millions of years, these ancient mountains eroded to form the Piedmont, and wide rivers carried sediment downstream to the Coastal Plain and, ultimately, into the Atlantic Ocean.

The rivers and streams of the Piedmont region are especially important ecologically. These waterways harbor a diversity of aquatic species, including some **endemic** organisms that exist nowhere else in the world. The Neuse River waterdog is an aquatic salamander whose entire earthly existence is concentrated in only fifteen individual populations in the Neuse River Watershed. The endangered Cape Fear shiner is a small fish that is known only from the Piedmont portion of the Cape Fear River drainage, relying on shallow turbulent waters for suitable nursery and spawning habitat. The endangered mussel species, the Carolina heelsplitter, is found only in the waters of the Catawba and Pee Dee **river basins**. The presence of rare and endemic fish, mussels, and amphibians in Piedmont rivers indicates that water quality here remains pristine enough to support these animals that are considered sensitive to pollution and sedimentation. The presence of these animals also indicates healthy ecosystems, where natural riparian zones, the borders between land and water, are functioning properly to protect water quality, reducing turbidity, erosion, and pollution.

At the southern border of the Piedmont and Coastal Plain regions, the Sandhills supports rare and endangered longleaf pine forests, one of the most richly diverse natural communities in the world. Longleaf pine forests historically ranged from northeastern North Carolina to Texas and depended on frequent, natural fires and wetland hydrology for survival. The fact that these sensitive species can coexist with North Carolina's largest cities within the same region is something of which North Carolinians can be proud. Careful planning of the economic growth and development of our state will allow us to achieve a sound, prosperous economy while still maintaining these important ecosystems.

Piedmont Geology

April C. Smith

The North Carolina Piedmont has a somewhat violent geologic history that might surprise you: ancient volcanoes and giant rift basins helped form what is now the center of our state. The Piedmont region is not as old as the Mountain region; the rocks that you find in the Piedmont are between 600 million and 200 million years old. Like the rocks in the mountains, the Piedmont rocks also are **igneous** and **sedimentary**, and most of them later underwent **metamorphism** from intense heat and pressure deep inside the Earth. About 500 million years ago an ancient sea called the Iapetus Ocean existed between what is now North America and Africa. Evidence of the ancient seashore sands can be seen at Pilot Mountain. Between 480 million and 260 million years ago, a series of three landmass collisions occurred where volcanic islands were caught and squashed between the landmasses. These collisions added blocks of crust to the eastern edge of North America, creating mountains and causing metamorphism. As these collisions brought North America and Africa together to form the supercontinent **Pangea**, the Iapetus Ocean was slowly being squeezed out of existence. Pangea existed for ~100 million years before breaking apart. As it did so, the land ripped, leaving giant ditches called Triassic basins stretched across the Piedmont. You can see where these basins existed on the Piedmont region map on p. 107. Today the Piedmont is rolling hills and plains, farmland and rivers. If you look closely, you will see that the extraordinary geologic history of the Piedmont has left us with hidden ecological gems that beg to be explored.

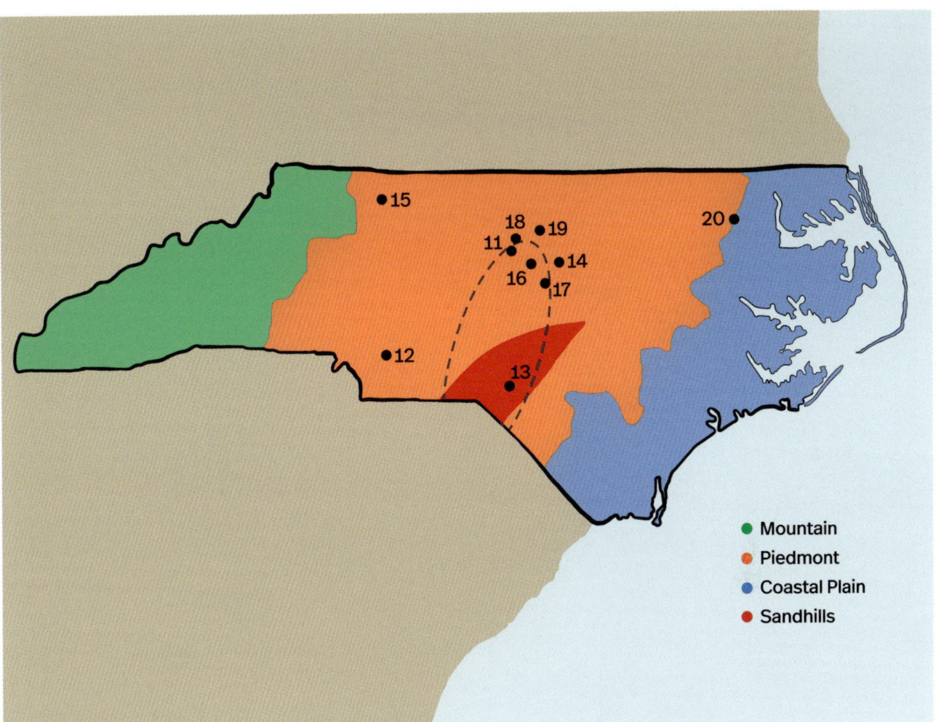

Map 3. Exploration locations in the Piedmont region of North Carolina. The dashed line represents the approximate location of the Triassic ditches that were ripped into the land when Pangea broke apart (see the Piedmont Geology section). Map by Ashleigh M. Smith.

11 Haw River

12 Reed Gold Mine

13 Sandhills

14 Prairie Ridge Ecostation

15 Pilot Mountain State Park

16 North Carolina Botanical Gardens

17 Hemlock Bluffs

18 Occoneechee Mountain State Natural Area

19 Eno River State Park

20 Medoc Mountain State Park

CHAPTER 11

Saxapahaw on the Haw River

Investigating Aquatic Insect Adaptations

CHRISTINE L. GOFORTH

SCIENTIFIC FIELDS OF STUDY: *Entomology, Aquatic Ecology, Evolutionary Biology*

The Haw River is 110 miles (177 kilometers) long and runs through eight counties, remaining entirely within the state of North Carolina. The first known villages around the banks of the Haw River were small bands of **Indigenous** peoples from the Sissipihaw tribe, the People of the Haw. They lived here sustainably, or in a manner than does not deplete natural resources, for thousands of years. As settlers arrived from Europe in the 1700s, they built gristmills and cut forests, and the larger **predators**, like bears, wolves, and eagles, began to disappear. Plantations were built in the area, and during the Civil War, the Haw River Watershed was the site of many Underground Railroad safe houses for sheltering escaped slaves. The Industrial Revolution brought tremendous growth to the area with the building of textile mills, and people began using water from the Haw River to power their machinery. Saxapahaw was the site of one of the most well-known mills of this type, churning out textiles along the banks of the river for 150 years. Although the community flourished from this commerce, the river and surrounding watershed area suffered ecologically. Today, the cleared forests along the Haw River are regrowing, the eagles are returning, and scientists know that there is tremendous **biodiversity** in the Haw **River basin**, which is home to a number of significant natural heritage habitats harboring rare and endangered species.

For many years, scientists and conservation groups have monitored changes in the environmental quality of the Haw River, including the Saxapahaw area. One of the methods commonly used for this is the identification of **indicator species**, or bioindicators. Ecologists also use bioindicators to help identify specific community types in nature, but for this particular application, bioindicators are used to reveal the health of an ecosystem because of how they react to the conditions within an environment. Aquatic insects are often used for this purpose, as some insect species are more sensitive to pollution, while others have been documented as more tolerant to contaminants. Insects are also extremely diverse organisms, and many spend some or all of their existence in water, making them a perfect model for examining the effects of **evolutionary** adaptation as well.

Evolutionary Adaptation

Let's start with a basic question. What is evolutionary adaptation and how has it affected the types of insects that we find in the Haw River? The first thing you should know is that adaptation is not an immediate process. It happens over time, and only the organisms that are capable of adapting in some way to their changing surroundings can pass those traits to future generations so that they not only survive, but thrive. Adaptation can occur due to a gene mutation, where a tiny change in the genetic code of an organism can cause it to grow or act differently than its predecessors. Adaptation can also occur because of a behavioral change that persists. For example, certain types of moths will avoid laying eggs on leaves that have been treated with insecticides. As a result, their adaptive behavior allows them to continue producing offspring successfully. An organism will only produce successful offspring if its adaptation, whether genetic or behavioral, is favorable in that particular environment. In this chapter we will explore various evolutionary adaptations of aquatic insects, some of which may have made them more or less susceptible to pollutants, thereby resulting in reliable bioindicators of environmental quality. Saxapahaw on the Haw River is a prime location for the study of insects and their fascinating adaptations, and afterward you will find an ample supply of local culture, food, and fun. So let's begin with a little insect introduction.

Aquatic Insects

Insects make up the largest group of organisms in the world. With 1.5 million described species and estimates of up to 10 million still left to be discovered, insects are found almost everywhere on our planet. Of the described species, about 40,000 are found living in or on or otherwise depend on the presence of fresh water at some point in their life cycles. These are the aquatic insects, and they have many amazing adaptations that allow them to live in their watery habitats.

While insects living in ponds, rivers, lakes, streams, springs, and other freshwater systems are abundant today, there haven't always been aquatic insects. Millions of years ago, insects first evolved on land, and the earliest species to appear in the fossil record were entirely terrestrial. This is important to consider when you think about insects living in water. Because early insects began life on land, they have body systems adapted for life on land. They developed a respiratory system, an extensive network of interconnected tubes that delivered oxygen from the air directly to their cells. They learned how to walk, and later to fly, on land. They learned to find mates, eat, and seek shelter on land. Their lives depended on easy access to air, easy movement through the air, and the ability to send signals on the wind, and they required terrestrial species of plants and animals as sources of food.

Let's consider for a moment what it would take for us, humans who live on land, to become an aquatic species. What would we need to survive? Obviously, our first concern would be getting oxygen. Assuming we could figure out a way to breathe underwater, we would also need to change the way we do almost everything. We would need to find or build new types of structures for shelter. We would need to learn to move differently, swimming instead of walking. We would need to change how and what we eat. We depend on electricity or fires to cook our food, and since neither is available underwater, we would have to eat raw foods.

These are problems similar to those faced by the first aquatic insects. Their systems were adapted to life on land, so why would insects move into an aquatic habitat at all? There are many possible scenarios. For example, a single gene mutation could have allowed for a single organism to be successful in the water, finding a surplus of food there and then producing a large number of offspring as a result. That gene would have been passed to the offspring, who also would have been successful in the water. If a mutation works to the benefit of the organism, evolutionarily it is worth keeping and, therefore, is passed on. Ultimately, living in water had advantages, such as new food sources and reduced predation, at least initially. Over the past 200 million years, insects have evolved many adaptations to aquatic habitats that have allowed them to use their terrestrial body plan in an aquatic setting. So let's talk about some of the adaptations required for survival in the water.

Getting oxygen is especially important for animals. We can survive without water for a few days and without food for a few weeks. We cannot, however, survive for more than a few minutes without oxygen. The very first aquatic insects probably held their breath underwater, coming back up for air whenever they needed it, just like marine mammals do. If you are a small aquatic insect, this is a very inefficient way to breathe, and it puts you at risk for being eaten by a great many predators at the surface. Because survival of a species requires adaptation to environmental change, more complicated respiratory adaptations began to evolve over time. Some insect body forms now include a snorkel, called a respiratory siphon. Early in the evolutionary process these insects had a small tube sticking out of their back end so that they were able to lurk underwater while keeping in contact with the air at the surface. Over time, insects with longer tubes were more successful, producing more offspring with longer tubes. As a result, breathing tubes increased in length, allowing insects to rest deeper in the water, find greater protection from predators, and perhaps even increase their ability to find food without giving up their connection to surface air.

As you imagine this change occurring over time, remember that any path of evolution is not a voluntary decision. The insects did not decide to grow a snorkel. This likely began as an unexpected mutation that worked, and so it was passed down to offspring who also were successful with that trait. Today, insects such as mosquito larvae, giant water bugs, and water scorpions use this type of system. They poke their long breathing tubes out at the surface to breathe more easily while remaining safely hidden underwater. Rat-tailed maggots (*Eristalis tenax*), the larvae of very beautiful flies, begin life in the muck at the bottom of stagnant waters. They extend a very long tube that is often several times the length of the insect's body so that they can breathe. Insects with snorkels often cannot stay completely underwater for more than a few minutes. As a result, they must remain fairly close to the surface so that they can extend their snorkels for air when needed.

Other insects get their oxygen another way: they take their air with them! These air bubbles are similar to SCUBA (self-contained underwater breathing apparatus)

Figure 11-1. Larval predacious diving beetle with a siphon for breathing at the surface. Photo by C. L. Goforth.

Figure 11-2. Adult predacious diving beetle showing the air bubble that it carries for breathing. Photo by C. L. Goforth.

tanks that human divers use, allowing the insects to remain underwater for much longer than their snorkel-breathing relatives. An insect with an air bubble might be able to stay underwater up to three hours. However, like a diver with a SCUBA tank, eventually the air in the bubble is used up, and the insect must return to the surface to get another bubble. Many aquatic beetles, including predaceous diving beetles, use this approach. Most aquatic bugs, like the water boatman and backswimmers, also carry bubbles of air with them while they are underwater.

Going to the surface is dangerous for many aquatic insects. They have to leave the safety of their hidden places to breathe, exposing themselves to potential predators. Many insects, over millions of years, have reduced their dependence on surface air by adapting their **exoskeletons**, or a rigid covering on the outside of the body for protection, so that they can remain underwater for longer periods. There are several methods by which this occurs: (1) Some insects have evolved with exoskeletons that are thin and soft, allowing oxygen to easily flow from the water through to their bodies. (2) Some insects have expanded the size of their exoskeletons by growing gills, creating a much larger body surface through which they can absorb oxygen from the water, because more surface area allows for greater oxygen exchange. Having gills virtually eliminates the need to go to the water surface because an insect can absorb all the oxygen it needs from the water. Many larval or juvenile, meaning immature, forms of winged insects, including dragonflies and damselflies, stoneflies, mayflies, caddisflies, and many true flies, use this method.

There are other problems that insects face in the water. Have you ever tried to run when you are chest deep in a swimming pool? If so, you know how much harder it can be to move in water than on land. The first aquatic insects likely moved awk-

Figure 11-3. Damselfly larva with gills at the end of its body. Photo by C. L. Goforth.

wardly and relied on walking around on the bottom to move. Some insects still walk most of the time, such as the family of crawling water beetles. However, today's aquatic insects show off a variety of adaptations that help them move more effectively through the water. Some insects body shapes have evolved to provide better underwater mobility. Predaceous diving beetles have a very elegantly curved, very smooth body surface that allows water to glide easily over their bodies as they swim. Backswimmers have developed a keeled upper body surface so that they literally cut through the water. This means they have a fin on their backs similar to the keel underneath a sailboat. They swim on their backs, so they are able to use this "keel" to cut through the water efficiently.

For other insects, the modification of only a few body parts can help them move better in the water. Water boatmen, giant water bugs, and water scavenger beetles have long hairs along one side of their hind legs. These help by giving each kick of the legs a more powerful stroke and pushing the insect through the water more quickly. Have you ever worn flippers while swimming? They work in a similar way. Dragonfly nymphs (juveniles) keep their gills tucked safely inside a chamber inside their bodies and must pump water in and out of their gill chamber to breathe. While this adaptation originally developed to help them breathe, dragonflies can also squirt water out of the gill chamber so quickly that they shoot forward in the water. This amazing jet propulsion method has prevented countless dragonfly nymphs from becoming a tasty meal.

We've discussed how movement in water can be difficult for a lot of aquatic insect species, but have you considered that staying in place could be tough as well? Stream insects are constantly at risk of being washed downstream. Staying in one place becomes more important than moving, and so there are a variety of adaptations that allow aquatic insects to avoid being washed away. Some aquatic insects simply grab a rock or other object in the stream tightly and hold on. Net-building caddisflies and hellgrammites have hooks at the back of their abdomen that they use to hold onto the underside of rocks. Blackflies weave a little pad of silk and connect themselves to it with a silken thread. If they are knocked off their rock, they can easily retract the silken thread and return to their rock. Case-building caddisflies build a kind of sleeve made of small rocks or plant materials that they live inside. This case weighs them down, so they can sink to the bottom and they won't float away. Many insects have flattened bodies so that water flows over them easily, providing less friction as

Figure 11-4. Caddisfly larva inside its protective casing. Photo by C. L. Goforth.

water flows downstream. One type of mayfly is incredibly flat and essentially crawls around on its belly when it wants to move about. There are even insects with suction cups! Both net-winged midge larvae and water pennies, a type of beetle larva, suction themselves onto rocks so tightly that it's hard to peel one off to take a closer look.

Finding Aquatic Insects

Many insect adaptations are very easy to look for in almost any freshwater habitat, but Saxapahaw on the Haw River is a marvelous place to look for them in the Piedmont region of North Carolina. There is easy access to shallow water at the boat launch.

Prepare for your trip by taking a few clean white yogurt cups with you. Greek yogurt cups work especially well because they are wide and shallow. Also, consider taking a metal kitchen strainer, a plastic spoon, and a magnifying glass. Once you arrive, fill your yogurt cups less than half full of water from the river. Swish the strainer through the river, scraping along the bottom a bit and up the sides of cattails and other aquatic plants. Then pull the strainer out of the water and look for movement. You will be able to carefully transfer any insects you see to your yogurt cups with the plastic spoon. Wade into the river and gently flip rocks upside down and look for insects on the bottoms. Make sure to put the rocks back where you found them. Use a magnifier if you have one to get a good, close-up look at the things you see. You'll likely be able to identify many aquatic adaptations in the insects you find.

When you are finished looking at your insects, it is good practice to put them back where you found them; they are likely to die if you don't. You are welcome to get into the river and look for aquatic insects, but remember that there is a no-collecting policy.

Before You Go

Pack your tools for exploring in a quick-dry or water-resistant bag, and plan to wear water shoes that will not come off. Wet rocks can be slippery.

After your aquatic insect adventures, consider exploring the area. Saxapahaw Island has a fun playground for kids. At the landing you can rent canoes and kayaks, or consider exploring the small but vibrant town around the river. The Old Dye House now houses a coffee shop and a general store with amazing food.

References and Resources

Bradley, T. J., A. D. Briscoe, S. G. Brady, H. L. Contreras, B. N. Danforth, R. Dudley, D. Grimaldi, J. F. Harrison, J. A. Kaiser, C. Merlin, S. M. Repppert, J. M. Vandenbrooks, and S. P. Yanoviak. "Episodes in Insect Evolution." *Integrative and Comparative Biology* 49, no. 5 (2009): 590–606.

"Haw River Trail." Alamance Parks, https://www.alamance-nc.com/recreation/outdoors/hrt/. Accessed October 28, 2018.

"Natural and Cultural History of the Haw River." Haw River Assembly, http://hawriver.org/about-the-river/history/. Accessed October 28, 2018.

"Saxapahaw." Map. The Haw River Canoe and Kayak Company. http://hawrivercanoe.com/saxapahaw-map/. Accessed October 28, 2018.

Website: Use any of the above websites for information regarding the Saxapahaw area specifically.

Contact: Chris Goforth—email: chris.goforth@naturalsciences.org

Address: Access at The Haw River Canoe and Kayak Company, 6079 Swepsonville-Saxapahaw Road, Graham, N.C. 27253; access at Saxapahaw Lake Paddle Access, 6096 Jordan Drive, Graham, N.C. 27253

GPS Coordinates: N 35°56.94, W 79°19.44

CHAPTER 12

Reed Gold Mine and Gold Hill Mines Historic Park

Gold Mining in the Piedmont

RANDY BECHTEL

SCIENTIFIC FIELDS OF STUDY: *Geology, Tectonics*

America's First Gold Rush

In 1799 Conrad Reed, a twelve-year-old boy, was playing in the creek on his family's farm in the rolling hills of the Piedmont between Charlotte and Asheboro. He spotted a 17-pound (7.7-kilogram) heavy, yellow "rock" and carried it home to his father. John Reed did not know what type of "rock" his son had found and used the unusually dense nugget as a doorstop. A few years later, the farmer decided to have the doorstop identified, so he took it to a jeweler in Fayetteville. In 1802 that sample became the first authenticated gold find in the United States. John Reed asked for a "big price" for the gold nugget. He accepted a week's worth of wages at about $3.50. The sample was actually worth a thousand times more than that, around $3,500, a value much lower than in today's dollars. Today, a gold piece of that weight would be valued at more than $300,000. There are reports that John Reed, realizing the error, returned to the jeweler and did receive further compensation for that nugget, but history does not record if he ever received the full value of his gold find.

The following year, John Reed partnered with some other local farmers and began mining gold on his land in Little Meadow Creek. The farmers mined during the off-season using pans or rockers, which were simply rocking boxes, to help sift through and wash sand and gravel, thereby concentrating the heavier gold flakes

Figure 12-1. Reed Gold Mine State Historic Site. This is the creek where gold was first discovered in the United States. North Carolina Department of Natural Resources. Courtesy of the Cultural Heritage Institutions of North Carolina, NC ECHO Project.

and nuggets in the bottom of the pan. This type of mining is called placer mining (pronounced plasser), and panning is one type of placer mining. Before the end of the first year, a slave named Peter had unearthed a 28-pound (12.7-kilogram) nugget. Worth $6,600 then, it would be worth more than $500,000 today. One story reported that Peter was offered a walnut-sized piece of the nugget before it was sent off for processing, but he declined, fearing that the offer was not sincere. As word spread around the Piedmont about the success of the Reed Gold Mine, many other farmers began part-time placer mining in their creeks. The success of these miners began the first gold rush in the United States.

Many nuggets were found on the Reed property; unfortunately, none of these nuggets remain for us to see what they look like or how big they are. A tennis-ball-sized sphere of gold would weigh about 5.7 pounds (2.6 kilograms). Can you imagine how big the 17-pound (7.7-kilogram) sample that Conrad Reed found would be? What about the 28-pound (12.7-kilogram) nugget that Peter found? In only twenty-five years, these part-time miners had discovered an estimated yield of $100,000 in gold according to 1824 gold values. Today, estimates of their find would have a value of over $1 million.

Panning is still a common, low-tech method of placer mining in the search for gold. The only requirements are a creek, a pan, and a scoop for shoveling sediment (gravel, sand, mud, etc.). The pan of sediments must be gently swirled in the water to separate different sediment sizes while also allowing heavy, dense gold to sink to the bottom of the pan. A slightly larger scale of panning uses rockers, which were made with half-barrels or hollowed out logs that were "rocked" back and forth to separate the creek sediment from the gold. Using these methods, many Piedmont farmers became quite adept at finding gold, but they were not familiar with the science of geology. They did not know why the gold was there or in which type of rocks it might be found. All they knew was that if they carefully sifted through stream sediments, they might find gold.

There was so much gold being discovered in North Carolina by 1823 that the state government commissioned Professor Denison Olmsted, from the University of North Carolina at Chapel Hill, to conduct geologic surveys determining the extent of gold deposits in the state. Olmsted's surveys revealed that gold deposits covered nearly half of the state throughout the Piedmont and Mountains. Today, the North Carolina Geological Survey still produces geologic maps and surveys for natural resources and other geologic studies.

When word spread about the presence of gold, North Carolinians had "gold fever" and were on the hunt for the precious metal. Gold was discovered northeast of the Reed Gold Mine in 1824 on nearby Gold Hill. Placer mining led to more extensive underground mining around Gold Hill in 1825 when an observant miner walking in a local creek made an interesting observation. Mathias Barringer noticed that past a certain spot in the stream, he could not find any more gold, but he also observed that gold existed in veins of the local white quartz rock. He found a white vein of quartz running from the creek. As the quartz weathered and was broken down by natural erosion, gold was released gradually from the vein and washed downstream, thus revealing to Barringer the source of the gold. Barringer's observations would change the course of gold mining in the area forever.

Realizing that gold could be found in quartz veins was both good and bad for the miners. The good news was that they found more gold. The bad news was that the gold was trapped in hard quartz veins. Miners had to determine how to excavate the veins and then process the rock to release the gold from the quartz. This type of hard-rock mining, or lode mining, took much more physical effort, money, machinery, and knowledge, so experienced English miners were consulted. These miners had deep-mining expertise. In North Carolina, they excavated shafts over 800 feet (244 meters) deep following the gold-rich quartz veins. Reed began digging deep on his property to excavate gold from quartz veins in 1831. The deepest shaft at the Reed Gold Mine is around 140 feet (42.7 meters).

As the miners dug deeper following the quartz veins, they built elaborate supportive structures of timber frames to reinforce the shafts and tunnels. Ladders, pulleys, and iron buckets, called kibbles, were used by miners to access the work area and to haul the raw ore, the rock containing **minerals**, that was being mined out of the ground. Miners worked by candlelight to pry rocks apart along their natural joints, or **fractures**, using chisels, picks, shovels, crowbars, and gunpowder.

Lode mining is dangerous even using modern techniques. There always have been concerns about underground tunnels collapsing, dangerous gases that contaminate the air and hinder breathing, and the need to pump out groundwater to prevent the tunnels and shafts from flooding. After the gold-bearing quartz was excavated from the ground, it had to be processed by crushing the ore into a powder with a special mill and then mixed with liquid mercury to separate the gold from the rock powder. Later, other chemicals, like chlorine and cyanide, were used to separate the gold. The mercury combined chemically with the gold, creating an amalgam, or a mixture of mercury plus a metal. The gold was separated from the amalgam by boiling away the mercury, leaving only gold. Mercury is poisonous; it strongly affects the nervous system, and in the past many people became sick by breathing mercury vapors during the boiling process. Although mercury is no longer used, there are reports of mercury in North Carolina streams as a result of historic gold mining.

The Gold Hill District mines produced about $7–9 million in gold and were some of the most productive gold mines in the South. The California Gold Rush of 1848 reinvigorated gold mining in North Carolina, and between 1853 and 1858 the Gold Hill mines were known as the richest property east of the Mississippi River. North Carolina gold mines continued to prosper and led the way in gold production until the beginning of the Civil War. When the gold rush was in full swing during the early to mid-1800s, these modern-day sleepy little hamlets were major employers in North Carolina's economic engine, second only to agriculture. The Reed Gold Mine operated until 1912 and is currently a North Carolina Historic Site. The Gold Hill mines operated until 1915 and are now a Historic Park. Almost 600 known inactive gold mines or prospects are located in the Piedmont and Mountains of North Carolina.

Although gold was first officially authenticated in the United States from the 17-pound (7.7 kilogram) sample found by Conrad Reed, this was probably not the first occurrence of gold being found. Native Americans searched for gold in what is now Cherokee County, and the first European to mine gold here was most likely Hernando DeSoto in 1540, also in Cherokee County near the town of Murphy.

Why Is Gold There?

Good question. The short answer is that hot fluids within the Earth, primarily **magma** and heated water, carrying lots of different minerals, including gold, flowed through cracks and pores in the rocks. As these fluids cooled, they could not hold the minerals and caused the gold, quartz, and other minerals to precipitate and fill in cracks in the rocks, forming deposits of gold-rich quartz veins.

The bigger question for geologists is why were there hot fluids flowing in and through the rock? This is a mystery that geologists want to understand. If they can understand why the gold is in certain places, they may be able to predict where more might be found. The surrounding rocks hold clues and many times tell a really interesting story, if geologists are able to decipher what is written in the rocks.

The key for our story is that the rocks in the rolling hills of the Piedmont are parts of ancient volcanoes. Actually, the area was part of a chain of volcanic islands, or a volcanic island arc. Volcanoes, in general, are really good at concentrating minerals into veins. This is because there is a hot magma chamber underground that is feeding the volcano. It heats the water and other materials, so they flow through the surrounding rocks. The hot water dissolves gold and other minerals from the rocks and then gradually cools, concentrating the minerals into veins. Also, when the volcano emits lava or ash clouds, it is spewing microscopic pieces of gold that are deposited in the surrounding sediments. So now we have gold deposited above and below the surface of the Earth.

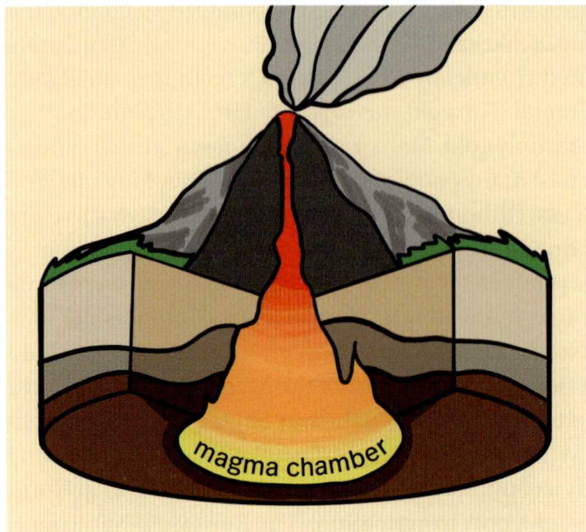

Figure 12-2. Cross-sectional illustration of an active volcano. Illustration by Ashleigh M. Smith.

The next part of our story involves massive collisions of two continents that eventually formed the supercontinent **Pangea** and the Appalachian Mountains that ran down the middle of the supercontinent. We have discussed this concept in various ways in previous chapters, but please see the Piedmont Geology section (p. 106) for a broad overview of the geologic history. For this particular story, the volcanic islands were erupting about 540 million years ago off the coast of one of these continents, called Gondwana, which included ancient Africa, South America, and Antarctica.

Why were there volcanoes erupting? That was due to plate **tectonics**. Gondwana was on a collision course with the continent of Laurentia, or ancestral North America, but there was an ocean, the Iapetus Ocean, caught in the middle. In Greek mythology, Iapetus was the father of Atlas, whose name is the basis for the name Atlantic Ocean, just as the Iapetus Ocean existed before the Atlantic Ocean. The ocean crust beneath the Iapetus Ocean had nowhere to go, so it dove, or subducted, under Gondwana. As the ocean crust dove deeper into the Earth, it started melting. Molten or melted rock, called magma, oozed up through the Gondwana crust and is the source of magma for the volcanic islands in our story. As the two continents got closer and closer, the ocean got smaller and smaller until there was no more room for our unlucky volcanic islands. They were squished, folded, and faulted as they were plastered, or accreted, onto Laurentia around 450 million years ago. Slowly, the Iapetus Ocean was squeezed out of existence as Laurentia and Gondwana collided to form the Appalachian Mountains and the supercontinent of Pangea ~300 million years ago. All of this occurred over a period of ~240 million years.

The Reed Gold Mine and the Gold Hill district are located in one of these ancient fault zones. At this point in our story, the gold deposits were still deep underground, beneath the huge mountains formed by the collisions. About 220 million years ago, Pangea began to rift, or split up, into numerous pieces, including the continents of North America and Africa. Both erosion and the rifting of Pangea have allowed the once-deep gold deposits to be uncovered and raised to the surface of the Earth, where humans could easily find them. These two modern continents are still spreading apart today, and the mountains are still eroding today. Twelve-year-old Conrad Reed was probably just having fun playing in a creek in the rolling hills of the Piedmont in 1799, but he made history when he found a 17-pound (7.7-kilogram) nugget of gold that was over 500 million years in the making.

Before You Go

Reed Gold Mine State Historic Site (Cabarrus County, N.C.)

At this state historic site there is a museum that focuses on the history of gold in North Carolina, including a twenty-three-minute historical film called *All That Glitters*. Portions of the underground tunnels at Reed Gold Mine have been restored for tours. Guided tours of a ca. 1895 restored stamp mill—a machine used to crush gold ore—are also offered. There are several picnic areas available, and vending machines are located outside the museum. All site activities, apart from panning for gold, are free of charge.

The panning area is open from April to November, weather permitting. Instructors give lessons on how to pan for gold in troughs set up next to historic Little Meadow Creek. For those not wanting to pan for gold, or for those under the age of eight, a panning demonstration by an instructor is available at no charge.

Websites: www.nchistoricsites.org/reed/reed.htm; www.facebook.com/reedgoldmineshs?ref=hl; twitter.com/reedgoldmine
Contact: phone: (704) 721-GOLD (4653)
Address: 9621 Reed Mine Road, Midland, N.C. 28107
GPS Coordinates: N 35°17.16, W 80°27.96

Gold Hill Mines Historic Park (Rowan County, N.C.)

As you may already know, Au is the chemical symbol for gold, and the Gold Hill Mines Historic Park offers an "Au-some" experience celebrating the gilded age of gold discovery in North Carolina—all puns intended. Today, the Barnhardt Gold Mine and the Randolph Gold Mine are two of four gold mines located on the 70-acre park.

Visitors will enjoy the great outdoors, as the park offers several miles of hiking/biking/equestrian trails and playground and picnic areas. This includes the Gold Hill Rail Trail, which is the railroad corridor right-of-way through the park that extends into Cabarrus County. It was added in 2005 as an additional hiking trail. All areas are pet friendly and kid friendly. Tours of the park and historic village are available for school groups, senior groups, church groups, civic organizations, etc.

Websites: www.historicgoldhill.com; www.facebook.com/pages/Historic-Gold-Hill-North-Carolina/163269537038650
Contact: email: vivian@HistoricGoldHill.com; phone: (704) 267-9439
Address: 735 St. Stephens Church Road, Gold Hill, N.C.
GPS Coordinates: N 35°30.78, W 80°20.64

References and Resources

Blakeslee, Sandra. "Fiery Volcano in Colombia Spewing Gold." *New York Times*, October 28, 1994, https://www.nytimes.com/1994/10/28/world/fiery-volcano-in-colombia-spewing-gold.html. Accessed October 29, 2018.

Carpenter, P. Albert, III. *Gold in North Carolina*. Information Circular no. 29 (2nd ed.). Raleigh: North Carolina Geological Survey, 1999.

Knapp, R. F., and B. D. Glass. *Gold Mining in North Carolina: A Bicentennial History*. Raleigh: North Carolina Office of Archives and History, 1999.

"Mercury Amalgam." M4V video, 1:56. YouTube, https://www.youtube.com/watch?v=gKxCw889qck. Accessed October 29, 2018.

Stuart, Doug. "Gold Element Facts." Chemicool, http://www.chemicool.com/elements/gold.html. Accessed October 29, 2018.

For a general geology guide with field trips that includes a chapter on Reed Gold Mine, see K. G. Stewart and M. R. Roberson, *Exploring the Geology of the Carolinas: A Field Guide to Favorite Places from Chimney Rock to Charleston* (Chapel Hill: University of North Carolina Press, 2007).

For a technical geologic field trip guide with scientific papers, see J. Hibbard and J. Pollock, *One Arc, Two Arcs, Old Arc, New Arc*, Carolina Geological Society, 2013, http://carolinageologicalsociety.org/CGS/Guidebooks.html (accessed October 29, 2018).

CHAPTER 13

Sandhills

The Making of a Forest

KIM HYRE

SCIENTIFIC FIELDS OF STUDY: *Geology, Forest Ecology, Mycology, Ornithology*

Take a walk in the woods of the Sandhills, and the first thing you might notice is the white sand underfoot and tall pine trees swaying over your head. The massive pine cones growing in these trees can be up to 10 inches in length, and they pack a punch when they hit the ground. Explore a little closer and you will notice the bases of all the pine trees are black and look as though they have lived through a wildfire, even though they are still green with growth in the branches. This is an environment very different from what you will find throughout the rest of North Carolina. The first thought that probably hits you is where does all this sand come from when the ocean is so far away? Welcome to the Sandhills, North Carolina's region of ancient ocean shoreline found right in the middle of the state.

The three geographic regions of North Carolina are the Mountains, the Piedmont and the Coastal Plain. The Sandhills area is sometimes discussed as its own geographic region, because most often it is included in the Coastal Plain or the Piedmont. In this book, it is treated as part of the Piedmont. The Sandhills is a small, skinny strip of land covering only about seven counties in the south-central region of North Carolina, wedged between the Coastal Plain and the Piedmont with very different environmental characteristics. If you were to look over a larger scale across the southeastern United States, you would see that the Sandhills is a unique geographic band that stretches southwest through South Carolina and Georgia.

The Sandhills area was once ancient sand dunes, but it is not all sand now; many different soil types are found in the area. At the surface, the top layer is bright white sand, but if we dig a hole to plant a tree, we may find different colors of sand, clay soils, or even pebbles. Because of the sand layers, we can infer that the ocean has been here, but we will have to turn to the study of geology to help us learn about the rest of the Sandhills formation.

Let us start when all the known land masses on the Earth's crust collided together forming a single land mass called **Pangea**. You can refer back to the Piedmont Geology introduction for dates if you're interested. This gradual action, occurring over three different collisions, pushed land together with such force that rocks were pushed upward to form North Carolina's mountains. At that time, the mountains were at a tremendous height of approximately 26,000 feet (7,925 meters) above sea level—roughly the same height as the Himalayas today. Today, our tallest mountain in North Carolina is Mount Mitchell, which now measures about 6,684 feet (2,037 meters) above sea level. So where did the tops of the mountains go? Downhill is the answer. Through erosion caused by **weathering** over 100 million years, all these newly exposed soils were carried downhill toward the ocean by rain, wind, and fast-flowing rivers.

Now, let us skip to ~200 million years ago as the continents moved away from each other, tearing and ripping the ground, forming three gigantic ditches just beyond our newly formed Piedmont. You can locate these ditches, called Triassic basins, by drawing an imaginary line on a map of North Carolina stretching from just south of Durham all the way to Wadesboro, with a width that includes Sanford to Troy. Triassic basins can be found up and down the Atlantic coast of the United States as evidence of when Pangea broke apart. They served as "catch basins" for the solid material rolling from the mountains toward the ocean, and they started to fill up with soils, rocks, and boulders. At this stage, the Sandhills was still just beyond the Piedmont and still underwater. Refer to Map 3 (p. 107) to see where North Carolina's Triassic basins are located.

Moving ahead in time to ~140 million years ago, the ditches were filled to the brim with sediments and rocks, making the land very level. The once fast-moving streams slowed down and meandered lazily to the ocean carrying lighter materials such as sand, clay, or small pebbles and depositing them into the shallow ocean at the Sandhills. This created a giant delta fan making new land spanning from North Carolina through South Carolina and into Georgia. The same thing is happening today on a much smaller scale near New Orleans, where the Mississippi River meets the Gulf of Mexico. Moving forward again in time, this new land eventually formed what is now the Coastal Plain, leaving lots of newly exposed land for animals and plants to occupy. If you look at the Piedmont map, you'll see that the Sandhills section is farther inland from most of the Coastal Plain. While, geographically, it sits directly south of the Piedmont, it maintains characteristics similar to those of the Coastal Plain region because of its origin (see Map 3).

This new land was sandy and shifted daily with high winds. New plants needed to be able to set their seeds quickly into the shifting sands and hold on to water any way they could. To survive in these conditions, the plants' root systems adapted in various ways. Some plants began to form shallow roots that held shifting sands in place and had water-storing roots as well. Others grew long roots straight downward into the ground to find water deep within the layers of soil. Many plants today still use these same root structures. The new plants that moved into the area came by wind from the southwest or from the land exposed around the Gulf of Mexico. A new type of grass, called wiregrass (*Aristida stricta*), spread in the newly exposed sandy soils by blowing its light seeds into the Sandhills. Wiregrass helped to stabilize the sand by forming the shallow spreading root system that secures the plants and soil and stores water, even in the driest of times. Wiregrass continues to serve this role today.

Arriving on that same wind were flying, helicopter-like seeds from a new kind of pine tree known as longleaf (*Pinus palustris*), which would begin to inhabit the new sandy land over time. Longleaf pines have adapted to survival in the harsh sandy soils by growing a long, deep-set taproot, which begins developing just days after the seed hits barren sand. Longleaf pines have an interesting and unusual growth

Figure 13-1. Longleaf pine in the mature stage, which lasts until the tree is 250 to 300 years old. Photo by Nancy Williamson.

Figure 13-2. Longleaf pine in the flat-top or old-growth stage. This stage occurs when the tree is between 300 and 500 years old. Photo by Nancy Williamson.

pattern. As seedlings, they grow 16- to 20-inch-long needles that seem to sprout right out of the ground, making them look like tall tufts of grass on the surface, while the roots move deep into the ground seeking water. This is called the grass stage, and it lasts 4 to 6 years. Once the long taproot has found water, a stem starts to grow, and the long needles stick directly out of the trunk with no branches. This is called the bottle brush stage. The third stage is called the mature stage. At this stage, the longleaf begins to grow straight limbs near the top of the tree and produce very large pine cones. Longleafs stay in this mature stage until they reach 250 to 300 years old.

In the final stage of growth, the limbs start to become crooked or mangled, and they look as if a giant sat on them, giving them a flat look on top. This is called the flat-top or old-growth stage. Longleaf pines live in this stage until they are around 500 years old.

While the forests develop, survival requires adaptation to a powerful force of nature: fire. Adaptations to fire include the many growing stages, as well as thick protective bark. Lightning is very common in the southeastern United States during the spring and summer months, and these bolts of electricity hit the ground with such force that fires can start quickly. During the early days of the developing longleaf pine forests, these natural fires would occur every two to four years, leaving very little fuel to burn, so the fires remained "low intensity," where they slowly creeped along the ground and could have burned for days without any interruption from people. When Native Americans inhabited the area, they probably helped these fires by letting them burn or possibly starting some themselves, because they learned that the results were magical. Fire added important nutrients to the soil and kept the landscape open for grazing animals, such as the woodland buffalo and white-tailed deer, making it a **productive** hunting ground for any **Indigenous** tribes. Refer to Chapters 14 and 16 to read more about how fire benefited Native Americans.

Still today when fire breaks out, a thick bark protects the longleaf pines from heat and flames, and wiregrass stays in a state of readiness for any chance to regenerate and produce new seeds. After fire has moved through a longleaf forest, the animals will return to the burned areas within hours, while wiregrass resprouts within forty-eight hours. Humans have interrupted the natural cycles of fire in many longleaf pine forests, so today highly trained personnel start fires called controlled burns in an effort to reduce underbrush and restore the natural renewing effects of fire. If you visit the Sandhills region in the spring or summer months, there is a good chance you will see recently burned areas.

Fire has helped to maintain an open forest for a few special animals that live in the Sandhills: the fox squirrel (*Sciurus niger*) and the red-cockaded woodpecker (*Picoides borealis*), in particular. Both of these tree-dwellers use the longleaf pines for food and homes. Fox squirrels are huge when compared with gray squirrels. They weigh about 2.5 pounds (1.1 kilograms) and have a very long tail. They can be all black or gray, but they can also be found with touches of red, brown, gold, and white on them. Normally, they have a white nose tip and white ears with a black mask across their face. They spend a majority of their time on the ground, and the Sandhills locals have nicknamed them "monkey squirrels" because of the fun they seem to have searching for foods on the forest floor. They have two primary food sources: pine nuts found in the longleaf cones and puffball mushrooms. Puffball mushrooms are round, white mushrooms containing millions of spores. If you touch the top of this soft fungus with your finger, a cloud of spores will shoot into the air from a hole in the top. This is one simple method of dispersal for growing new mushrooms. Fox squirrels prefer to eat puffball mushrooms when the flesh is bright white and they are shaped like small balls lying on the ground. The squirrels eat the entire mushroom, spores and all. Once these spores have gone through a squirrel's digestive system, they come out as scat, or poop. This is a second method of dispersal for growing new mushrooms. The spores work their way into the ground during rain events and attach themselves to longleaf pine roots. Newly attached spores grow into the longleaf pine root system, helping the tree to absorb extra nutrients, especially phosphorus, needed to survive the dry, sandy soils. The tree's roots then deliver food in the form of sugars to the fungus. New fruiting bodies, like mushrooms, then form under the tree ready to release new spores. This type of relationship is called a mycorrhizal symbiosis, and neither the fungus nor the tree could thrive without the other.

The red-cockaded woodpecker is an endangered species with fewer than 10,000 individuals remaining in the wild. This bird never flies south for the winter but, instead, makes its home in live pine trees year-round. Most woodpeckers prefer dead standing trees; however, red-cockaded woodpeckers choose live pine trees because, once a tree has been excavated to make a home, small holes pecked underneath each entrance allow sap to drip down the trunk, providing a sticky protective barrier from climbing **predators**. Inside this pine tree home lives a family with one male

Figure 13-3. Red-cockaded woodpecker (*Picoides borealis*). This particular bird has been banded to help the forestry service keep track of a dwindling population. The red-cockaded woodpecker is considered a keystone species in southern pine forests because many different types of animals use the cavities that they make in the trunks of pine trees. A keystone species refers to an organism on which many other organisms depend for survival. Photo by Scott Hartley.

and one female who are the only mating pair. The rest of the family is made up of the previous season's offspring, mostly young males, who remain in the family tree to help raise the newest family members by gathering food and cleaning the nest. This makes them cooperative breeders. Every one of the family members has its own tree cavity within the same tree to roost, or sleep, in at night. Young females tend to leave the family home during the first winter to look for a mate and start a family of their own.

It can take several years to create these cavities in a living tree because the birds must fight sticky pine sap. For this reason, red-cockaded woodpeckers prefer to use trees that are in their last stage of life, the old-growth stage, and are infected with red-heart fungus. The fungus makes the center of the tree soft for easier excavation, and in this older stage sap is found only a few inches under the bark, so that the entire center of the tree holds no sap. This makes a nice dry cavity for sleeping and raising a family.

Longleaf pine forests thrived in the Southeast at one time and formed one giant forest that was around 93 million acres. It stretched west from the coastline of Virginia through the Southeast to Texas. As far as the eye could see in all directions, the forest floor was an open savanna with grasses on the ground and tall pines overhead. After the Civil War (1861–65) many large stands of longleaf pines were cut for development, homebuilding, and shipbuilding. At that time, Americans could not imagine such a large resource ever disappearing. Yet today there are only about 4 million acres of longleaf pine forest remaining across the southeastern United States. It is now broken up into many small segments, and this loss of habitat is the main reason why the red-cockaded woodpecker and nearly thirty other species that live there are endangered or threatened. Conservationists are working hard to bring back longleaf pine forests by planting saplings and reintroducing controlled burning. Controlled burns capitalize on fires' regenerative benefits and prevent **understory** growth that serves as fuel causing fires to burn so hot they damage the trees.

Before You Go

There are two North Carolina state parks, both located in the Sandhills, that have good examples of a longleaf pine forest: Carvers Creek State Park and Weymouth Woods–Sandhills Nature Preserve. These parks are open every day of the year except Christmas Day, and they provide free public programs. All programs are advertised on the North Carolina State Parks website. While visiting both of these parks, be sure to bring water, bug spray, and binoculars to hike along the trails investigating the world of longleaf pines. Look for evidence of fire, watch for fox squirrels or red-cockaded woodpeckers, and enjoy walking on the sandy trails.

Carvers Creek is a new park located in Spring Lake, north of Fayetteville and Fort Bragg Military Reservation on Manchester Road. Carvers Creek State Park has many educational programs available, but only two require a reservation: the canoe hikes and the tour of the James S. Rockefeller home.

Website: https://www.ncparks.gov/carvers-creek-state-park
Contact: Park office at (910) 436-4681 daily from 8:00 A.M. to 5:00 P.M., or by email at carvers.creek@ncparks.gov.
Address: 2505 Long Valley Road, Spring Lake, N.C. 28390
GPS Coordinates: N 35°12.24, W 78°58.62

Weymouth Woods–Sandhills Nature Preserve is just outside Southern Pines on Fort Bragg Road. There are 4.5 miles of hiking trails as well as an educational public program every Sunday at 3:00 P.M.

Website: https://www.ncparks.gov/weymouth-woods-sandhills-nature-preserve
Contact: Park office at (910) 692-2167 daily from 8:00 A.M. to 5:00 P.M., or by email at weymouth.woods@ncparks.gov.
Address: 1024 Ft. Bragg Road, Southern Pines, N.C. 28387
GPS Coordinates: N 35°8.82, W 79°22.14

References and Resources

Haywood, James D. *Prescribed Fire—A Necessary Management Tool for Longleaf Pine*. USDA Forest Service Southern Research Station, https://www.srs.fs.usda.gov/longleaf/products/brochure-files/Prescribed_Fire_in_LLP.pdf. Accessed October 30, 2018.

Kendrick, Bryce. "Chapter 17: Mycorrhizas-Mutualistic Plant-Fungus Symbioses." In *The Fifth Kingdom*. 3rd ed. Indianapolis: Focus Publishing, 2001.

Red-cockaded woodpecker: Picoides borealis. U.S. Fish and Wildlife Service, 2005, https://www.fws.gov/northeast/pdf/rcwood.fs.pdf. Accessed October 30, 2018.

CHAPTER 14

Prairie Ridge Ecostation

Prairie in the City

KATHRYN STEVENSON

SCIENTIFIC FIELDS OF STUDY: *Ecology, Zoology*

Close your eyes and think of a prairie . . . switchgrass and wildflowers flowing in the wind, butterflies and bees feasting on abundant nectar, bobwhite quail fluttering away as you walk along, a hawk swooping low looking for mice to eat, and even a small herd of buffalo in the distance. Where are you? Kansas? The Wild West of the 1800s? Or could you be in Raleigh, North Carolina?

Prairie ecosystems were abundant throughout the Piedmont regions of the eastern United States as recently as 1750, including an area that is presently one of the fastest-growing urban centers in the country, the Research Triangle in North Carolina. Imagine that instead of looking out to see the concrete of a mall parking lot, or even a forest in a North Carolina state park, you could stand atop a hill and see acres and acres of prairie adjacent to thick forests. Historical records suggest that both forests and prairies were abundant in the Piedmont, so this is exactly what you might see. Prairie ecosystems thrived because of grazing animals like bison and elk, naturally occurring wildfires, and fires set by Native Americans to maintain grazing lands. These fires killed young trees and shrubs that might have encroached on the prairie. The network of rivers here would act as firebreaks, so North Carolina prairies were probably much smaller than those in the Midwest; but as early as 1540 settlers wrote of the "savannahs" here, suggesting that we had big prairies. Yet the land of savannahs changed after most of the Native Americans were forced to leave the Carolinas and the bison and elk were hunted to extinction, so now only remnants of Carolina prairies remain. But you have the chance to see what this landscape may have looked like with a visit to Prairie Ridge Ecostation in Raleigh.

Just off Reedy Creek Road, near the North Carolina Art Museum, Prairie Ridge occupies 38.5 acres of prairie grassland and bottomland forest, with ponds and a stream. At one time, the site was part of a prison farm owned by the North Carolina state prison system where prisoners were required to farm the land. Afterward, the

Figure 14-1. The prairie at Prairie Ridge Ecostation. Photo by C. L. Goforth.

land was used for grazing cows. When the North Carolina Museum of Natural Sciences established the ecostation in 2004, the maintained cow pasture was allowed to return to a more natural state, and the prairie was created so that today we can experience a prairie as we would have long ago. The switchgrass that dominates the prairie grassland came from North Carolina seed stock, and a variety of wildflowers were planted or brought in by birds or wind-driven seed dispersal. The bottomland forest is now a healthy and mature wooded area, including an impressive arboretum, an area of various types of trees and shrubs, that features breeding pairs of as many as 90 percent of the tree species native to North Carolina. Because some tree species grow male and female flowers on completely separate plants, known as dioecious breeding, a breeding pair is required to fertilize the female plant, grow seeds, and then form new trees. These rich and diverse ecosystems attract a wide array of wildlife including birds, amphibians and reptiles, fish, mammals, and an enormous number of **invertebrates**, including terrestrial, winged, and aquatic species. Invertebrates are animals without backbones, comprising approximately 95 percent of all animal species on Earth. The invertebrates you most likely will see at Prairie Ridge include

- arthropods (insects including bees, butterflies, beetles, grasshoppers, and flies; centipedes; millipedes; arachnids like spiders and ticks);
- mollusks (snails);
- various types of worms.

Figure 14-2. Eastern bluebirds (*Sialia sialis*). Photo by C. L. Goforth.

Figure 14-3. A purple martin (*Progne subis*) singing near its gourd-shaped house. Photo by C. L. Goforth.

Prairie Ridge maintains a species list that you can find on its website. Download it and see how many you can find when you visit. It's an impressive list for an area tucked into a major urban center.

Exploring Prairie Ridge through the Seasons

One of the best things about the mild climate in the North Carolina Piedmont region is that any time of year is a good time for getting outside to explore. Just about the time we switch to daylight saving time in March, you might start noticing that the birds are particularly loud in the morning—this is called the dawn chorus. Springtime is when birds use songs to attract their mates and begin making nests to lay eggs. The open grasslands at Prairie Ridge are a great place to look for birds in the spring. You might hear the "tru-al-ly, tru-al-ly" song of the eastern bluebird (*Sialia sialis*) and see its unmistakable bright royal blue feathers flying in a wave motion. Bluebirds eat insects and fruit, nest in cavities in trees or boxes, and live near open fields.

You might also see the purple martins (*Progne subis*) that migrate through North Carolina at the beginning of March from their winter homes in South America. Purple martins eat mosquitoes, termites, and other insects and nest in groups in open areas. You might notice some white, gourd-shaped houses hanging over the fields near the Neighborhood Garden—those have been placed there for purple martins. While these birds usually nest in tree cavities, the gourds have been installed at Prairie Ridge to encourage nesting and offer shelter to attract an even greater number of birds.

Figure 14-4. Maypop, or passionflower (*Passiflora incarnata*), grows in every county in North Carolina. Photo by C. L. Goforth.

While you are at the garden, keep your eye out for crossvine (*Bigonia capreolata*), a large, climbing native vine that attracts hummingbirds. As you walk down toward the lowland forest, look up for the eastern tent caterpillar (*Malacosoma americanum*) nests. They look like big webs and keep the eggs safe and warm. These caterpillars are blue, black, orange, and white with a yellow-and-white stripe down their backs. They will become moths after a few months inside their nests. Along the lowland forest trail, keep an eye out for **vernal pools**, which are temporary pools that occur only in the spring when we get lots of rain. The word "vernal" refers to the spring season. Salamanders and frogs lay their eggs in these pools, and that is a brilliant ecological strategy; since the pools are temporary, there are no fish to eat the eggs. See Chapter 17, "Hemlock Bluffs Nature Preserve and the Stevens Nature Center," for a photo of salamander egg masses (Figure 17-3). Listen for the Cope's gray treefrog (*Hyla chrysoscelis*), which has a short, shrill trill, or call: "Whrrrrrrr!!"

In the summer, head across the prairie trail to the pond. Keep an eye out for the green darner (*Anax junius*), which is a dragonfly known as the "mosquito hawk." It eats mosquitoes and other flying insects and migrates all the way from Mexico. You may also see and hear red-winged blackbirds (*Agelaius phoeniceus*) calling. The males are easy to spot; they are all black with a flash of red on their shoulders that is visible when they fly. The females are brown and can also be found hanging out around the pond. Along the trail, keep an eye out for the passionflower (*Passiflora incarnata*), with exotic blue, pink, and white flowers. This vine has three- to five-lobed leaves, can grow 25 feet in length, is native to every North Carolina county, and blooms May through July.

In late June, also watch out for the blackberry patch where you can stop and try a few. If you continue on the Prairie Trail toward the arboretum and the lowland forest, you will pass Rat Snake Junction, a spot where you can often see the eastern rat snake (*Pantherophis alleghaniensis*) sunning itself. It is nonvenomous and a good climber, and it eats small mammals, birds, eggs, and lizards. If you don't spot it here, head up toward the classroom, where it is sometimes sunning itself near the steps. Feel free to step into the cool shade, use the restroom, and fill up your water bottles if there are no programs in session. As you head up toward the classroom,

Figure 14-5. Monarch butterfly (*Danaus plexippus*). Photo by C. L. Goforth.

Figure 14-6. The prairie in the fall when the switchgrass starts to brown. Photo by C. L. Goforth.

look for common milkweed (*Asclepias syriaca*) growing in tall green stems with flowers in purple bunches. Milkweed is host to a variety of insects, including monarch butterflies (*Danaus plexippus*). The adult monarchs lay their eggs on the milkweed leaves, then the hatched larvae (or caterpillars) feed exclusively on milkweed—it is required for their survival.

The fall is one of the best times of year to appreciate the beauty of the prairie. The switchgrass (*Panicum viratum*) (Figure 14-6) displays its feathery plumes and turns a golden brown. It is more than just beautiful; it provides seeds and cover for

Figure 14-7. A controlled burn occurs in the winter. Photo by C. L. Goforth.

native birds as well as erosion control during the winter rains because its roots hold the soil in place. Recently, scientific researchers have been considering the potential for growing switchgrass to be used as a **sustainable** biofuel. Watch for the American bird grasshoppers (*Schistocerca amricana*), which are about 2 inches long, as you walk through the prairie. In the demonstration garden, you might notice the black swallowtail butterfly larvae (*Papilio polyxenes*). These caterpillars of green or white, yellow, and black will hatch into beautiful adult swallowtail butterflies. As you head toward the lowland forest, you will likely spot a tree bearing orange fruits and with bark that is grooved and blotchy. This is the common persimmon (*Diospyros virginiana*), which provides tasty treats for raccoons, possum, deer, and other animals. If you can reach one of the soft, wrinkly fruits, feel free to try it. Just note that they can be very astringent, or sharp, until after the first frost. Next to the outdoor classroom you'll find the beautyberry (*Callicarpa americana*) shrubs. We don't recommend eating these, but they do provide food for insects and birds all winter and are lovely to look at. If you would like to grow these at home, they are available for purchase at most garden centers. Make sure to keep an eye to the sky for the red-tailed hawk (*Buteo jamaicensis*), which is one of the largest hawks you will see on the prairie. It has a reddish tail and can be as long as 18 inches (46 centimeters) with a wingspan of 4.0 feet (1.2 meters).

Figure 14-8. An American bullfrog (*Lithobates catesbeianus*) enjoying the pond. Photo by C. L. Goforth.

Winter is a great time to explore the prairie and see some of the features that you might not see the rest of the year. Winter is a time for restoration on the prairie, so you may be able to observe the particularly renewing practice of prescribed fire. Fire is a natural process, and fires are beneficial to the land because they serve to renew natural resources. These natural fires help provide good food-hunting opportunities for birds, limit overgrowth of vegetation, and provide important nutrients for the soil. In the wild, fire often occurs because of a lightning strike; however, in many locations, years of preventing wildfires have led to a dangerous buildup of underbrush. The excess fuel allows fires to burn hotter than regularly occurring natural fires, and these extremely hot fires can damage mature growth and spread rapidly. One solution to maintaining a healthy ecosystem is to schedule prescribed, or controlled, burns. Prescribed fire is a fire that is set by experienced firefighters to help reduce that excess natural fuel or underbrush, so that when a fire burns through an area, it is not catastrophic. Instead, it contributes to the natural process of renewing the land by allowing for the regrowth of native vegetation. Fires are an important part of natural ecosystems, and every year, about one-third of the prairie at Prairie Ridge undergoes a prescribed burn to help maintain a healthy prairie ecosystem. To read more about the role of fire in the Piedmont region, please refer to the Sandhills chapter (Chapter 13), the Pilot Mountain chapter (Chapter 15), the Botanical Garden chapter (Chapter 16), and the Medoc Mountain chapter (Chapter 20).

Every year, about one-third of the prairie at Prairie Ridge undergoes a prescribed burn that creates good hunting opportunities for birds, clears out underbrush, and creates fertile soil for the prairie to grow back even stronger. Naturally occurring fires caused by lightning were common several hundred years ago, and fires were also set by Native Americans who understood the importance of maintaining the prairies by setting fire that cleared land to support good habitat for the American bison (*Bison bison*). You can spot the bison sculptures at Prairie Ridge and imagine what it must have been like to see live bison roaming here in the 1700s.

With a winter walk to the pond, you will spot the cattails (*Typha* sp.), which have fluffed out so that the wind will disperse their seeds. You may hear the white-throated sparrow (*Zonotrichia albiocollis*) singing a tune, "Old Sam Peabody, Peabody, Peabody." It has a gray belly, a brown back, and a black-and-white head. Also keep an eye out for pileated woodpeckers (*Hylatomus pileatus*), red-bellied woodpeckers (*Melanerpes carolinus*), great horned owls (*Bubo virginianus*), mourning doves (*Zenaida macroura*), and white-breasted nuthatches (*Sitta carolinensis*) perched on the many snags, which are standing dead trees. Some people see snags as unsightly, but they are an incredibly important habitat for birds, insects, spiders, bats, treefrogs, and other wildlife. You may also see the winterberry (*Ilex verticillata*), a deciduous holly that provides food for birds and deer in the lowland forest.

Upon the first glance at the prairie, it looks like a field of swaying grasses. Yet you can see that the prairie is a rich and varied ecosystem filled with a huge variety of plants and animals that change with the seasons and with nature's important cycles of life.

Before You Go

Prairie Ridge is largely a place to explore on your own, but there are a few things that will maximize your visit. First, Prairie Ridge is open daily from 9:00 A.M. to 4:30 P.M. It is located very close to the Raleigh Greenway system, so it would be a great place to ride to on your bike. It is worth checking the Prairie Ridge website before you visit to see what events may be occurring. For instance, you can participate in **Citizen Science** projects or go on a guided nature walk, or little ones can enjoy a Nature Storytime at the nature playspace in the lowland forest. The website also has a map to get you oriented, more background on the green architecture, a history of the site, and even a video tour. When you do visit, please keep in mind that this site receives around 30,000 visitors a year. Help others enjoy Prairie Ridge for a long time by observing the "Leave No Trace" policy. Please leave your dogs at home so as not to disturb the natural wildlife and be respectful of other visitors. Have fun exploring!

Visit Prairie Ridge's website under the "Resources" tab to obtain of a map of the ecostation, species lists, and colorful guides for visiting during each season.

Website: http://naturalsciences.org/prairie-ridge
Contact: phone: (919) 707-8888
Address: 1671 Gold Star Drive, Raleigh, N.C. 27607

CHAPTER 15

Pilot Mountain State Park

Exploring a Sauratown Mountain Monadnock

JESSE A. ANDERSON

SCIENTIFIC FIELDS OF STUDY: *Geology, Ecology*

Introduction

As you drive toward Pilot Mountain State Park, you begin to understand where the name "Pilot" came from. Imagine yourself as a Native American: no access to GPS, no Google Maps, and no developed roads, road signs, or place names. Imagine using the sun primarily for navigation, with its ever-changing location in the sky due to the Earth's rotation. And because the sun is often obstructed by clouds, you would have to be very skilled to use it as your primary measure for finding direction. Having the use of local landforms could make a huge difference. Lakes and rivers would be invaluable for guidance, but a mountain with an unusual shape, like Pilot Mountain, likely would get you home every time.

Today, Pilot Mountain is 2,421 feet (738 meters) above sea level and stands over 1,400 feet (426.7 meters) above the surrounding landscape. The shape of Pilot Mountain is iconic and identifiable from any nearby hilltop, ridgeline, or large open prairie. If you are in the Yadkin Valley, Winston-Salem, or the nearby Blue Ridge Mountains of Virginia, you can see Pilot Mountain from more than 60 miles away. For this reason, Pilot Mountain was important not only to the local Native American tribes. The first European settlers in the area, the Moravians, wrote about Pilot Mountain's importance for their travels as well. In Powell's *Encyclopedia of North Carolina*, it is documented that they wrote of reaching the top of the Blue Ridge Escarpment, where the mountains are reduced to foothills, and they finally "saw the Pilot Mountain in North Carolina and rejoiced to think that [they] would soon see the boundary of Carolina and set foot on [their] own dear land."

Pilot Mountain is considered a **monadnock**, which is an isolated hill or mountain that is resistant to erosion because the rock is harder than that around it and does not break down as easily from **weathering**. This mountain of rock stands above the gently rolling hills of the peneplain, an area of plains created from many millions of years of erosion, thus creating the beautiful farmlands in the Yadkin Valley. From the mountainous scenery to the wide diversity of species, many features of Pilot Mountain provide an exciting opportunity to visit southern Appalachia without traveling to western North Carolina.

Exploring Pilot Mountain

Visiting Pilot Mountain can be exciting any time of year, and your interests will guide the timing of your trip. Geologists can study and observe the geology of Pilot Mountain any time of year. If you are interested in seeing native wildlife and wildflowers in bloom, then early April through May is the best time to visit. If you want a wide variety of leaf color, visiting in mid-to-late October provides stunning views of fall foliage.

The most interesting features of Pilot Mountain discussed in this chapter can be accessed by hiking the Little Pinnacle Overlook, the Jomeokee Trail, and the Ledge Springs Trail. The Little Pinnacle Overlook is a "must-do" for any visitor to the park. It provides the best views of Pilot Mountain with a panorama of the surrounding landscape. Standing at the "little pinnacle" of elevated land and looking east toward Pilot Mountain, or the "big pinnacle," provides a good understanding for how this area was named, as it is not as high as the very top of Pilot Mountain. Standing at the little pinnacle, behind Pilot Mountain, you will see three other prominent peaks. The closer mountain (and farthest left) is Sauratown Mountain, named after the Saura tribe that primarily inhabited this area. This peak is also identified by the presence of large radio towers on its summit. To the right of Sauratown Mountain stand two other peaks. These two peaks are part of Hanging Rock State Park—Moore's Knob (left) and Cook's Wall (right). Including Pilot Mountain, these three peaks are all part of the Sauratown Mountain formation.

The Jomeokee Trail (pronounced JOE-me-O-kee) is 0.8 miles (1.2 kilometers) long and wraps completely around Pilot Mountain. The word "Jomeokee" is a Native American word meaning "Great Guide" or "Pilot." By hiking the Jomeokee Trail, you will be able to completely immerse yourself in exploring the geology that made Pilot Mountain what it is today and witness the rich diversity of plants and animals of this region. From the Jomeokee Trail, you can also access the Ledge Spring Trail. At 2.2 miles (3.5 kilometers) round-trip, the Ledge Spring Trail is the longest and most strenuous of the three trails suggested and will provide a more complex look at the geology associated with Pilot Mountain.

After the first 500 feet (152.4 meters) on the Jomeokee Trail, the trail levels out on a low point, called the saddle, between the little pinnacle and the big pinnacle. This area has been less resistant to physical weathering and has eroded away into the valley below. At this point on the trail you can see the large **quartzite** cliffs of Pilot Mountain.

Figure 15-1. Pilot Mountain at sunset from the Little Pinnacle Overlook, with Cook's Wall, Moore's Knob, and Sauratown Mountain (*right to left*) in the background. Photo by Jesse Anderson.

Geology of Pilot Mountain

The presence of Pilot Mountain rising high among the surrounding landscape is a sign of strength and perseverance. For the Sauratown Mountains, that existence is due solely to the composition of the rock. To understand where the strength comes from, you must understand the unique story and take a walk down the geologic timeline of Pilot and the surrounding Sauratown Mountains.

Pilot Mountain is composed of the **metamorphic** rock quartzite, which is made from sand deposited when this part of North Carolina was covered by an ancient sea, called the Iapetus Sea, about 500 million years ago. We previously discussed the Iapetus Sea in the Piedmont Geology section (p. 106) but also when we learned about gold mining at Reed Gold Mine (Chapter 12). Thanks to the presence of the Iapetus Sea here, sand was deposited, much as it is on the shores of North Carolina beaches today. The sand on our beaches today contains a mixture of mostly quartz, with some feldspar, other heavier **minerals**, and calcium carbonate from broken-down shells. During the time of the Iapetus Sea, the sand being deposited was a very fine-grained sand made of pure quartz, so the beaches would have been pure white. When this sand was buried deep within the Earth, it underwent metamorphism and was then pushed back up again in the form of the quartzite rock that now composes Pilot Mountain. We know that the primary mineral in quartzite is quartz, and we know that quartz is very resistant to weathering and erosion. After millions of years of rain, snow, wind, and water, Pilot Mountain remains a lone-standing formation

Figure 15-2. An example of cross-bedding along the Jomeokee Trail. Take note of the near-horizontal layers toward the top, intersected by layers below at a 30° angle (toward the bottom of the scale card). Photo by Jesse Anderson.

today because the surrounding rock, which was not as strong as the rock on Pilot Mountain, was worn and eroded over time, leaving the monadnock of quartzite towering above the rest of the land. For more information about the processes of metamorphism, uplift, and erosion, see the Blowing Rock Gneiss chapter (Chapter 8) and the Elk Knob chapter (Chapter 9).

While hiking the Jomeokee Trail and the Ledge Springs Trail, pay attention to the patterns and colors in the rock to help you understand what geologists have learned about Pilot Mountain's quartzite deposition, which refers to how the sediments were layered over time. Close observation of these rocks reveals examples of cross-bedding (Figure 15-2). Cross beds are sediment layers that are slightly tilted, or inclined, within the many horizontal layers, often due to water movement. When sediment particles are pushed along by water or air, they tend to form a steep slope. When the slope becomes unstable, a thin layer of sediment falls down the slope. These layers build over time, creating the cross-bedding patterns seen in the rock along the trails at Pilot Mountain. Try to imagine the gentle waves of a shallow sea depositing sand along its shores in this manner. These cross beds may have formed as dunes on the ancient beaches or offshore in tidal channels.

In addition to cross beds, many areas of the exposed rock are intersected by thick, shiny, dark bands of another rock type. These bands are comprised of **mica schist**, a metamorphic rock formed from a different sediment type—mud. Under what circumstances today would you see a thick layer of mud deposited on top of pure sand? Perhaps during a large rainstorm or flood. Floods are well-known forces of nature that can move heavy sediments around quickly and easily. The layers of

Figure 15-3. Wavy, folded layers of mica schist bordered by the lighter Sauratown quartzite. Photo by Jesse Anderson.

mud set down here from floods were subjected to the same metamorphism as the surrounding quartzite; however, they were affected quite differently by temperature and pressure. Look closely at the bands of mica schist. You will see strange patterns of wavy dark lines (Figure 15-3). The mica schist rock is a softer rock that folded due to stress during the mountain-building events that caused the **uplift** of the Appalachian Mountains, while the hard quartzite rock layers remain mostly flat. You may also remember from Chapter 1 on the Rock Garden that the softer features of mica have allowed its use in a variety of modern products, including makeup, lotion, potting soil, and drywall. Conversely, the strength of quartzite makes it an ideal building material.

Ecology of Pilot Mountain

Walking around Pilot Mountain, you are surrounded by visible geologic features. With large cliffs of quartzite and bands of folded mica schist, it can be hard to remember to stop and admire the plant and animal life in the area. Many species of plants and animals around Pilot Mountain are reminiscent of western North Carolina and southern Appalachia, yet the combination of elevation and soil mineral composition allows these plants and animals to be successful here as well. While walking the Jomeokee Trail along the shaded, north side of Pilot Mountain, you will be surrounded by Catawba rhododendron (*Rhododendron catawbiense*) and mountain laurel (*Kalmia latifolia*). These can be identified any time of year, as they are broadleaf evergreen shrubs. The mountain laurel has small, pointy leaves,

Figure 15-4. Pitch pine (*Pinus rigida*) showing its adaptation to fire. Note the needles coming out of the trunk of the tree, also called epicormic branching. Photo by Jesse Anderson.

compared with the broad, oblong, rabbit-ear-shaped leaves of the rhododendron. Identifying them in the spring can be a treat when they are in bloom, as the Catawba rhododendron blooms are violet-purple, compared with the light pink or white flowers of the mountain laurel. Interspersed among the shrubs are tall pitch pine (*Pinus rigida*) and Table Mountain pine (*P. pungens*) trees.

As you walk around the often sunny, south face of the mountain, you will begin to see trees that are black around their bases from fires. We have discussed the importance of fire in previous chapters, and Pilot Mountain is another example of how fire helps to maintain a healthy and balanced natural ecosystem. Pitch pines are another plant species that has adapted to the benefits of fire. You can easily identify pitch pine by the presence of epicormic branching (Figure 15-4), or abundant needles coming out of the bark or trunk of the tree. These branches are a response to fires and other environmental stresses here at Pilot Mountain. The growth of new needles on the tree trunk after a fire provides more energy to the tree, helping it to flourish in this fire-adapted habitat.

Another adaptation that helps pitch pine and Table Mountain pine trees benefit from fire is serotinous pine cones, which means they are covered in resin, or pine sap. Knowing that the seeds of the pine tree are stored in its cones, how could fire benefit these trees? Serotinous cones open only when they are exposed to extreme heat during fire, which melts the coating of resin. After opening, cones release their seeds onto the freshly burned, nutrient-rich soil, where sunlight is now abundant because the fire has removed excess vegetation. You can see that fire is essential to the reproduction and survival of the pitch pine and Table Mountain pine trees, like many other pine species throughout North Carolina that we have discussed in this book.

While you are on these trails, it is important that you stay on the path because the plant life is very fragile. The soils around Pilot Mountain are xeric soils, which are shallow, dry soils, that can be disturbed easily, thereby harming the delicate plants. Hidden among the cliffs and slopes of the Jomeokee Trail and Ledge Spring Trail you may find plants that are rare in North Carolina, such as bear oak (*Quercus ilicifolia*), named after its sharp and pointed oak leaves. Bear oak is a shrubby oak species that is more commonly found in the mountains of Virginia. Because of its growth habits, bear oak also benefits from fire that burns off **understory** plants to allow more sunlight to shine through the sub-**canopy**. You can also find Greenland sandwort (*Minuartia groenlandica*), dwarf alum-root (*Heuchera parvifolia*), and ashleaf goldenbanner (*Thermopsis fraxinifolia*) nestled in cracks of the quartzite cliffs, seeking shelter under overhangs and in small gullies. These are also considered rare and/or threatened plants in North Carolina.

An animal of the slithering type to watch for, but not encountered commonly, is the timber rattlesnake (*Crotalus horridus*). Remember, snakes try to avoid encounters with you, so this animal is best observed from a distance and left alone. These snakes have a small **population** at Pilot Mountain State Park and are a species of concern in North Carolina. If you look to the sky, you may see some of our resident ravens. The common raven (*Corvus corax*) occasionally nests along the cliffs of Pilot Mountain. At one time, the Sauratown Mountains served as the only nesting area for ravens in North Carolina's Piedmont. Listen for the raven's distinct call that sounds like a crow with a sore throat. Many times of the year you can watch ravens playing in the sky as they fly and tumble in the uplifting winds created by the sun's warmth on the rock.

If visiting in September, be sure to stop by the Little Pinnacle Overlook to check in with the annual hawk migration and Forsyth Audubon volunteers. These hawk-watching events have taken place at Pilot Mountain since the 1970s. Every year, thousands of broad-winged hawks (*Buteo platypterus*) migrate past Pilot Mountain during their journey toward Central and South America and can be seen flying in large groups called kettles. These kettles of hawks are following conditions that are favorable for easy migration. Winds moving across the nearby valleys eventually run into the mountain and are forced upward, creating updrafts that support the birds' soaring patterns. Migrating raptors look for warm rising air currents, or thermals, in addition to updrafts. These thermals are created by the sun's warmth on the rock of Pilot Mountain, causing the surrounding air to rise high into the atmosphere. On any given day in mid-September, a patient visitor can be fortunate to witness thousands of migrating hawks over the course of a few hours.

Before You Go

Whether your interests lie in exploring the geologic past of North Carolina or visiting a mixture of Mountain–Piedmont wildlife close to home, Pilot Mountain State Park is worth the trip. Approximately 25 miles (40 kilometers) north of Winston-Salem or 15 miles (24 kilometers) south of Mount Airy, you will take exit 131 off US 52. Centrally located in the state, the park is within a 1-hour drive from Greensboro, a 2-hour drive from the Raleigh-Durham area, and approximately 2.5 hours from Asheville. If climbing is your forte, consider an experienced outfitter who offers guided trips to Pilot Mountain. There is a climbing access map posted on the Pilot Mountain website. If you are interested in camping, ranger-led programs/events, or more general information, it is all listed on the North Carolina State Park's website below. While visiting, feel free to ask a park ranger more questions about the geology and ecology of Pilot Mountain.

References and Resources

Powell, William S., ed. *Encyclopedia of North Carolina*, p. 886. Chapel Hill: University of North Carolina Press, 2006.

Website: https://www.ncparks.gov/pilot-mountain-state-park
Contact: Park Office phone: (336) 325-2355; email: pilot.mountain@ncparks.gov
Address: 1792 Pilot Knob Park Road, Pinnacle, N.C. 27043
GPS Coordinates: N 36°20.52, W 80°28.56

CHAPTER 16

North Carolina Botanical Garden

ELISHA TAYLOR

SCIENTIFIC FIELDS OF STUDY: *Botany, Ecology, Environmental Engineering*

Have you ever dreamed of exploring across the entire state of North Carolina, from the mountains to the coast, in just one day? Well, you can try it at the North Carolina Botanical Garden (NCBG) in Chapel Hill. The NCBG habitat gardens display the fantastic diversity of plants and plant communities that naturally occur in the state. As you know, there are three major geographic regions in North Carolina, each making up about one-third of the state: the Mountains, the Piedmont, and the Coastal Plain. Each of these regions is represented at the Garden, so you can stroll through pine savanna and discover Venus flytraps in the Coastal Plain Habitat, sit in the cool shade of rhododendrons and waist-high ferns in the Mountain Habitat, and wander trails through Piedmont forest towering with 100-foot oaks and tulip trees . . . all in one visit.

Part of the University of North Carolina at Chapel Hill, the NCBG is a "conservation garden" that celebrates and protects native plants and habitats. The Garden's guiding mission is to inspire understanding, appreciation, and conservation of plants and to advance a **sustainable** relationship between people and nature. What's so special about native plants, you ask? A native plant is considered native to an area because it was present when European settlers arrived more than 500 years ago. This means that these plants have been here long enough to have evolved with the local climate, soil types, and native animals to form important and complex relationships. Take, for example, eastern columbine (*Aquilegia canadensis*), whose red, nectar-rich flowers bloom just in time for the arrival of hungry ruby-throated hummingbirds from Mexico and Central America in early spring. The hummingbirds return the favor by pollinating the flowers. It is a special kind of symbiotic relationship, called mutualism, where both organisms benefit. The plant provides food; the hummingbird helps distribute pollen that fertilizes to make new plants. They need each other. Our native plants are the foundation of our ecosystems. They provide the best food and shelter for animals, as well as a natural beauty that is truly unique to North Carolina.

Figure 16-1. A ruby-throated hummingbird takes nectar from a cardinal flower. Photo by Mike Dunn.

Throughout the Garden, you can discover stories of interdependence between native plants, people, and wildlife. This means that we all need one another. Look for the blackened bark on the longleaf pines (*Pinus palustris*) as you make your way down the boardwalk through the Sandhills Habitat. The Sandhills is a subregion of the state between the Piedmont and the Coastal Plain, as described in Chapter 13. The Garden includes the Sandhills as part of the Coastal Plain Habitat. Longleaf pines get their name from having the longest needle leaves of any eastern pine—up to 18 inches (46 centimeters) long. This area is burned yearly by Garden staff to simulate natural fires caused by lightning strikes that are required by the endangered longleaf pine ecosystem. In previous chapters, we have discussed numerous ways that fires help an ecosystem, such as burning away leaf litter and shrubs to maintain a sunny, open environment conducive to growth, while also leaving behind a layer of ash that adds nutrients to the low-nutrient sandy soils. Longleaf pine seeds must come into contact with soil to take root, and longleaf pines are notorious for having very low seed production; however, fire does help facilitate seed dispersal. Longleaf pine has adapted to this harsh habitat with thick, scaly bark that protects the inner living tissue and makes it fire-resistant. See Chapters 13, 14, and 15 for more information about how fire benefits natural ecosystems.

Spicebush (*Lindera benzoin*) can be found in the Mountain Habitat Garden and Piedmont Forest Garden. When crushed, the aromatic leaves and stems of this shrub smell lemony and can be used to make a tea. The glossy red fruit also is edible by humans, although it can be quite astringent, and can be used to make a delicious tea or dried and used a spice. The berries are packed with energy and one of the favorite foods of fall migrating and overwintering birds that need the extra calories. The birds help scatter the seeds hidden within the fruit when they poop them out along their way. Shiny black and blue spicebush swallowtail butterflies lay their eggs on spicebush. Look for rolled up leaves where the caterpillars, with large false eyespots, might be hiding while they munch. If you disturb a larva, don't be surprised

Figure 16-2. A controlled burn in the longleaf pine habitat of the Garden. Photo courtesy of North Carolina Botanical Garden.

Figure 16-3. Spicebush swallowtail caterpillar. Photo by Mike Dunn.

Figure 16-4. The sassafras tree, with three differently shaped leaves. Photo courtesy of North Carolina Botanical Garden.

if forked yellow glands pop out from behind its head, putting off a strong odor like stinky cheese that serves to keep away **predators**.

In the Native American Garden, explore plants used for medicine, ceremonies, cleaning, cooking, and other daily needs by Native Americans of the Southeast and visit a replica ati, or Occaneechi hut. Look for the tall reddish stalks and skinny seedpods of Indian hemp (*Apocynum cannabinum*). It is poisonous to eat but was often collected in the fall as a natural plant fiber to make exceptionally strong cordage, or rope, for nets, bowstrings, and sewing. Also see if you can spy the sassafras tree (*Sassafras albidum*), which has three differently shaped leaves: oval, mitten-shaped, and three-lobed. The leaves and twigs have a fruity smell, and the roots have been used to perfume soaps and flavor root beer.

Figure 16-5. The carnivorous plant garden. Many types of carnivorous plants live here, including the Venus flytrap. Photo courtesy of North Carolina Botanical Garden.

The NCBG is home to one of the finest carnivorous plant collections in the Southeast. These meat-eating plants live in boggy habitats with poor soil, so they have adapted incredible strategies to "catch" bugs to obtain the additional nutrients they need. Venus flytrap (*Dionaea muscipula*) might be the most famous carnivorous plant, but did you know that it is also a native plant? In the entire world, Venus flytraps occur naturally only within a 70-mile area in the Coastal Plain of the Carolinas. For more information on the Venus flytrap, see Chapter 24. You also can see many other **carnivorous plants** here in the Garden, including pitcher plants, sundews, and butterworts, and discover the different ways they lure bugs to their traps.

Don't miss the Water Garden, where you can be wowed and grossed out at the same time by touching the super-slimy underside of the floating leaves and stems of watershield (*Brasenia schreberi*). The jellylike coating protects it from drying out and probably from plant-eating animals. American lotus-lily (*Nelumbo lutea*) flowers are as big as your face. They bloom in summer and last for only two days. Sprinkle water on their basketball-sized, waterproof leaves and watch the silvery droplets bounce and roll right off. The huge, banana-shaped root can be baked and eaten like sweet potato. Visit with the tadpoles, dragonflies, snails, fish, and even the occasional great blue heron that also live here.

Keep your eye out for a basking snapping turtle (*Chelydra serpentina*) or a red-bellied water snake (*Nerodia erythrogaster*) at the Coastal Plain pond, and, in late winter, look for grapefruit-sized egg masses floating in the nearby **vernal pools**, also called ephemeral pools. These are temporary pools that form after a wet period and are dry during other times. They are important habitats for organisms like the

Figure 16-6. The giant leaves and stems of the American lotus-lily. Photo by Elisha Taylor.

Figure 16-7. The American lotus-lily flower is as big as your face! Photo by Elisha Taylor.

Figure 16-8. The LEED Allen Education Center. Photo courtesy of North Carolina Botanical Garden.

secretive spotted salamander (*Ambystoma maculatum*), an amphibian that migrates from its forest burrow to mate and lay eggs in the fish-free pond each year. By choosing a location with no fish, this salamander is helping to ensure that its offspring survive and grow to become mature salamanders. To read more on vernal pools, see Chapter 14, "Prairie Ridge Ecostation."

After all your outdoor exploring, be sure to stop in to visit the certified Platinum-LEED (Leadership in Energy & Environmental Design) James and Delight Allen Education Center. Full of environmentally friendly, or "green," features like solar panels, a geothermal heat-exchange system that reduces energy use for heating and cooling, and cisterns that collect rainwater to supply landscape irrigation, the education center houses an exhibit hall, an art gallery, a library, a gift shop, a plant sale, and the Peacock Discovery Room. This is an excellent location to learn about "green" efforts that can help make your home and classroom planet-friendly.

Before You Go

The NCBG also manages several other properties, including Coker Arboretum and Battle Park on the UNC-Chapel Hill campus, and Mason Farm Biological Reserve. Just 1.0 mile (1.6 kilometers) down the road from the Garden, you can visit Mason Farm with a permit available at the education center. This amazing 367-acre property is home to a greater number of animal species than any other comparably sized location in the entire Piedmont. Hike the Old Farm Trail loop through old-growth forest with 300-year-old trees, swamp, and open fields to see how the Garden is preserving and restoring native plant habitat in this special place.

The North Carolina Botanical Garden is free and open to the public Tuesday through Sunday. A variety of programs and events are available to schools, children, and adults throughout the year. Visit the website below or call the NCBG for any questions before you visit. Directions are available on their website.

Website: http://ncbg.unc.edu
Contact: phone: (919) 962-0522; email: ncbg@unc.edu
Address: 100 Old Mason Farm Road, Chapel Hill, N.C. 27517
GPS Coordinates: N 35°53.94, W 79°1.98

CHAPTER 17

Hemlock Bluffs Nature Preserve and the Stevens Nature Center

MARK JOHNS & LAURA K. WHITE

SCIENTIFIC FIELDS OF STUDY: *Forest Ecology, Botany*

Natural History of the Nature Preserve

Hemlock Bluffs Nature Preserve, located in south Cary, Wake County, is approximately 140 acres of unusual and storied land situated along Swift Creek. Its vegetation and topography, or features of the land, are more typical of the western part of North Carolina. The keystone to the interesting natural history of the nature preserve is a system of north-facing bluffs, or broad, rounded cliffs, running along Swift Creek that support a very small but rare and disjunct **population** of the eastern hemlock tree (*Tsuga canadensis*), a coniferous (cone-bearing) evergreen tree native to the eastern United States. "Disjunct" means that this particular population of trees is separated from all other hemlocks in the state, as the closest naturally occurring eastern hemlock populations live in the foothills of North Carolina.

So how did the hemlocks get there? The origin of the eastern hemlocks can be traced back roughly 10,000 years to a time when sheets of ice were common to the north and west portions of North Carolina and the temperatures were much colder, on average. Fossil evidence from this period indicates that plant species, such as the eastern hemlock, that were more typical of the northern United States and the mountains of North Carolina were once widespread in the central Piedmont of our state. As glaciers from the north receded, a warming trend began that evidently caused these plant communities to disappear gradually in the Piedmont; however, a few rare isolated groupings were left behind. The hemlock trees at Hemlock Bluffs

Figure 17-1. The floodplain forest as seen from the Swift Creek Loop Trail. Photo courtesy of Hemlock Bluffs.

are believed to be one of these unique relics of the ancient past, surviving in this particular site due to the protective nature of the north-facing bluffs, Swift Creek below, and the geology of the actual bluff system. There is a cooler, moister microclimate along the bluff face that allows the hemlocks to be competitive with other plant species.

Hemlocks are currently under dire threat due to an **invasive** insect called the **hemlock woolly adelgid**. You will recall from previous chapters that invasive species are **nonnative** organisms that spread rapidly because they lack natural **predators** and cause environmental and economic harm. This insect is killing hemlocks at a rapid rate in the northeastern United States and in western North Carolina. The hemlock woolly adelgid was first detected in the western United States in 1924, but its origin was a mystery for many years. The insect spread rapidly, and by 1951 it was detected in the eastern United States, near Richmond, Virginia. The first positive identification of hemlock woolly adelgid in North Carolina occurred in 1995, and by 2005 nearly half of the hemlock populations in the eastern United States, from Georgia to Maine, were infested by these tiny aphidlike organisms. They were detected at the Hemlock Bluffs Nature Preserve in 2010 and again in 2014 and 2015. Systemic insecticides have been used to treat the hemlock woolly adelgid infestation, and extensive checks for these insects are now conducted twice each year at Hemlock Bluffs Nature Preserve. Managing the invasive insect will be important in the years to come to ensure the survival of this rare and isolated population of trees.

The nature preserve is an island of extremely important habitat for wildlife,

Figure 17-2. The boardwalk at Hemlock Bluffs can take you through delicate ecological habitats. Photo courtesy of Hemlock Bluffs.

plants, and fungi in the suburban landscape of the town of Cary. It is also a living educational laboratory for environmental education programs conducted by staff year-round. Within the 140-acre tract there are several historically and scientifically significant finds. There is an extensive **floodplain** system with a complex of temporary pools along Swift Creek where early settlers built a gristmill for grinding wheat and corn. Sections of the dam for the mill are part of the lower trail system, and one of the millstones is on exhibit in the nature center. There are intact remnants of **Oak-Hickory Forest** that would have existed when settlers first began to live and farm here more than 200 years ago. There are also relic longleaf pines (*Pinus palustris*) that have disappeared from much of the rest of North Carolina. Evidence remains here showing that there was an active turpentine products industry operating on the site many years ago. Certain types of living pine trees, like loblolly and longleaf, would have been "chipped into" to form a wound on the surface of the tree bark. The resin, exuded by the tree as a healing mechanism, was then collected in buckets. Turpentine was made from pine tree resin that was distilled, where repeated boiling and cooling of a substance separates its chemical components. For many generations, turpentine has been used as a solvent for paints and as a protective coating on wood surfaces.

Even before the site was made into a state nature preserve, Hemlock Bluffs was well known for its eastern hemlocks, some of which are hundreds of years old, and for other notable flora, or plants. Visitors come from all around to experience the extraordinary and extensive spring wildflower populations. There are also relic old-growth chestnut oaks (*Quercus montana*) that require more than two people to reach all the way around the trunk. Large tulip trees (or yellow poplar) (*Liriodendron tulipifera*) live in the floodplain, and the American beech trees (*Fagus grandifolia*) and northern red oaks (*Quercus rubra*) found along the slopes are a testament to the fertile soils of the floodplain and its terraces that support incredibly diverse plant communities throughout the nature preserve.

Research at the Nature Preserve

Research on the natural communities at the nature preserve began in the 1950s, and researchers from many universities and organizations continue to study the area. More extensive biological surveys were conducted beginning in the 1970s. In the 1990s, staff at the nature preserve began a thorough inventory of many of the natural components of the nature preserve, and this work continues today. Over the past few decades, Hemlock Bluffs has been a valuable research site for many kinds of studies, including a systematic survey of reptiles and amphibians conducted by researchers from North Carolina State University (NCSU), inventories of rare plant species by several area universities, a documentation of nonnative forest ants through the PULSE survey program with NCSU, and a dendrochronology of some of the trees in the nature preserve (a scientific method for dating tree rings) in conjunction with UNC-Greensboro. Biologists from the North Carolina Department of Transportation have surveyed for bats, and biologists from the North Carolina Wildlife Resources Commission have documented turtles and salamanders. Researchers at Duke University began conducting salamander and songbird research in 2013, and scientists from the NCSU CAMCORE Program have run genetics testing on the eastern hemlock trees themselves. These researchers also help with spot checks for the hemlock woolly adelgid in large heritage trees.

Plants, Fungi, and Slime Molds, Oh My!

At least 58 species of trees have been documented at the nature preserve since the 1990s. Approximately 154 woody plant species (**shrubs**) and 168 species of **herbaceous** plants (small plants with no woody parts, such as grasses, sedges, ferns, and wildflowers) have been documented by staff. Extensive populations of spring wildflowers exist at the site, including spectacular numbers of trout lily, spring beauty, spicebush, serviceberry, giant chickweed, jack-in-the-pulpit, hepatica, windflower, and mayapple. The uncommon pink and yellow lady slippers have also been documented.

Over 150 species of fungi (mushrooms, wood polypores, etc.) have been documented at the nature preserve, and slime molds also are found at Hemlock Bluffs. Slime molds were once considered to be fungi, like mushrooms, but now they are classified separately because they are pretty unusual. Slime molds are fascinating organisms like no other in nature. Individual cells live separately in soils, but when the need arises, these individual cells find one another, congregate into a giant blob of goo, and then function as a single organism for mating or finding food.

Figure 17-3. Spotted salamander eggs can be found in vernal pools in the winter months. Photo by Mike Dunn.

Birds and Other Living Critters

Currently over 130 species of birds have been documented on the 140-acre site. The nature preserve serves as an important wintering, breeding, and migration stopover habitat for many birds in an increasingly urban Wake County landscape. At least 39 species of birds have been documented nesting at the nature preserve, including 12 neotropical migrants, which are birds that breed in North America in the summer but migrate to the tropics during the winter. Nesting habitats are augmented by staff with a system of nest boxes that target barred owls, eastern screech-owls, wood ducks, eastern bluebirds, great crested flycatchers, and other cavity-nesting species. Habitat management to increase nesting bird diversity and success is conducted by staff, as well as periodic surveys for birds, amphibians, and reptiles year-round. Wildlife boxes are maintained and checked annually.

Many insects have been identified and documented at the nature preserve, including 109 species of butterflies and moths, 29 species of dragonflies and/or damselflies, and hundreds of other species of insects, representing dozens of families. In Swift Creek and its tributaries, 22 species of fish, 5 species of snails, 4 species of crayfish, and 3 species of freshwater mussels have been documented, but we still need a systematic survey of the aquatic organisms living in Swift Creek, the small streams, and the temporary pools and hillside seeps. There also have been 29 mammals, 27 amphibians, and 29 reptiles documented, including 17 species of snakes. Salamander diversity is very high at this site, considering that the size of the property is only 140 acres and it is located in Wake County.

Education at Hemlock Bluffs

Perhaps the greatest value for the town of Cary, the community, and the Triangle region lies in the use of the nature preserve as a living educational laboratory both during staff-led programs and for groups visiting on their own. Within the borders of the nature preserve, patrons of all ages are introduced to the history, culture, and ecology of the central Piedmont of North Carolina from indoor and outdoor exhibits,

Figure 17-4. A staff member shows kids how and where to look for different types of forest critters because exploring the grounds at Hemlock Bluffs means you never know what you may find around (or underneath) the next bend. Photo courtesy of Hemlock Bluffs.

kiosks and bulletin boards, and self-guided trails. In addition, the staff conducts hundreds of environmental education programs for all ages year-round, targeting thousands of participants each year. Visitation is increasing at the nature preserve, so staff must work on plans to accommodate more visitors.

Hemlock Bluffs is a window into the ecological, geological, and cultural past of Cary, and the Piedmont in general. On its trails can be seen the patterns and evidence of how early settlers used the local land, including homesteads, farms, gristmills, logging operations, and an active turpentine industry. It is also a glimpse into how natural communities transition over time. Spend a day at the nature preserve and step back in time as you experience relics of the ecological past.

The nature preserve holds relic plants on the edge of their natural ranges from both northwestern North Carolina (eastern hemlocks) and the Sandhills region (longleaf pine). It provides important habitat for forest birds, salamanders, and wildflowers in the heart of busy, crowded Wake County. At the same time, easy access for study by visitors of all ages, abilities, and interest levels is provided while the diverse habitats present are still protected.

Get Involved

Community involvement and volunteers are the backbone of natural resource management, operations, and nature programming at the Stevens Nature Center and Hemlock Bluffs Nature Preserve (Figure 17-5). Without the assistance and involvement of local scout troops, Eagle Scout candidates, and Girl Scout Gold participants,

Figure 17-5. Stevens Nature Center. Photo courtesy of Hemlock Bluffs.

the conservation projects and environmental efforts of the nature preserve would not be a success. Teens from local high school environmental clubs and from the Cary Teen Council volunteer their time year-round to maintain the trails, gardens, and amenities at the preserve. They provide volunteer labor and hundreds of service hours to keep the preserve maintained and beautiful for visitors. Teens who have participated in Hemlock Bluffs camps and programs volunteer their time as camp counselors during summer camps. They give back the knowledge they have learned at nature camp and instill a love of nature in the next wave of children attending summer camp at Hemlock Bluffs.

Before You Go

Whether you would like to attend a nature program to learn more about birds, plants, or salamanders; help on a workday to maintain the trails; or join the Friends of Hemlock Bluffs to assist on a long-term basis, there is a place for you at Hemlock Bluffs. You can also visit Hemlock Bluffs anytime on your own for a quiet bit of solitude in the forest. Before you visit, find out more about the programs being offered each day and how to get involved at the websites listed below. Contact Stevens Nature Center for group visits.

References and Resources

Van Driesche, Roy G., Joseph H. LaForest, Charles T. Bargeron, Richard C. Reardon, and Megan Herlihy. *Forest Pest Insects in North America: A Photographic Guide.* September 2013. USDA Forest Service Forest Health Technology Enterprise Team. Publication no. FHTET-2012-02, https://www.fs.fed.us/foresthealth/technology/pdfs/Forest_Pest_Insects_Photo_Guide_508.pdf. Accessed October 31, 2018.

WEBSITES:

Town of Cary site: https://www.townofcary.org/recreation-enjoyment/parks-greenways-environment/parks/stevens-nature-center-at-hemlock-bluffs-nature-preserve

Friends of Hemlock Bluffs site: https://www.hemlockbluffs.org

Contact: Stevens Nature Center Staff, phone: (919)387-5980; email: mark.johns@townofcary.org

Address: 2616 Kildaire Farm Road, Cary, N.C. 27518

GPS Coordinates: N 35°43.44, W 78°46.98

CHAPTER 18

Occoneechee Mountain State Natural Area

LIZ STABENOW

SCIENTIFIC FIELDS OF STUDY: *Geology, Ecology*

History of Occoneechee Mountain

In the heart of the relatively flat Piedmont, there is a mountain you can climb perched along the Eno River. The peak of this mountain rises more than 350 feet (106 meters) above the river and 867 feet (264 meters) above sea level, providing rare aerial views of Orange County from a spot that is the highest point in North Carolina between Hillsborough and the Atlantic Ocean. This state natural area is managed by North Carolina State Parks.

The name Occoneechee comes from the first people to call this area their home. The Occaneechi Band of the Saponi Nation, sometimes spelled Occoneechee, is a Native American tribe that lives along the Eno River. Today, you can learn more about the Occaneechi people at their annual powwow, where dancing, drumming, and singing of traditional songs celebrate Occoneechi culture. The history of the area coalesces beautifully with local ecology and geology to explain why Occoneechee Mountain and the Eno River are important locations in North Carolina for the Occaneechi people and for all North Carolinians.

Geology Rocks!

When you explore this mountain, you will see some of the amazing history of the Earth written in its rocks and landscape. Occoneechee, like Pilot Mountain in Chapter 15, is a **monadnock**—a mountain that was formed when the rest of the land was eroded away and now rises above the relatively flat area around it. The rocks that make up the mountain are more resistant to erosion and have remained, while other

Figure 18-1. A view of the Eno River from Occoneechee Mountain, the highest point east of Hillsborough, N.C. Photo by Annie Planck Howell.

Figure 18-2. Along the hiking trail on Occoneechee Mountain.
Photo by Annie Planck Howell.

rocks were worn down and washed away over many years by **weathering**. Most of the hard, erosion-resistant **minerals** that form the mountain are quartz, which is easy to spot as you hike along the trails of Occoneechee. White and smoky quartz are most common. Keep your eyes open, and you might see a line, or vein, of quartz inside another rock.

This Piedmont mountain was formed perhaps 500–600 million years ago in an area with a lot of volcanic activity. Long ago, Occoneechee was part of the curved chain, or island arc, of volcanoes that we discussed in Chapter 12 on Reed Gold Mine. If you recall, hot **magma** from deep below the Earth's surface rose up through those volcanoes. Water entered through cracks and was heated, only to return to the surface as geysers and hot springs. All of this hydrothermal activity, referring to water heated deep inside the Earth, formed concentrated gold veins in the Gold Hills area, but here at Occoneechee it formed some truly beautiful rocks with fantastic colors. Many people call these "rainbow rocks." Most of the colors found in the rocks are due to the presence of various iron-containing minerals that are exposed to weathering, staining the rocks red, orange, and purple. You can see them along the trails as you hike.

We discussed above that much of the rock on the mountain is hard quartz that was formed by a volcano, but Occoneechee is also home to some very special soft minerals. If you hike around the bottom of the mountain, you can enter the old quarry, where people once mined rocks and even had a small railroad line to carry the rocks out. What were they mining? An amazing mineral called pyrophyllite.

Figure 18-3. Rhododendron found on Occoneechee Mountain. Photo by Annie Planck Howell.

The rocks containing this mineral are so soft, you can crumble them in your hands. As they were mined from the quarry, the rocks were ground up to make a very fine powder. This powder was used as a lubricant to make parts of machinery run more smoothly by reducing friction, which is the amount of resistance that occurs when machine parts move past each other. As more modern lubricants were discovered, pyrophyllite was no longer needed, and the mine was closed around 1906. You can still find pyrophyllite here, and it has quite an interesting **texture**. Feel free to pick it up and crumble it in your hands.

Ecology—Mountains as Islands

On the mountain, there are some amazing living creatures as well. Because it has remained at a higher elevation while the rest of the land around it has eroded away and changed over time, Occoneechee is like an island. If you recall our discussion of Mount Mitchell, an island can be any defined area that is isolated in some way. Occoneechee Mountain's elevation of 867 feet (264 meters) is the highest point in Orange County, North Carolina, and this distinction makes it an ecological island. Refer to Chapter 5, "Mount Mitchell," for a discussion of **island biogeography** and the positive and negative issues associated with living on an island.

With five distinct ecological zones that you can visit all on one 3.5-mile (5.6-kilometer) loop trail, Occoneechee has unique plants and animals that usually are found farther west in the Smoky Mountains. One of the notable species here is the

Figure 18-4. The varied terrain at Occoneechee Mountain is ideal for hiking and exploring. Photo by Annie Planck Howell.

small brown elfin butterfly (*Callophrys augustinus*), which is separated from other **populations** of brown elfins by about 100 miles (161 kilometers). They have been living on Occoneechee Mountain since the Ice Age. When ice began to retreat from North Carolina and the surrounding land changed, Occoneechee Mountain was the only habitat remaining in the Piedmont that could still support the brown elfin butterfly. The best time to see the brown elfin is in the spring, and there is even a hiking trail named after it. If you don't see a brown elfin, there are plenty of other interesting butterflies to observe, so bring a field guide for butterflies on this exploration.

In the spring, you also can see blooming wildflowers almost everywhere you look. Some of these species have beautiful blooms and are most often found in the mountains: mountain laurels (*Kalmia latifolia*), Catawba rhododendron (*Rhododendron catawbiense)*, wild sarsaparilla (*Aralia nudacaulis*), and the rare purple fringeless orchid (*Platanthera peramoena*). But on Occoneechee Mountain they are found on a special ridge overlooking the Eno River, where they are well protected.

Before You Go

While you are out hiking, make sure you stop at the top—there is a great view of the old quarry, the Eno River, and the town of Hillsborough. If you want to learn more, there are educational programs at Occoneechee Mountain year-round. Check out the website below for Occoneechee Mountain State Natural Area for more information and to sign up for an educational geology program.

References and Resources

Occaneechi Band of the Saponi Nation, http://obsn.org. Accessed October 31, 2018.

Website: https://www.ncparks.gov/occoneechee-mountain-state-natural-area/history
Contact: phone: (919) 383-1686; email: eno.river@ncparks.gov
Address: 625 Virginia Cates Road, Durham, N.C. 27705-9275
GPS Coordinates: N 36°3.66, W 79°7.02

CHAPTER 19

Eno River State Park

Exploring the Eno

LIZ STABENOW

SCIENTIFIC FIELDS OF STUDY: *Aquatic Ecology, Invertebrate Zoology, Limnology*

The Eno River is a major tributary, a river that flows into a larger river, to the Neuse **River Basin**, which supports one of the most **productive** waterways in the state of North Carolina. Because the Neuse River Basin contains one-sixth of the state's **population**, the tremendous population growth over the past two decades has led to concerns over the runoff of pollutants into these river systems. At this time, water in the Eno River is clean, but continued development and large withdrawals of water upstream give cause for concern over future water quality in the Eno. How can we monitor water quality to ensure that our rivers are staying healthy and clean? And why is it important that we know that?

If you live in the Piedmont, you or someone you know probably uses the Eno River as a public water supply or for recreational swimming, fishing, and playing. Both the Eno River State Park and West Point on the Eno, a Durham city park, host a number of rare or endangered species of organisms that only exist in this part of North Carolina. We discussed in the Haw River chapter that some organisms can help determine if their water habitat is clean. These are **indicator species**, or bioindicators, and they are tremendously valuable in the Eno River as well for helping to monitor water quality over time. See Chapter 11 for more information on bioindicators and water quality.

When evaluating water quality, pollution can come from different sources. Scientists call these **point** and **nonpoint source pollution**. Point source pollution refers to a specific location that can be pinpointed as a source of pollution, like a factory or a farm. Nonpoint source pollution refers to general runoff into the river that originates from many different sources. When you visit the Eno River, see if you can locate areas of potential point and nonpoint source pollution that could affect the water quality in the Eno River.

Figure 19-1. Summer on the Eno River. Photo by Annie Planck Howell.

Water Wonders

Macroinvertebrates are key indicator species in aquatic ecosystems. "Macro" indicates that we can see them with our eyes; no microscope needed. **Invertebrates** have no backbone, but they often will have an **exoskeleton**. For examples of these organisms, see the figures in Chapter 11. These organisms can tell us a lot about water quality because they typically possess many of the traits, but not always *all* of the traits, required for an indicator species. These traits include the following: (1) They are long-lived, so they show a response to changes in water conditions over time. (2) They are found in many different aquatic systems, so they allow for comparisons between sites. (3) They have several different types of life history strategies, or characteristics that help with survival and growth, like respiration, reproduction, and feeding. Finally, (4) they can be sampled easily and efficiently without much cost.

Part of living responsibly within a river basin is learning about the other organisms that live in that basin. A solid understanding of what organisms need to survive allows us to make smart decisions about the health of the ecosystem. An initial path to learning involves careful observations, so that you must use your senses to collect and record data. Bring along a net and a bucket, bowl, or ice cube tray. Put some river water in your container and place it in a shady location near the water so that it will not float away. Then, grab your net and start sweeping for animals that live underwater. One of the first things you might catch with your net is a crawfish, which is also called a crayfish or crawdad. The net will make it easy, but you can pick crawfish up with your bare hands if you are careful. You will want to grab them gently on the dorsal side, which is their back, in between the tail and the head. This area is called the cephalothorax, and it is a safe location to hold them so that their claws cannot pinch you. You might notice while you are out crawfish hunting that the best way to catch them is from behind because they will often swim backward.

They can use their tails like a paddle and shoot backward if you surprise them. Place your net behind them, and they are likely to swim right into it. Crawfish are fun to watch, and if you have a container of water, they can be gently placed in it for closer observation. Although they spend a lot of time in the water, they can also crawl out onto land and build chimneys, or mud castles, along the banks of the river. Crawfish are common in the Eno River and are important indicators of water quality because they are sensitive to water pollution. If you can find a crawfish, it means the water is relatively clean. After you have caught and closely observed a crawfish or two, release them back into the water and continue your search for other river critters.

If you look back at Chapter 11, "Saxapahaw on the Haw River," you will remember that many types of insects, or their immature forms, live in the water as aquatic macroinvertebrates. Look for the larvae of mayflies, caddisflies, stoneflies, and water pennies. Mayfly larvae have three tails but are long and thin. Along the abdomen, near the tail, they have gills waving in the water. When these strange-looking larvae develop, they will become adult mayflies and will leave the safety of the water, as will the other larval flies that we are discussing here. Stonefly larvae are larger and flat with two tails. Caddisfly larvae are greenish/bluish and wormlike, with small frilly gills. Caddisfly larvae usually make a tube to live in for protection and to move water over their gills. Look for a tube made of sticks or smalls rocks attached to the bottom of a rock. If you are really lucky, you may find a water penny. These do not turn into flies, like the others, but into beetles. While they are young, they lie flat against a rock and are curiously round, similar to a flat roly-poly with little legs underneath. Water pennies are another indicator of great water quality.

Take a Closer Look

On many of the rocks in the Eno River, you will find snails, or gastropods, attached. Gastropods are a type of **mollusk**, soft-bodied animals that often have a shell for protection. Pick up a few and take a closer look. There are live animals inside these snail shells. In fact, there are three different kinds of snails that are often found in the Eno. One looks like a ram's horn, which is why it is called a ramshorn snail (*Planorbella* sp.). The other two types of snails have a point at one end and an opening at the other. Find one of these pointy snail shells, hold it pointy end up, and observe whether the aperture, or the opening where the snail comes out, is on the left side or right side. If the aperture is on the left, you have a lunged snail, which means it breathes directly from the air. This is a type of common pond snail. Because they have lungs, both the ramshorn and pond snails can live in a variety of water conditions, including muddy puddles, and are not affected by the quality of the water. However, you may find a pointy snail shell that opens on the right, and this is a rare gilled snail, known as the panhandle pebblesnail (*Somatogyrus virginicus*). It is very small at approximately 0.14 inches (3.6 millimeters) long. This snail has an operculum, or a little door, that can close over the opening for protection or to prevent the skin from losing too much water. Because these snails have gills to breathe air from the water, they are much more sensitive to changes in water quality. If there is too much pollution in the water, you won't find any gilled snails, and for this reason, the panhandle pebblesnail also is an ideal indicator species. Fortunately, the Eno River has been fairly well protected by the surrounding parklands, so the water is clean, and it is a great habitat for gilled snails and other river critters. For feeding, snails have a sharp tongue, called a radula, which they use to scrape up algae and decaying matter.

As you hunt around in the water, you will probably see several different kinds of shells. Collect some in your water container and make observations on the shapes and details of your shells. Keep your eye out for those that are hinged together so that they look like a butterfly. This is another type of mollusk, called a bivalve because it has two shells attached in the middle. Some may even be tightly closed together, and this that means there is a live animal inside. Examine the shells you find. For these particular species, if the hinge, the piece holding the two shells together, is in the middle and the shell is small, it is a type of clam. If the shell is larger and elongated with the hinge off to one side, it is a type of mussel. These animals are filter feeders. They get food (and oxygen) by pumping water through their bodies and filtering out the food, so they are also found in clean water and can serve as an indicator species for water pollution. The Asian clam (*Corbicula fluminea*) is often seen in the Eno River. It was introduced to the river and is an invasive species. The most common type of mussel is the eastern elliptio (*Elliptio complanata*), but the Eno is also home to rare and endangered species of mussels, like the dwarf wedgemussel (*Alasmidonta heterodon*). You might be holding one of these rare or endangered animals in your hands as you explore in the Eno. Please remember to be gentle, and always return these live animals to the river where you found them.

You can also look for vertebrate aquatic creatures, including the Neuse River waterdog (*Necturus lewisi*), also known as the Carolina mudpuppy. This organism is a primitive aquatic salamander, meaning that it is an early **evolutionary** form of salamander. They are extremely fast, but with a keen eye you may actually see one. This mudpuppy only exists in North Carolina, nowhere else in the world, and only in two river systems in the Piedmont and Coastal Plain: the Neuse River basin and the Tar-Pamlico River basin. The Carolina mudpuppy is sensitive to water quality, requiring clean and moderate- to fast-moving water for survival and reproduction. Fast-moving water provides the necessary high oxygen levels required by this organism in its water home. When water moves rapidly and is churned, there is more water surface area and greater pressure for oxygen to diffuse across the air-water surface, providing a higher level of dissolved oxygen, which is the amount of oxygen in the water. Mudpuppies generally choose to live under rocks or in crevices. If you are lucky enough to catch a mudpuppy, hold it gently behind the gills. They are not poisonous, as some people believe, but they are slimy, so they can slip out of your hands if you're not prepared. One of the benefits of catching a mudpuppy is that you might hear it "bark." The ability to make sound is unusual for salamanders, but it is the reason that mudpuppies or "waterdogs" have their name. After you have carefully examined your mudpuppy, gently place it back in the water.

Learning More

Are you fascinated by limnology? A limnologist is a scientist who studies inland waters as ecological systems. If you would like to learn more about limnology, take your observations from this chapter and research a little further. Ask questions about the organisms that you're finding: Do they emerge from the water as adults? What

Figure 19-2. Take a picnic lunch for a nice day along the Eno River. Photo by Annie Planck Howell.

do they look like when they emerge? What would you find at a different time of year? Create your own questions according to your specific interests.

A trip to the Eno will always be more fun and more successful if you bring along a few key items. Water shoes that secure onto your feet or old muddy sneakers are a great idea. If it is chilly, rubber rain boots work best. Avoid wearing flip-flops in the water because they will not stay on when wet and will cause you to slip. Consider bringing a notebook, pencil or pen, and field guides that represent your interests. A hand lens or magnifying glass is a great tool to bring along for making observations of both smaller organisms and the small details of larger organisms. Always bring plenty of water to drink, a snack, sunscreen, and bug spray.

There are miles of trails along the riverbanks. In Durham, you can head to West Point on the Eno City Park and see the historic mill grinding corn and wheat into flour. Kids will enjoy splashing and playing below the dam.

Eno River State Park is another great place to hike and explore along the river. There are several entrances and many trails to discover. One great place to start is the main entrance at the end of Cole Mill Road, called Few's Ford. A ford is a shallow place in the river where people cross, or ford, the river. At Few's Ford, you can imagine a time not too long ago when people crossed on horseback or in wagons. Today, people come to the ford to play, relax, or even go trail running through the river. Whether you like to run or just float, the ford is a nice place to visit. Looking upstream, you can see the cascades, a small waterfall on the Eno. There are picnic tables, a picnic shelter with a stone fireplace, an exciting suspension bridge to cross over the river, a wilderness cabin to relax in, and campgrounds to spend the night with family or a group. Wherever you go, the river is cool, rippling, and inviting. There are only a few deep spots, or swimming holes, along the Eno, and most of it is fun, safe, and easy to explore, even for little ones.

Before You Go

Want to learn more? There are educational programs available at the parks year-round. Check out the websites of the Eno River Association, Eno River State Park, and West Point on the Eno (Durham Parks and Recreation) to find out more and sign up for a program on water bugs, birds, or whatever other wonderful things pique your interests.

References and Resources

"Dwarf Wedgemussel (I. Lea, 1830)." North Carolina Wildlife Resources Commission, https://www.ncwildlife.org/Learning/Species/Mollusks/Dwarf-Wedgemussel. Accessed October 31, 2018.

Neuse River Basin. Raleigh: Office of Environmental Education and Public Affairs, 2013, https://files.nc.gov/deqee/documents/files/neuse.pdf. Accessed October 31, 2018.

WEBSITES:

Eno River Association: www.enoriver.org; Eno River State Park: http://www.ncparks.gov/eno-river-state-park

West Point on the Eno City Park: https://durhamnc.gov/Facilities/Facility/Details/West-Point-on-the-Eno-158

Contact: phone: (919) 383-1686; email: eno.river@ncparks.gov

Address: Few's Ford: 6101 Cole Mill Road, Durham, N.C. 27705

GPS Coordinates: Few's Ford: N 36°4.74, W 79°0.42

CHAPTER 20

Medoc Mountain State Park

JOEL JAKUBOWSKI

SCIENTIFIC FIELDS OF STUDY: *Geology, Ecology, Forest Management*

If you began a journey in search of fine wine, your adventures could take you to faraway lands in France and Italy, or perhaps even keep you a bit closer to home in California. However, there was a time when your voyage would have ended in Halifax County, North Carolina, where you would have found Sidney Weller and his vineyard located on Medoc Mountain. Weller, born in 1791, was raised in Montgomery, New York, and eventually earned a master's degree from Union College in Schenectady. In 1829, he and his wife, Elizabeth McCarrel, moved to Halifax County, where he purchased approximately 300 acres of land to experiment with new farming techniques. The soil was of poor quality, but Weller, a self-proclaimed "book farmer," read and implemented agricultural techniques such as crop rotation, plant propagation, and waste matter distribution to improve the soil's condition. Eventually the soil grew so rich he was able to establish a vineyard. By 1840, the vineyard was the largest in North Carolina, producing popular wines and helping the state become the largest wine producer in America.

Weller called his vineyard Weller's Vineyard, which included a unique section of rocky land that he named Medoc as an homage to the famous Médoc region of Bordeaux, France, known for its vineyards. When Weller died in 1854, his vineyard was purchased by Charles and F. M. Garrett, who changed the name to Medoc Vineyards and expanded operations to both California and New York. In the early 1900s, Prohibition was established, making the production and sale of alcoholic beverages illegal, and around the same time a devastating fire put an end to the vineyard and all wine production. Soon after, a Boy Scout camp was established at the peak of the mountain, where a stream was impounded to create a swimming pond. The camp closed in the 1950s, but remnants of its operations are still found in the park today.

Geology

From a geological and environmental standpoint, Medoc Mountain State Park sits in a distinctive location where the Piedmont and Coastal Plain environments meet along the fall zone, or fall line. The fall zone is a narrow region, running north and south, where soft sediments from the Coastal Plain meet harder rocky sediments from the Piedmont. The fall zone can be observed all along the east coast of the United States and is particularly easy to identify where rivers cross the zone, because there will be rapids at that location. When explorers were first visiting North Carolina, they took boats up the rivers from the coast, only to find that they could not pass the rapids at the fall zone.

Medoc Mountain is a **monadnock**, like both Pilot Mountain (Chapter 15) and Occoneechee Mountain (Chapter 18). Monadnocks, a name that originated with the Native Americans, are isolated rocky ridges that rise abruptly from the flat, low-lying surroundings. The Medoc Mountain monadnock rises to an elevation of 325 feet (99 meters) and is comprised mostly of **granite**, formed when a pocket of **magma**, or molten rock deep inside the Earth, slowly cooled and hardened. The granite rocks in the park were formed when Africa collided with North America about 300 million years ago. Refer to the Piedmont Geology section (p. 106) for more details of this history. During this collision, as the two **tectonic** plates moved toward each other, the oceanic crust between them was squeezed and forced deep within the Earth. Portions of this deep oceanic crust and the continental crust were heated and melted at more than 1200°C, turning into magma. The magma rose within the crust, stopped when still deep below the surface, and then slowly cooled and solidified into hard granite, leaving plenty of time for large crystals to form. Over time, erosion wore away the rocky material above the granite, until eventually the hard granite was exposed at the Earth's surface.

Millions of year later, the Atlantic Ocean's water levels rose to their highest point, covering most of what is now eastern North Carolina. Sediments were deposited on the seafloor in the vicinity of what is now Medoc Mountain State Park. When the water levels receded, a very thin layer of this Coastal Plain sediment was left behind over the igneous rock base of biotite granite, a granite containing black mica. In some locations, the soil is so thin that large rock exposures protrude out of the ground, leaving no signs of the Coastal Plain environment. Once the sandy soil layers eroded away, the granite again became exposed, leaving the rock that we see today.

Rocks even older than the 300-million-year-old granite forming the monadnock are also present in the park. More than 500 million years ago, layers of volcanic ash and silt were deposited on the flanks of an ancient volcanic island. As the continents were shifting, this volcanic island, along with others forming an "island arc," was caught in the middle of the two continents and was squished between them. The rocks from this volcano are now represented by metamorphosed tuff, which was once volcanic ash, and siltstone in the southwestern part of the park along Little Fishing Creek. These rocks attest to a violent volcanic chapter in the geologic story of the park.

The rocks in the park are made up of many types of minerals. The granite in the park is comprised mostly of feldspar, quartz, and mica (Figure 20-1). These minerals are randomly dispersed, giving them a "salt-and-pepper" look, very similar to what we discussed in Chapter 8, "Blowing Rock Gneiss." Molybdenite, or molybdenum

Figure 20-1. The primary minerals found in the granite rocks in the park are quartz, feldspar, and mica. Pyrite, or "fool's gold," is often found in small amounts. Photo by Joel Jakubowski.

disulfide, is also found in the park. It is the most common molybdenum ore, meaning a rock from which a metal can be mined. In the early 1940s, the park was explored to locate significant sources for mining. Molybdenum is a strengthening element that is added to iron ore during the smelting process to increase the strength of steel. Just after World War II, there was a steel shortage in the United States, and all possible mineral sources were being examined to help resolve the issue; but no mining ever took place in Medoc Mountain State Park.

Pyrite, or "fool's gold" is commonly found in the park. Occasionally pyrite pebbles and small cubic crystals have been found along Little Fishing Creek, giving rise to tales of gold in the park. Although several true gold deposits have been found within a few miles, no gold has ever been found in the park itself.

Forest Communities within the Park

Due to its uniqueness, the 185-acre parcel of land that encompasses Medoc Mountain has been designated as a registered Natural Heritage Area to ensure it is managed in the best interest of the land.

The park contains six different natural communities that can be visited and explored, all providing valuable habitats for many different plant and animal species. These include (1) the **Piedmont Alluvial Forest**, (2) the **Piedmont Monadnock Forest**, (3) the **Mesic Mixed Hardwood Forest**, (4) the **Piedmont/Coastal Plain Heath Bluff**, (5) the **Dry-Mesic Oak-Hickory Forest**, and (6) the **Dry Oak-Hickory Forest.** Feel free to bring along a botanical field guide to help you identify which type of community you are exploring.

Figure 20-2. The Piedmont Alluvial Forest occurs along Little Fishing Creek. Photo by Joel Jakubowski.

The Piedmont Alluvial Forest (Figure 20-2) occurs along Little Fishing Creek, its tributaries, and the surrounding **floodplain**. In this area, **understory** trees, such as ironwoods, red maples, and flowering dogwoods, grow beneath the taller water oaks, swamp chestnut oaks, sweet gums, and river birch trees. At ground level, there is a mixture of viburnum, speckled alder, orange-flowered jewelweed, mayapple, false Solomon's seal, poison ivy, and atamasco lilies. Speckled alder trees (*Alnus incana*) are known for having special bacteria associated with their roots. Inside root nodules live nitrogen-fixing bacteria that convert inert, or nonreactive, forms of nitrogen into ammonia-nitrogen that can be used by plants and other bacteria, making the soil healthy and rich. This process is very similar to planting legumes in an agricultural field to enrich the soil for growing other crops, so we know that the speckled alder trees have a very important role in this environment.

The second community type of interest in the park is a Piedmont Monadnock Forest, which occurs on both the low northern slopes and the southern/southwest-facing middle and upper slopes of Medoc Mountain. These natural communities are very common in the Piedmont, but they are not common in the eastern part of the state, serving as a reminder that the park sits on the fall line between the Piedmont and the Coastal Plain regions. A Piedmont forest like this can be difficult to identify, so you will need to look for the trees that comprise the forest as an indicator of community type. The forest layer is comprised of white oak, northern red oak, black oak, mockernut hickory, and loblolly pine trees in all stages of growth. Chestnut

Figure 20-3. The Bluffs is a Mesic (moist) Mixed Hardwood Forest on the lower slopes of the steep, north-facing ravines along Little Fishing Creek. Photo by Joel Jakubowski.

oak (*Quercus montana*) is also present here, marking the easternmost occurrence of this hardwood tree in North Carolina. Smaller trees such as mountain laurel, pinxter azalea, fringe tree, sparkleberry, squaw huckleberry, dwarf huckleberry, and dangleberry are also common in this area.

The Mesic Mixed Hardwood Forest of the Piedmont subtype (Figure 20-3) found along Little Fishing Creek is referred to at Medoc Mountain as The Bluffs. "Mesic" indicates that this habitat is moist, and the trees that grow here are mostly hardwoods of varying types. This community occurs on the lower slopes of the steep, north-facing ravines along Little Fishing Creek and is dominated by American beech trees (*Fagus grandifolia*), often of great age and size. Other trees common to this area are white oak, black gum, tulip tree, willow oak, and sourwood. Mountain laurel and pinxter azalea are extremely common, with small pockets of wild ginger, wood-rush, and Christmas fern present as well. The Bluffs is a registered Natural Heritage Area covering 20 acres, with slopes in some areas exceeding 70 percent grades. A "natural area," as defined by the Natural Heritage Program in North Carolina, is a site of significant **biodiversity** due to the presence of rare species, unique habitats, or important groupings of certain animals. Many years ago, this area served as a dumping site for local residents, which greatly affected the growth of the understory vegetation. The creation of the state park in the mid-1970s provided protection for this unique habitat, and efforts to restore the natural vegetation have been successful.

Figure 20-4. Because of fire suppression in the past, stands of loblolly pine now inhabit this forest, blocking out the light and preventing the establishment of ground cover that once grew in this forest. Aggressive management plans have been implemented to revert the forested landscape to its previous state. Photo by Joel Jakubowski

The fourth community type in this park is a Piedmont/Coastal Plain Heath Bluff that is found just above Little Fishing Creek on the lower northwest-facing slopes of Medoc Mountain. This area is dominated by a dense **shrub layer** of heath species that thrive in infertile, **acidic** soils where tall trees cannot grow. Look for mountain laurel, sparkleberry, deerberry, hillside blueberry, and pinxter azalea as common understory trees, while galax, trailing arbutus, teaberry, wintergreen, and partridgeberry plants can be found along the ground.

Another community type found in the park is the Dry-Mesic Oak-Hickory Forest. These forests occur on the midslopes of ridges and typically consist of large white oak, northern red oak, black oak, mockernut hickory, pignut hickory, and sweet pignut hickory trees, with understory trees of red maple, dogwood, sourwood, black gum, and American holly. Wild blueberries, strawberries, and grapes can also be found growing in this area, along with the low-growing forest floor plants downy rattlesnake plantain, spotted wintergreen, beggar's lice, rattlesnake weed, and Lewis's heartleaf. Lewis's heartleaf (*Hexastylis lewisii*) is a very rare small fern that is **endemic** to North Carolina and Virginia.

Dry Oak-Hickory Forest occurs on the ridgetops directly north and east of Medoc Mountain. While similar to Dry-Mesic Oak-Hickory Forest, this community type is dominated by oaks adapted to dry soils, such as white oaks and southern red oaks, with chestnut oak, scarlet oak, black oak, black jack oak, and several hickory species present as well. The understory and the forest floor are often sparse, with the occasional needle grass, oat grass, goat's rue, and spotted wintergreen present.

During the 1930s, a shift occurred in the use of land in and around the park, and personal homesites and farms were sold off to logging companies that harvested pine trees from plantations. As seen throughout much of North Carolina, logging removed many of the tree communities growing at that time, and they were replaced with loblolly pines that were native to our state but not typically abundant here (Figure 20-4). Loblolly pines (*Pinus taeda*) prefer wet areas where fire is not a factor, and because fire suppression practices became more popular throughout the years, the loblollies now commonly grow throughout the park, but mainly on the slopes of Medoc Mountain. Because of the abundance of loblolly pines in the park, the six community types described above can be a bit difficult to detect with the naked eye when you visit Medoc Mountain State Park. Bringing along a botanical field guide will help you discover these natural places a little more easily. The park has implemented management plans to restore the forested landscape to its state prior to the logging of the 1930s and the fire suppression activities that followed. The park's volunteer program allows visitors to assist with management plans by actively participating in removing unwanted species.

Land Management and Forest Restoration

Staff from the Division of Parks and Recreation, the North Carolina Forest Service, and Medoc Mountain State Park have reintroduced fire into the ecosystem through prescribed burns and implemented land management plans for the park. Fire is an important element of forest ecosystems, and the repeated discussions of fire in this book for different locations throughout the Piedmont should indicate the role it plays in this part of the state. As discussed in Chapters 13 through 16, fire reduces fuel loads, eradicates misplaced vegetative species that have been brought in by birds or even humans, and promotes healthy growing communities. Land management plans involving prescribed burns at Medoc Mountain State Park may take over twenty years, with four or five burns undertaken in that time, to achieve a rediscovered state of diversity in the forests where oak and hickory species dominate again. Results from recent prescribed fires can be noticed along the Stream, Loop, and Discovery Loop Trails. The thick layer of ground cover has been burned away, allowing for more herbaceous vegetation to grow in its place. Furthermore, many of the sweet gum, American holly, and young loblolly pine trees that served as understory vegetation because of years of fire suppression were affected drastically by the recent prescribed burns and have since died, making more room for a new forest community to establish.

Another approach to restoring the landscape involves timber harvesting. The areas of the park dominated by loblolly pine trees often have no understory trees growing, and ground-level shrub or herbaceous plants can barely survive. In order to reestablish an oak-hickory type community here, land management procedures are calling for the removal of loblolly pine trees, which, in combination with prescribed burns, will allow other fire-tolerant species to repopulate. The immediate impacts seem drastic and may appear detrimental to many; however, the benefits

Figure 20-5. Little Fishing Creek has excellent water quality, which allows for high biodiversity, providing homes to many species of fish and invertebrates that may not be seen in other aquatic environments. Photo by Joe Shimel, Medoc Mountain State Park.

to the landscape will be tremendous. In forty to fifty years, visitors to the park will be enjoying the newly established forests for themselves. If you have questions about the land management and restoration plans at Medoc Mountain, please feel free to engage a park ranger at any time or arrange for a ranger-led guided tour highlighting current restoration activities.

Notable Creatures

Little Fishing Creek has been designated a Nationally Significant Aquatic Habitat by the National Heritage Program due to excellent water quality and biodiversity (Figure 20-5). Over 50 **invertebrate** species call the creek home, as well the Neuse River waterdog (*Necturus lewisi*), which is a candidate species for endangered protection status from the U.S. Fish and Wildlife Service. Other rare, threatened, and endangered species that occur in the creek are the Roanoke bass, the North Carolina spiny crayfish, the notched rainbow mussel, the squawfoot mussel, the Atlantic pigtoe, the yellow lance, the yellow lampmussel, and the eastern lampmussel. These species need excellent water quality for survival, which Little Fishing Creek provides. Protection of the water quality in this creek was one of the primary reasons that this land was acquired and the park was established in 1973.

Figure 20-6. Medoc Mountain State Park has nearly 30 miles of trails for hiking, biking, and equestrian activities. Photo by Joel Jakubowski.

Before You Go

While Medoc Mountain State Park has outdoor activities that appeal to everyone, most visitors that explore the park spend the day hiking the vast network of trails. The trail system is nearly 30 miles (48.3 kilometers) long and contains 15 different sections. The Pyrite and Saponi Loops, the two newest trails, are open to mountain bikers and hikers (Figure 20-6). All the trails in the southern end of the park are open for equestrian riders, with a total of 11 miles (17.7 kilometers) for riding. The Bluff Loop Trail meanders through the forest and along Little Fishing Creek, giving visitors a firsthand look at The Bluffs rock outcrop. The Dam Site Loop trail takes visitors past the remnants of the old Boy Scout camp swimming pond and buildings. The park also boasts three different types of camping options: a family campground with designated camping spots, both with and without electricity; a primitive group campground facility for organized groups like Boy Scouts, Girl Scouts, or other organizations; and a primitive equestrian campground for self-contained equestrian riders. While you're encouraged to make reservations for overnight camping, they are not required. Campers can guarantee a campsite by contacting the reservation company at 1-877-CAMP-NC (877-722-6762) or visiting the website at www.ncparks.gov.

The park also features an exhibit hall inside the visitor center, showcasing the history of the area and the natural resources in the park. There is a large public picnic area as well as a picnic shelter adjacent to a large grassy field that can be rented for private gatherings. Aquatic adventurists can launch their canoes or kayaks and float Little Fishing Creek for approximately 2.5 miles (4.0 kilometers) to a takeout point at Medoc Mountain Road. The park does not rent boats; however, arrangements to borrow canoes may be possible with advanced notice. The park plans to incorporate an interactive, handicapped-accessible habitat adventure trail, as well as a community building. Call for more information about the status of these projects.

Park rangers offer interpretive and educational programs throughout the year on various topics for the public to attend free of charge. Groups may request specific ranger programs, such as tree identification, animals in the park, or general nature hikes, by contacting the park office for advanced arrangements. For more information about programming, volunteering, or anything else the park offers, visitors can contact the office at (252) 586-6588 or visit our website by selecting Medoc Mountain State Park at www.ncparks.gov.

References and Resources

Biggs, W. C., and J. F. Parnell. *State Parks of North Carolina*. Winston-Salem: J. F. Blair, 1989.

Brady, N. C. *The Nature and Property of Soils*. Upper Saddle River, N.J.: Prentice Hall, 2002.

Jones, H. G., ed. *Sketches in North Carolina, USA, 1872 to 1878: Vineyard Scenes by Mortimer O. Heath*. Raleigh: Division of Archives and History, 2001.

Nesom, Guy, comp. *Plant Guide: SPECKLED ALDER Alnus incana (L.) Moench ssp. rugosa (Du Roi) Clausen*. U.S. Department of Agriculture, 2006, https://plants.usda.gov/plantguide/pdf/cs_alinr.pdf. Accessed March 6, 2018.

"Neuse River waterdog: *Necturus lewisi*." U.S. Fish and Wildlife Service, https://www.fws.gov/southeast/wildlife/amphibians/neuse-river-waterdog/. Accessed February 21, 2018.

"North Carolina Wine Pioneer Sidney Weller," https://www.ncdcr.gov/blog/2017/03/01/north-carolina-wine-pioneer-sidney-weller. Last modified March 1, 2016. Accessed February 14, 2018.

Roberts, D. C. *A Field Guide to Geology*. Boston: Houghton Mifflin, 1996.

Schafale, M. P. *Guide to the Natural Communities of North Carolina*. Fourth Approximation ed. North Carolina Natural Heritage Program, 2012, https://files.nc.gov/dncr-nhp/documents/files/Natural-Community-Classification-Fourth-Approximation-2012.pdf. Accessed February 14, 2018.

Shearin, S. "History of the Medoc Vineyards." Unpublished report, 1981.

Website: https://www.ncparks.gov/medoc-mountain-state-park
Contact: phone: (252) 586-6588; email: medoc.mountain@ncparks.gov
Address: 1541 Medoc State Park Road, Hollister, N.C. 27844
GPS Coordinates: N 36°16.44, W 77°53.28

Part III
Coastal Plain Region

Introduction

Overview

Misty Buchanan

Many of you likely have been to the beautiful beaches on North Carolina's coast, but there are so many more highlights to explore on North Carolina's Coastal Plain. Sure, North Carolina has wonderful beaches. When the weather is just right, the water is the perfect temperature, and the uncluttered view stretches all the way to the horizon, it is easy to see why some people call North Carolina "the southern part of heaven." Jockey's Ridge at Nags Head is the tallest natural sand dune on the U.S. east coast. Sea turtles come from halfway around the world to lay their eggs on North Carolina beaches, including Fort Fisher and Hammocks Beach State Park. Peregrine falcons come from the mountains to winter in open areas of the Outer Banks, like Cape Hatteras. And rare seabeach amaranth plants cling to survival at the base of sand dunes. But if you ever get a chance to travel down some of the backroads of the Coastal Plain, you'll see many other reasons why this region is such an exciting place. After all, this is home to the Venus flytrap, which Charles Darwin called "the most wonderful plant in the world," and Linnaeus (considered the father of taxonomy) called it a wonder of nature (in Latin, *miraculum naturae*).

The Coastal Plain Province occurs in the eastern third of North Carolina, and the boundary between the Coastal Plain and the Piedmont, as discussed in Chapter 20, "Medoc Mountain State Park," is often called the fall line. This is due to a general vertical "fall" or drop that is most noticeable in rivers, but it is also due to a change in the rock type from a harder crystalline rock in the Piedmont to a softer **sedimentary** rock type in the Coastal Plain. Where the water "falls" from the Piedmont to the Coastal Plain, there are often rapids that would have made early navigation difficult by watercraft. From the fall line and Sandhills on the western border, the Coastal Plain region covers the eastern part of the state, all the way to the maritime strand, the **estuaries**, and the **barrier islands** bordering the Atlantic Ocean.

The Coastal Plain was created over geologic time as sand and clay from the Mountains and Piedmont eroded, washing downstream to be deposited in an ancient sea that once covered the area. This region is known for wide, flat expanses, sandy or silty soils, and a shallow water table that often creates large **wetlands** that are great places for reptiles, amphibians, and breeding birds. The clear, shallow waters of Lake Waccamaw support the greatest concentration of rare and **endemic** animal species of any of North Carolina's waterways. The formation of Lake Waccamaw and other Carolina bays has been the subject of great scientific discussion for many years.

In addition to these show-stoppers, the Coastal Plain hosts some environments that are less endearing for the humble wanderer. To many people, coastal swamps and other wetlands, such as **pocosins**, appear to be inhospitable environments, infested with snakes, bears, and ticks, but these wild places are vitally important for the health and diversity of North Carolina's Coastal Plain. Take a little time to explore these areas for yourself to see that the Coastal Plain is much more than just beautiful beaches.

Coastal Plain Geology

April C. Smith

In the two previous sections of this book, we have discussed the continental collisions that formed **Pangea**. The final collision of landmasses ~335–260 million years ago completed the formation of the supercontinent and closed the Iapetus Ocean. Pangea existed as a supercontinent for ~100 million years before it broke apart, tearing and ripping the Earth and leaving giant ditches that began to fill with soil, rocks, and boulders from the eroding mountains. As North America and Africa moved farther apart, the Atlantic Ocean formed in between. The mountains continued to erode, sending more sediment downstream over hundreds of millions of years and leaving a layer of sediments thousands of feet thick to form our coastline. Because of this action, the rocks of the Coastal Plain are different from those of the Mountain and Piedmont regions. They did not form there as the result of heat and pressure but instead were moved there over time, and they are much younger in age, ranging from ~145 million years to 25 million years old. The Coastal Plain is a highly dynamic environment. It is low-lying with frequently flooded wetland areas, and it is affected by currents, tides, winds, and other natural forces causing constant change to the lay of the land. You can experience the dynamics of this environment in its most extreme forms by visiting Jockey's Ridge (Chapter 25) and Cape Hatteras (Chapter 30). You'll notice a stark contrast between the ecology of coastal environments versus those in the mountains, where geologic history has outlined a very different set of rules for habitats and the living things that reside there.

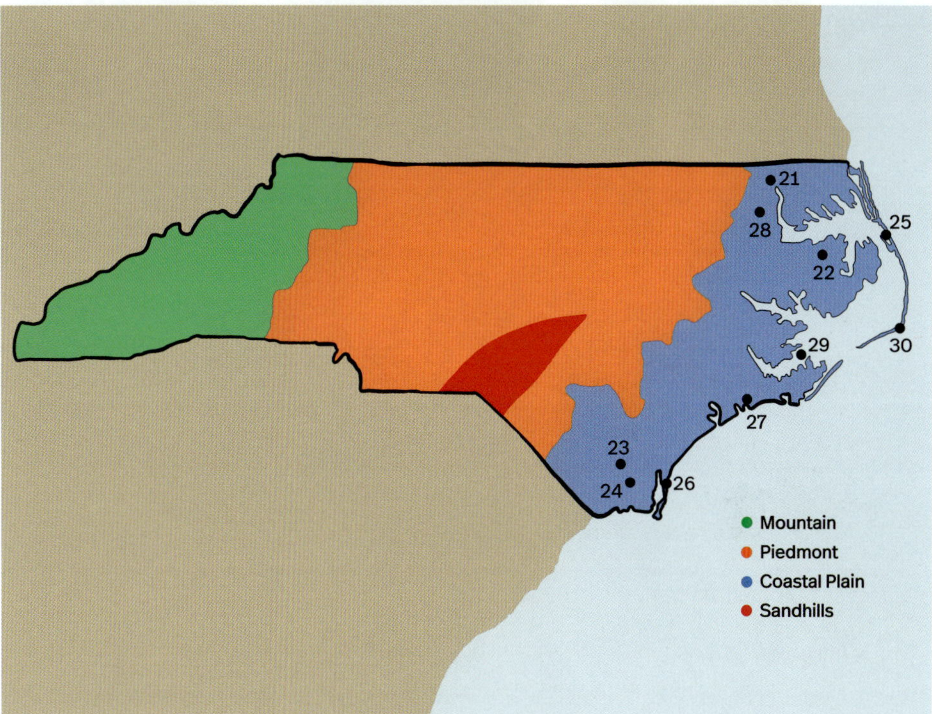

Map 4. Exploration locations in the Coastal Plain region of North Carolina. Map by Ashleigh M. Smith.

21 Merchant's Millpond State Park
22 Pocosin Lakes National Wildlife Refuge
23 Lake Waccamaw State Park
24 Carolina Beach State Park/Green Swamp
25 Jockey's Ridge State Park
26 North Carolina Aquarium at Fort Fisher
27 Hammocks Beach State Park, Bear Island
28 Roanoke River System
29 Pamlico Sound/Neuse River Estuary
30 Cape Hatteras Lighthouse

CHAPTER 21

Merchant's Millpond

A Cypress Swamp

APRIL C. SMITH

SCIENTIFIC FIELDS OF STUDY: *Wetlands Ecology, Herpetology*

In 1660, only seventy-five years after the first English settlers set foot in North Carolina, the area now known as Gates County was settled. This was a difficult region to explore because of the wet, muddy swamps and dense wooded forests. Most settlers would venture far south to avoid crossing this tough land, but a few chose to stay and make it home, recognizing they could harvest wood to sell for growing settlements. Most of the early rural communities that sprung up in Gates County survived by farming and selling lumber, and a few decades later, millponds were being established as regional marketplaces for families to sell produce and buy goods for survival. Millponds are bodies of water used as reservoirs to provide water energy to power mills. In 1811, Norfleet's Millpond was built on Bennett's Creek and became a bustling social center. A gristmill for grinding corn and a sawmill for cutting lumber also were established, along with a number of other supply stores, providing a center for commerce in Gates County.

For a little over a hundred years, Norfleet's Millpond remained a busy marketplace, but in the late 1930s the millpond businesses all closed, and the surrounding land was sold to developers. In the 1960s, a nature lover by the name of A. B. Coleman of Moyock, North Carolina, purchased the land. He believed the land was too beautiful to develop and decided instead to donate 919 acres of the property, including the millpond, to the state. The name was changed eventually to Merchant's Millpond to reflect the history of the site. In 1973 Merchant's Millpond State Park was established on this land, and the Nature Conservancy donated another 925 acres of woodland to the park.

Today, Merchant's Millpond State Park is known as one of the rarest ecological communities in North Carolina, where southern cypress swamp converges with hardwood forest and coastal pond. Bald cypress and water tupelo trees, some nearly

1,000 years old, are draped with Spanish moss, creating a scene out of storybooks. The number of online and print references calling Merchant's Millpond a "magical place" highlights that it is certainly a place not to be missed.

What Makes a Swamp a Swamp?

In the most basic sense, a swamp is an area with low-lying ground where water pools for at least part of the year but soils remain waterlogged for most of the year. If this sounds to you like a wetland, you are correct. Other chapters in this book discuss various types of **wetlands** in North Carolina: bogs and fens in Chapter 3, **pocosins** in Chapter 23, and **salt marshes** in Chapters 26 and 27. What is it about a cypress swamp that is so different from these other types of wetlands? The trees.

Most trees' roots cannot withstand waterlogged soils, never mind full-water immersion. Trees need oxygen, and since water contains less oxygen than air, trees that grow in the water must adapt to growing in low-oxygen environments. Bald cypresses (*Taxodium distichum*) and water tupelos (*Nyssa aquatica*) have adapted to such conditions and thrive here. They only require a dry period long enough for their seeds to germinate before flooding. Both types of trees have a wide swollen base and special root systems that provide a firm hold in soggy soils.

Bald cypress trees give Merchant's Millpond its unique character. They are the trees that are most recognized in this type of landscape, but cypress trees are best known for the "knees" that grow nearby. They, of course, are not actually knees at all, but a special kind of root called a pneumatophore, which means "air bearing." It is thought that the pneumatophores probably are responsible for taking air from above the water line down to the trees' horizontal roots located under waterlogged soils. It would be a safe bet to assume that cypress knees also provide a little extra support for the trees from which they sprout. In this case, perhaps the term "knees" fits after all. Bald cypress trees are deciduous conifers, which is unusual. Conifers are cone-bearing trees with needles, such as pine trees. Conifers usually stay green all year long, losing only part of their needles. But the bald cypress is deciduous, which means it actually loses all of its needles every year, giving it a "bald" appearance in the winter.

Tupelos are also adapted to growing in standing water, but they are not as well known as the bald cypress. Tupelos exist as separate male and female trees, a reproductive method known as dioecious reproduction, which we discussed in Chapter 14, "Prairie Ridge Ecostation." The females have small, green, pollen-producing flowers that are pollinated by bees before becoming a pulpy purplish-red fruit much loved by swamp wildlife, although a little bitter for people. The juice from the tupelo fruit is very sour and can be used as a substitute for lime juice. In some places in the southeastern United States, bee boxes are brought into the swamp and placed on platforms next to tupelo trees to make a special type of rare honey called tupelo honey.

Merchant's Millpond State Park has a terrific Kids in Parks TRACK Trails Program where you can learn more about these trees and others in the park as you hike through the forest. Your tree search should include red maple (*Acer rubrum*), tulip tree (or yellow poplar) (*Liriodendron tulipifera*), American holly (*Ilex opaca*),

Figure 21-1. A bald cypress tree growing in Merchant's Millpond. Photo by Jane Wyche, NC State Parks.

Figure 21-2. An up-close view of the bald cypress tree's trunk as it grows in the water. Photo by Jane Wyche, NC State Parks.

Figure 21-3. If you look at the bottom of a cypress trunk you will see its "knees" sticking out of the water. Photo by Stephen Smith.

sassafras (*Sassafras albidum*), and American beech (*Fagus grandifolia*). Each of these trees has a special function in the forest, and many have interesting stories as well. For example, in North Carolina, nectar from tulip trees is an important source for another unique and delicious type of honey, while sassafras was once used to flavor candy and root beer.

Who Else Lives Here?

If you are looking to immerse yourself in a herpetology paradise, this is the place for you. Herpetology is the study of reptiles and amphibians. Of all the reptiles and amphibians that live in and around Merchant's Millpond, most visitors tend to come looking for the alligators. Merchant's Millpond State Park is the northernmost boundary for the American alligator (*Alligator mississippiensis*). A small cluster resides within the boundary of the state park, but until recently most people thought that alligators were not able to survive this far north. About twenty-five years ago a fisherman caught a baby alligator within the state park boundary, and state officials have been watching this cluster of ancient reptiles ever since. Because the weather can get cooler here than in more southerly parts of North Carolina, alligators have a shorter growing season and reproduce much less frequently. As a result, the cluster that lives here will not expand rapidly but appears to have a stable **population**.

Figure 21-4. Water tupelo trees in the swamp. Photo by Jane Wyche, NC State Parks.

Figure 21-5. American alligator (*Alligator mississippiensis*) close-up. Photo by Mike Dunn.

Now I bet you're thinking, why does the weather restrict an alligator's ability to live farther north of Merchant's Millpond? Let's talk a little about alligator biology. American alligators exhibit a fascinating trait, where the sex of the eggs in a nest is determined not by genetics, as in mammals, but by the temperature of the surrounding environment during incubation. So, if Mama alligator lays approximately fifty eggs, and the temperature in the nest is lower than ~86°F (30°C), all of the babies will be female. If the temperature of the incubating eggs is higher than ~93°F (34°C), all of the babies will be male. Usually in a nest, the incubating temperature varies, and the hatching baby alligators will be both male and female; but in northern North Carolina, the temperatures are more consistently cool, thus affecting the eggs. The closer we get to the Virginia border, temperatures during the early part of the sixty-five-day incubation period in May–June hover precariously around that 86°F (30°C) boundary. Some years the temperatures do not rise above the magical 80°F (27°C) survival mark for either gender, which means none of the eggs will develop at all. But between 80°F (27°C) and 86°F (30°C), all the offspring are females, limiting the alligators' future reproductive potential in the region because there are no males for mating. It is for this reason that the alligator cluster living at Merchant's Millpond is so very special. Here is something for you to ponder: what happens when climate change increases the late spring temperatures along the mid-Atlantic coastline? These impacts are already happening. Some types of animals are already expanding their habitat ranges due to changing temperatures. It is possible that, in your lifetime, we will see alligators in Virginia after all.

The alligator population, small as it might be, is really good for the aquatic environment at Merchant's Millpond. Because alligators are apex **predators**, meaning they are at the top of the food chain, they help maintain healthy populations by preying on other animals in the swamp, including amphibians, snakes, turtles, birds, fish, and any mammal that does not move fast enough. The baby alligators, called hatchlings, will often feed on snails, spiders, and worms. The role than an organism fills in a natural environment is called its niche, and apex predator is a very important niche. When the population of an apex predator declines, the populations of its food sources begin to grow uncontrollably unless another predator moves into its place. In the case of a cypress swamp, secondary predators capable of filling

Figure 21-6. Pinewoods tree frog (*Hyla femoralis*). Photo by Jane Wyche, NC State Parks.

this coveted ecological niche might include foxes, large birds of prey, or even large snakes. Eventually, if no suitable predator can fill the niche, overgrown populations of organisms will not have enough food to eat, and the food web can collapse.

Alligator movements throughout the water column also serve to stir the water, keeping it oxygenated and preventing **eutrophication**. This is a term used to indicate an excess of nutrients in the water, such as nitrogen and phosphorus, from fertilizers. Phosphorus is a common ingredient in many detergents as well, so it is easy for it to make its way into aquatic ecosystems when it is washed down drains and sewers. When extra nutrients enter an aquatic system, the immediate result is rapid plant and algae growth, just as if you were to add fertilizers to your garden at home. But excessive growth will cause plants to compete for space and light, eventually leading to die-offs. Plant and algae die-offs result in oxygen depletion in the water, which then causes the aquatic animal life to die. Eutrophication is a type of water pollution that can be mediated by smart consumer choices like purchasing detergents less harmful to the environment. In this particular circumstance, the alligators' movements help support the health of the aquatic system.

And Other Than the Gators . . .

In the winter, Merchant's Millpond is a bit quieter than in spring and summer. When it's cold outside, cold-blooded amphibians, like frogs and salamanders, spend the season in a slow, relaxing state of hibernation. Aquatic species will sit mostly motionless on the pond bottom, while terrestrial species generally will bury themselves to hibernate on land. Frogs and toads have special "antifreeze" that keeps their bodies from freezing during winter. High concentrations of glucose, or sugar, in their vital organs, like the heart and lungs, protect them from freezing. Other parts of the body may freeze, and the heart and lungs may stop working; but when the temperature rises, the body will thaw, and the heart and lungs will start working again. When the weather warms, frogs emerge from their long rest, and after spring and summer rains, they make their presence known to mates with a loud frog chorus that you definitely will want to experience. Merchant's Millpond is home to

Figure 21-7. Black rat snake (*Pantherophis obsoletus*) on a cypress trunk. Photo by Jane Wyche, NC State Parks.

approximately 22 species of frogs and toads, as well as 12 species of salamanders. Contact the Merchant's Millpond visitor's center below to ask for the best times and locations to visit.

Other animals that you might see in Merchant's Millpond include 11 turtle species, with the 2 most common being yellow-bellied sliders and box turtles. If you are interested in participating in the box turtle survey, please see a ranger for more information. Two species of primitive fish, the bowfin and the longnose gar, can often be seen from a canoe on the water. These fish have remained unchanged for millions of years and can grow to be very large. Some reports indicate that the bowfin can grow to approximately 2.0 feet (0.6 meter), while the longnose gar can grow to be over 6.0 feet (1.8 meters). Snakes are also abundant here—22 different species to be exact. Sightings of cottonmouth, water snakes, kingsnakes, timber rattlesnakes, and copperheads indicate a healthy terrestrial ecosystem in the park.

Before You Go

There are many fascinating things to see at Merchant's Millpond. It is truly a relic of the past and harbors numerous living organisms as evidence. Lassiter Swamp sits at the far north end of Merchant's Millpond. It has an ancient landscape displaying the cypress and tupelo trees in all their glory and begging to be explored by canoe. There are incredible scenic hiking trails here, ranging from a 0.3-mile (0.5-kilometer) trail that is handicap accessible and great for young kids, to the popular 6.0-mile (9.7-kilometer) Lassiter Trail. But without a doubt, the best way to see the area is by canoe. It takes about two hours to paddle across. Bring your own or rent one at the park for the day. Camping is also available at Merchant's Millpond State Park. Call ahead for reservations. Consider attending a ranger talk while you're visiting. There are numerous programs to provide you with more information about herpetology, plant life, and the history of Merchant's Millpond.

References and Resources

"Bald Cypress: *Taxodium distichum*." National Wildlife Federation, https://www.nwf.org/Educational-Resources/Wildlife-Guide/Plants-and-Fungi/Bald-Cypress. Accessed November 7, 2018.

Emmer, Rick. "How Do Frogs Survive the Winter? Why Don't They Freeze to Death?" *Scientific American*, November 24, 1997, https://www.scientificamerican.com/article/how-do-frogs-survive-wint/. Accessed November 7, 2018.

Ferguson, Mark W. J., and Ted Joanen. "Temperature of Egg Incubation Determines Sex in *Alligator mississippiensis*." *Nature* 296 (April 29, 1982): 850–53, https://doi.org/10.1038/296850a0. Accessed November 7, 2018.

"The History of Gates County." GatesCounty.gov, https://gatescounty.govoffice2.com/index.asp?Type=B_BASIC&SEC=%7B9FA438DA-A6A9-48BA-B015-DBA6C392FF0D. Accessed November 7, 2018.

Lewis, J. D. "A History of Gates County." Carolana.com, http://www.carolana.com/NC/Counties/gates_county_nc.html. Accessed November 7, 2018.

"Merchant's Millpond State Park." Kids in Parks, https://www.kidsinparks.com/merchants-millpond-state-park. Accessed November 7, 2018.

Powell, William S., ed. *Encyclopedia of North Carolina*. Chapel Hill: University of North Carolina Press, 2006.

"Tupelo Honey." Honey Traveler, http://www.honeytraveler.com/single-flower-honey/tupelo-honey/. Accessed November 7, 2018.

Website: https://www.ncparks.gov/merchants-millpond-state-park
Contact: phone: (252) 357-1191; email: merchants.millpond@ncparks.gov
Address: 176 Millpond Road, Gatesville, N.C. 27938
GPS Coordinates: N 36°26.22, W 76°41.94

CHAPTER 22

Mattamuskeet and Pocosin Lakes National Wildlife Refuges

A Walk on the Wild Side

MIKE DUNN

SCIENTIFIC FIELDS OF STUDY: *Wildlife Conservation, Geology, Ornithology, Ecology*

The U.S. Fish and Wildlife Service manages 150 million acres of National Wildlife Refuge lands nationwide. Its mission is the conservation, protection, and enhancement of our nation's wildlife and fish **populations** and protection of their habitats. These and other public lands are important for other reasons, too. They help keep air and water clean, offer outdoor recreation opportunities, and bring visitors to vacation in nearby communities. North Carolina has eleven national wildlife refuges, mostly found in the Coastal Plain. For anyone wanting to experience the thrill of seeing a variety of wildlife, two of the best locations to explore are Mattamuskeet and Pocosin Lakes in eastern North Carolina. These are great places to learn about the science of wildlife biology and the important science practice of making observations and wildlife identifications. These two wildlife refuges are close to each other and could be visited in one day. Before visiting, consider participating in programs such as E-bird, Nature's Notebook, or a host of other **Citizen Science** projects.

Mattamuskeet National Wildlife Refuge

Mattamuskeet National Wildlife Refuge is centered on Lake Mattamuskeet, which is the largest natural freshwater lake in North Carolina. Like other natural lakes in the region, Lake Mattamuskeet is believed to be a complex set of Carolina bays. Carolina bays are elliptical topographic depressions in the Earth along the eastern U.S. Atlantic Coastal Plain, and many of these depressions are elongated in a northwest to southeast direction. For many years the origins of Carolina bays were disputed, and a number of explanations were proposed, some of them a bit mysterious in nature. Ideas such as meteorite or comet impacts, **peat** fires leading to soil instability and collapse, and targeted wind erosion have all been proposed as mechanisms for forming Carolina bays. After many years of drilling, coring sediment, and age dating, most scientists believe that these depressions, or oriented lakes, formed between 10,000 and 100,000 years ago during transition periods from cooler, dryer weather to warmer, wetter weather. As the frozen ground began to thaw, layers of soil collapsed to form topographic depressions. Prevailing winds pushed water and sediment into these depressions, scouring the edges of the lake until an elliptical shape evolved and sediment was deposited on the downwind margins of the depressions.

Let's put this into perspective. Imagine a hose being placed at the edge of a pool, such that the water projected directly across the pool hits the opposite side and forms a current within the pool. As the water current hits the far side of the pool, it has to go somewhere, and so it is deflected both to the right and to the left along the pool walls. Thousands of years of wind movement in the same direction, pushing water and sediment in the same direction, would eventually cause the pool to lengthen into an oblong, elliptical shape. Data on oriented lakes all around the world indicate that similar wind and water movements lead to the same results. There is still a great deal to learn regarding Carolina bays, and the collection of more data only helps to clarify the true nature of similarly complicated systems. If you're interested in the origins of Carolina bays and want to read more, then see the references at the end of this chapter. Lake Waccamaw is also a Carolina bay, and we explore some of its interesting inhabitants in Chapter 23.

When you first look out across Lake Mattamuskeet, it is hard to believe that early European settlers in North Carolina dreamed of draining it for farmland, but this was quite common and has happened to a number of Carolina bays. In 1837, a 7.0-mile (~11-kilometer) canal was dug from the lake to the **sound**. When the gates were opened, the water in the lake above sea level flowed out of the lake and reduced its size by about half.

The newly drained lands proved to be **productive** farmland. In the early 1900s, there were other schemes to further drain the lake for farming purposes. At one point, a pumping station, which was the largest in the world at that time, was built to pump water into canals to drain the entire lake. Eventually, the lake property was sold to the federal government, and the lake was restored to create a refuge for migratory waterfowl. For many years, the lake was known as the "goose hunting capital of the world." The pump station was converted to a lodge for visitors that operated for thirty-seven years. When changes in goose migration patterns and declines in the goose population greatly reduced the numbers of geese wintering at the wildlife reserve, the lodge closed, and it has been vacant since 1974. Many people hope that

Figure 22-1. Snow geese (*Chen caerulescens*) taking flight. Photo by Mike Dunn.

with public or private funding, the lodge will someday be reopened as an environmental education facility. While population numbers for migratory waterfowl do tend to fluctuate year after year, the overall trend seems to show an increase in the number of birds visiting the refuge along this migratory route.

Today, Mattamuskeet National Wildlife Refuge is considered one of the best birding spots in North Carolina, especially in winter, when tens of thousands of ducks, geese, and swans make their way here from their breeding grounds farther north. Some, such as the tundra swans (*Cygnus columbianus*) and snow geese (*Chen caerulescens*), may migrate as far as 3,000 miles (4,828 kilometers) from nesting areas above the Arctic Circle to spend winters in eastern North Carolina. Bird migration refers to the seasonal journey that birds take each year as the weather changes. Across the United States, birds migrate in four major flight paths known as flyways. The Atlantic flyway goes along the east coast through North Carolina. Biologists estimate that up to 75 percent of the Atlantic flyway population of tundra swans and the majority of the flyway population of snow geese spend the winter in the Albemarle-Pamlico region that includes Mattamuskeet and Pocosin Lakes National Wildlife Refuges. Waterfowl, or water birds like ducks, geese, and swans, begin arriving in November and usually stay through February, with peak populations often exceeding 200,000 birds in December and January. It is quite an impressive sight to see.

Figure 22-2. Great blue heron (*Ardea Herodias*) in the fog on Lake Mattamuskeet. Photo by Mike Dunn.

Visit Mattamuskeet National Wildlife Refuge

Bring a pair of binoculars or a spotting scope and a field guide and spend time on the refuge observing and identifying the large variety of waterfowl that can be found here in winter. There are numerous vantage points on the refuge where viewing waterfowl is relatively easy.

- Pull-outs along the 5 miles (8 kilometers) of Highway 94 that crosses the lake, including an observation platform near a small cypress island out in the lake. These are great for sunrise photographs.
- The marsh impoundment near the refuge Entrance Road off Highway 94. There is a loop road around the impoundment and an observation platform for easy viewing.
- East Canal Road (across a bridge near the lodge) and along the south shore of the lake for about 2 miles (3.2 kilometers). A short trail at the end allows views of some marsh and swamp habitats and associated animals.

There is still plenty of wildlife to see during other times of the year when most of the visiting waterfowl are absent. Over 240 species of birds have been observed here! Herons and egrets hunt the shoreline and marshes for prey throughout the year, and the refuge is a hot spot for migratory songbirds in spring and fall. Shorebirds are also abundant during the spring and fall migrations and are observed easily along the lakeshore, on mud flats, and in the managed impoundments. Impoundments are

Figure 22-3. Green heron (*Butorides virescens*) sitting on reeds. Photo by Mike Dunn.

areas where a dike, like a dam, is put up to maintain a higher water level, and they provide great habitats for birds and wildlife. Be sure to take the time to get out of the car. Look around and listen carefully, and you will certainly experience wildlife.

The 0.5-mile (0.8-kilometer) loop of the New Holland Trail, across the canal from the lodge, provides a boardwalk through a cypress swamp and is a good place to see songbirds and other wildlife such as white-tailed deer, gray fox, and raccoon. Several species of turtles are common along the canal edges, such as snapping turtles, yellow-belly sliders, and eastern box turtles. Native muskrats and their larger **nonnative** cousins, the South American nutria, can be seen swimming near the lakeshore or feeding along the canal banks. Nutria are considered an **invasive** species in North Carolina. Invasive species are defined as organisms that cause harm to an area where they are not native; this harm can be environmental or economic in nature. In North Carolina, we are mostly concerned that nutria will cause damage with their burrowing activities, consume too much marsh vegetation, and outcompete our native muskrat.

In warm weather, listen for various frogs and toads, watch for snakes, and look for abundant insect life, especially butterflies and dragonflies. Be alert for mounds of dirt that are home to invasive fire ants and avoid stepping on or near them, as the ants can inflict a painful sting. Your visit to this special area of North Carolina can focus on observing a species of interest or exploring the variety of wildlife in the area.

Figure 22-4. Yellow-bellied sliders (*Trachemys scripta scripta*) enjoying the sun. Photo by Mike Dunn.

Figure 22-5. Rat snake (Family: Colubridae). Photo by Mike Dunn.

Figure 22-6. Swallowtail butterfly (Family: Papilionidae). Photo by Mike Dunn.

Pocosin Lakes National Wildlife Refuge

While Mattamuskeet is a great place to see and learn to identify a variety of birds, nearby Pocosin Lakes National Wildlife Refuge, with over 110,000 acres of protected land, is a place where you can get a feel for the wild side of North Carolina. An area called the Pungo Unit was originally established in 1963 by the U.S. Fish and Wildlife Service as an important wintering habitat for migrating waterfowl. Although limited hunting is available around Lake Mattamuskeet, waterfowl in the Pungo Unit are protected from hunting and disturbance. In the early 1990s, the larger Pocosin Lakes National Wildlife Refuge was created to conserve some of the remaining unique wetlands of the Southeast known as **pocosins**.

Many sources indicate that the meaning of the word "pocosin" is "swamp on a hill," but William Tooker's original etymology of the term "pocosin," or "poquosin," from 1899 indicates a different origin, with the meaning of the Native American (Algonquin) word actually being "marsh or low ground." Pocosins typically have a thick **understory** of evergreen shrubs, mostly in the blueberry family, growing low to the ground with interesting names such as fetterbush, titi, gallberry, inkberry, and wax myrtle. There are also scattered clusters of trees, including pond pine, Atlantic white cedar, red maple, loblolly bay, red bay, and sweet bay. The thick vegetation makes it a difficult place to walk but provides valuable habitat for species that need large areas of land without much human disturbance, such as black bears, the red wolves that have been reintroduced to their natural habitat here in recent years, and many species of migratory songbirds.

Although the land on Pocosin Lakes National Wildlife Refuge is only a little above sea level, 20–25 feet (6.1–7.6 kilometers) at the highest point, it is higher than the surrounding swamps and marshes. Over thousands of years, as the dense vegetation has died, it has accumulated into thick layers of peat soil. Peat forms in wet areas, where **organic matter** decays, or breaks down, much more slowly than normal. Over time, the peat builds into domes where dense plant communities thrive, providing rich habitats for many plants and animals. Much of the area was previously ditched and drained with hopes of farming. However, the heart of the pocosin was impossible to drain, and efforts to farm failed. The wetland habitats that were drained lost their original character, along with many plant and animal species. This happened because when water fills the spaces between individual sediment particles, it pushes air out, causing bacterial decay to slow down. When the water is drained, air fills those spaces again, giving bacteria more energy to break down organic matter. If bacteria are working faster to break down the built-up peat, the land starts to sink. Even though North Carolina's Albemarle-Pamlico peninsula contains the largest acreage of pocosins in the United States, 70 percent of the pocosins in North Carolina have been lost in the past fifty years.

Pocosin Lakes National Wildlife Refuge was created to help conserve and restore this valuable wetland type. Conservation efforts include plans to rewet thousands of acres of these drained soils, adding water back into the soils to restore the natural **hydrology**, which is the movement of water. Refuge managers also manage both naturally occurring wildfires and prescribed fires on the landscape, as was discussed previously in Chapters 13 through 16. Peat fires also may be an issue in pocosins and are a concern. Peat can serve as a natural fuel, smoldering for up to 15 feet (4.6 meters) deep in the ground and lasting for weeks or sometimes months. Peat burns very

Figure 22-7. A young American black bear (*Ursus americanus*) in a soybean field. Photo by Mike Dunn.

hot and is very difficult to extinguish, often leaving billowing smoke covering large areas of land, affecting both humans and the resident animals. As in other habitats, prescribed fires help reduce the aboveground fuel load by removing dead shrubs that could burn extremely hot, but caution must be used when setting prescribed fires near peat so that the underlayers of the soil do not catch fire. Benefits of the management efforts in Pocosin Lakes National Wildlife Refuge include improving wildlife habitat, reducing the frequency and intensity of wildfires, and conserving the peat soils that keep water clean and hold extra water from storms.

Visit Pocosin Lakes National Wildlife Refuge

The vast areas of swamp and pocosin here are best viewed by driving south from the town of Columbia on Highway 94. At the Frying Pan Road intersection (mile 7.0), turn right onto Northern Road, which is currently unmarked and unpaved, and drive about 0.5 mile (0.8 kilometer) until you enter the refuge—signs indicate refuge land. With a map (see url below), you may want to follow refuge roads all the way to the south shore of Lake Phelps. Look for various species of wildlife and their signs along the way, including black bear, raccoon, muskrat, white-tailed deer, and

Figure 22-8. Bobcat (*Lynx rufus*). Photo by Mike Dunn.

bobcat. Wild turkey, northern bobwhite, great blue herons, and numerous songbirds are also abundant in the pocosin habitat and along the roadside canals.

The most popular area for wildlife viewing is the Pungo Unit, surrounding 2,800-acre Pungo Lake. Driving around this part of the refuge can lead to numerous wildlife surprises any time of year, so please drive slowly and keep an eye out for wildlife. Roads on the Pungo Unit can be very muddy in inclement weather.

In winter, you can hear the sounds of thousands of tundra swans resting on the water or flying to and from the fields to feed. Huge flocks of 30,000 or more snow geese may descend into a farm field next to the road or fly overhead as they go to and from the lake. Swarms of red-winged blackbirds (*Agelaius phoeniceus*) move as one as they feed in the cornfields or evade a hawk or falcon. Bald eagles, red-tailed hawks, great horned owls, northern harriers, and many other birds of prey are common. Keep your eyes open for large, dark shapes out in the fields or along the edges of the road ahead; this area has one of the densest populations of black bears (*Ursus americanus*) in the southeastern United States. You might even spot one in a large tree, where they often sleep or feed.

In warmer weather, watch for snakes and turtles crossing the road, songbirds in the trees and fields, and beautiful insects such as palamedes (*Papilio palamedes*) and zebra swallowtail butterflies (*Protographium marcellus*). Red bay (*Persea borbonia*) and pawpaw trees (*Asimina trilobal*) are the host plants for these beautiful butterflies and are very common plants in the low growth of the forests here.

Even if you don't see a bear or bobcat, you almost certainly can find evidence

Figure 22-9. Bald eagle (*Haliaeetus leucocephalus*). Photo by Mike Dunn.

Figure 22-10. Timber (canebrake) rattlesnake (*Crotalus horridus*). Photo by Mike Dunn.

in the form of scat (animal feces), tracks, and claw marks on trees. Try comparing a bear paw print to your foot print! Animal tracks are abundant on many of the dirt roads and in mud along the edges of the fields and canals. Consider bringing a journal for sketching or a track guide to help you identify who has recently been visiting. Also, try taking photos of tracks to help you learn which animal has passed through recently. If you visit at different times of the year, keep your observations in a notebook to compare which animals are more active in the cold versus warm months.

The best times for viewing wildlife are generally shortly after sunrise and before sunset, but you may get lucky almost any time of day. A short hike along North Lake Road is one of the best places to look for evidence of animals. Check the trunks of large trees along the way to look for bear claw marks. A few words of caution: please do not feed any of the wildlife or approach them too closely, especially bears. Be very aware that this area has a healthy population of snakes; most are harmless, but there are a few species of venomous snakes. You may come across the eastern form of timber rattlesnakes (*Crotalus horridus*), often called canebrake rattlesnakes, so watch where you are walking.

The sights and sounds of a day at Pungo can be one of the most memorable outdoor experiences anyone can have in North Carolina. Watching and hearing thousands of swans and snow geese flying overhead and maybe seeing a black bear feeding out in a nearby field is something you will never forget.

Before You Go

Mattamuskeet has excellent fishing and crabbing in warm months, and boating on the lake from March through October is a great way to spend the day. Boating is prohibited when the waterfowl are on the refuge in November through February. Hunting is permitted at certain times and in certain areas, so make sure to check hunting schedules before you go. Each December, the refuge sponsors an annual Swan Days educational event with lots of fun activities to celebrate the return of thousands of tundra swans that migrate from the arctic tundra to the refuge. A wonderful visitor center near the lodge has exhibits, a small gift shop, and restrooms. It is usually open on weekdays, as well as on weekends during the winter waterfowl season. This is a great place for learning about migratory waterfowl and the habitats they need for survival.

The Pocosin Lakes Visitor Center is located in Columbia, North Carolina, and is generally open on weekends. Take a walk on the Scuppernong River Interpretive Boardwalk located behind the visitor center. The boardwalk begins directly behind the Walter B. Jones Sr. Center for the Sounds and the Tyrrell County Visitor Center. It follows along the edge of the Scuppernong River for a short distance before entering a cypress swamp. Interpretive signs along the trail explain the unique features and characteristics of the area. The entire boardwalk is 0.75 mile (1.20 kilometers) in length.

References and Resources

Grant, John A., Mark J. Brooks, and Barbara E. Taylor. "New Constraints on the Evolution of Carolina Bays from Ground-Penetrating Radar." *Geomorphology* 22 (1998): 325–45.

Moore, Christopher R., Mark J. Brooks, David J. Mallinson, Peter R. Parham, Andrew H. Ivester, and James K. Feathers. "The Quaternary Evolution of Herndon Bay, a Carolina Bay on the Coastal Plain of North Carolina (USA): Implications for Paleoclimate and Oriented Lake Genesis." *Southeastern Geology* 51, no. 4 (March 2016): 145–71.

"Pocosin Lakes National Wildlife Refuge." Map. U.S. Fish and Wildlife Service, http://www.fws.gov/southeast/pubs/pocosin-lakes-tearsheet.pdf. Accessed November 8, 2018.

Swezey, Christopher S. "Carolina Bays of the U.S. Atlantic Coastal Plain Are Relict Thermokarst Lakes That Formed Episodically during the Last Glaciation." *Geological Society of America Abstracts with Programs* 50, no. 3 (2018), https://doi.org/10.1130/abs/2018SE-310370. Accessed November 8, 2018.

Tooker, William W. "The Adopted Algonquian Term for 'Poquosin.'" *American Anthropologist* 1, no. 1 (January 1899): 162–70, https://doi.org/10.1525/aa.1899.1.1.02a00120. Accessed January 23, 2019.

Ward, Sara, comp. *Benefits of Wetland Hydrology Restoration in Historically Ditched and Drained Peatlands: Carbon Sequestration Implications of the Pocosin Lakes National Wildlife Refuge Cooperative Restoration Project.* 2010. U.S. Fish and Wildlife Service, https://www.fws.gov/raleigh/pdfs/PeatlandRestoration_CSeqBenefits_Jan2010.pdf. Accessed November 8, 2018.

WEBSITES:

Mattamuskeet NWR (MNWR): https://www.fws.gov/refuge/mattamuskeet/
Pocosin Lakes NWR (PLNWR): https://www.fws.gov/refuge/pocosin_lakes/

CONTACTS:

(MNWR): phone: (252) 926-4021
(PLNWR): phone: (252) 796-3004

ADDRESSES:

(MNWR): 85 Mattamuskeet Road, Swan Quarter, N.C. 27885
(PLNWR): 205 South Ludington Dr., Columbia, N.C. 27925

GPS COORDINATES:

(MNWR) Visitor Center: N 35°27.06, W 76°10.62
(PLNWR) Visitor Center: N 35°54.9, W 76°15.24

CHAPTER 23

Lake Waccamaw

Studying Freshwater Mussels in Eastern North Carolina

ARTHUR E. BOGAN & JAMIE M. SMITH

SCIENTIFIC FIELDS OF STUDY: *Invertebrate Zoology, Ecology*

Have you ever been walking on the beach and looked down to see clam shells, oyster shells, or blue mussel shells? What about along the sandy beach of a riverbank or lake? It might have been more of a surprise to see shells there. Freshwater mussels are quite common worldwide, and they all belong to the class Bivalvia in the phylum Mollusca. Mussel is a common name used to refer to several members of several families of bivalves from both salt water and fresh water. Mussels occur in rivers, creeks, and lakes, as well as in the ocean, and they come in all shapes, colors, and sizes.

North America has the richest mussel fauna worldwide, with more than 300 species, and the southeastern United States has the greatest diversity of freshwater mussels in the world. Freshwater mussels are found in all 17 **river basins** of North Carolina (Map 5). There are over 60 species found throughout the state, with one species that is **endemic**, as it is found only in North Carolina: the Tar River spinymussel, which resides in the Neuse and Tar River basins. There are several different groups of bivalves in North Carolina that can be found only in fresh water. These include the very small fingernail or pea clams (Sphaeriidae), the introduced Asian clam (*Corbicula fluminea*), and our native freshwater mussels, which are classified within the family Unionidae, or the freshwater mussel family.

In Columbus County, North Carolina, a very special tea-colored lake is home to a healthy **population** of freshwater mussels. Although shallow, Lake Waccamaw is known for approximately 15 different species of mussels. The lake has a very high alkalinity, or calcium content, which is needed for the production of the mussel shells. Lake Waccamaw is a unique geological feature called a Carolina bay, which we also discuss in Chapter 22, "Mattamuskeet and Pocosin Lakes National Wildlife Refuges." These elliptically shaped and often similarly oriented (northwest to southeast) Carolina bay lakes are quite shallow, with a maximum depth of approximately 50 feet (15.2 meters), and are extremely rich in **biodiversity**, which is expressed quite beautifully by the mussels one can find here. Please refer to Chapter 22 for a detailed discussion of the origin and evolution of Carolina bays and to find further references for this fascinating topic.

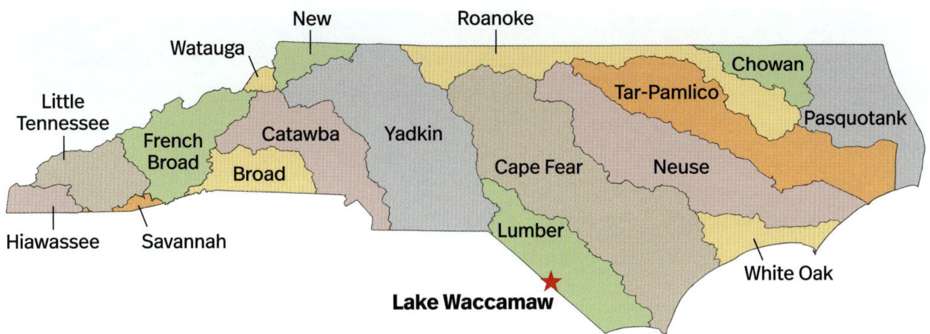

Map 5. North Carolina has seventeen river basins throughout the state. Lake Waccamaw is located in the Lumber River basin.

Figure 23-1. Eastern lampmussel (*Lampsilis radiate*), mantle flap and apertures. Photo by Brian Watson.

What Do Mussels Do?

Freshwater mussels live partially or completely buried in the bottom of rivers, creeks, and lakes with their posterior exposed. The head end is buried in the sand. However, mussels do not have a head or a brain, just a good nervous system. On the exposed posterior end of the animal are two openings, or apertures, where the water enters through the bottom aperture (incurrent) and exits through the top aperture (excurrent) (Figure 23-1). The two valves are slightly open, allowing water to circulate across the gills to absorb oxygen and to trap fine bits of food. Mussels are omnivores, which means that they eat both plants and other animals, including algae, diatoms, bacteria, dissolved organic matter, and **detritus**, which is decaying organic matter.

Mussels are Mother Nature's filters because they pump a substantial amount of water though their bodies via their incurrent apertures where water comes in, as described above. The volume of water pumped depends on the size of the animal, population density, water temperature, and the species itself.

Not only do mussels filter our waters, but when the animals die, their used empty shells provide a habitat for other organisms like mites, tardigrades, and insect larvae

Figure 23-2. Two aquaria, one on right with ten freshwater mussels. Photo by John Alderman.

Figure 23-3. Same two aquaria, fifteen minutes later, showing the impact of mussel filtration. Photo by John Alderman.

Figure 23-4. The typical life cycle of a freshwater mussel. Drawing by Virginia Greene.

such as caddisflies and midges. Some organisms may even nestle themselves inside the shell with a living mussel. It seems like a pretty safe spot. Spent, or empty, shells are imperative in areas where other hard substrates, like rocks, are unavailable. A substrate is the surface upon which an organism lives. Freshwater snails find that spent shells are a great place to lay their eggs. Several recent studies have shown that firmly burrowed mussel shells stabilize streambed sediments.

Freshwater mussels in the family Unionidae have a remarkable life cycle unlike that of any other group (Figure 23-4). They have a larval stage that requires some time attached as a parasite to the gills or fins of fish. The larvae are microscopic and are called glochidium or (plural) glochidia (Figure 23-5). Some mussel species can use a variety of fish species as hosts for the larvae, while others are limited to one or very few. In most species of mussels, the sexes are separate. The male releases gametes into the water column, and the female siphons them in with water and food items. Fertilization occurs internally, and the developing embryos are held in all or part of her two pairs of gills. She releases them when they are mature. They can be released in a cloud when a host fish is close, or she may release them in gelatin-like packages imitating fish food items such as larval fish, fish eggs, or various types of flat worms. Some species have evolved a remarkable reproductive strategy where the edge of the female's mantle protrudes from the shell when she is ready to release glochidia and forms the shape of a small fish, crayfish, or other prey (see Figure 23-1). These structures move in the current and attract the attention of the potential host fish. When a fish bites the lure, the glochidia are released, giving them a chance to attach to their host.

Once the glochidia are attached to the fins or gills of a host fish, a cyst forms around them. While they are attached, the gills, the foot, and the intestines develop within the glochidia. After a period of a week to several months, depending on the

Figure 23-5. The larva, or glochidium, of a freshwater mussel, the dwarf wedgemussel (*Alasmidonta heterodon*). Photo by Barry Wicklow.

Figure 23-6. A freshwater mussel moving through a sandy bottom and leaving a trail. Photo by Art Bogan.

species, they detach from their host, settle to the bottom, and if they land in a suitable habitat, begin life as juvenile mussels.

The ride that the glochidia get while attached to their fish host allows them to migrate to a new habitat. Some mussels will sit in the same spot where they landed when they dropped off the host fish. Other species actively move and can be followed by the tracks they leave in the sand (Figure 23-6). To move, mussels extend their foot out of their shell, into the substrate. Then they retract the foot and pull themselves along.

What Will You See?

The most common species that you will see in Lake Waccamaw is the Carolina slabshell (*Elliptio congaraea*) (Figure 23-7). This mussel is elliptical in shape with a prominent angular ridge. The outside of the shell, or periostracum, is light to dark brown. The inside of the shell, or nacre, is white to bluish. Another common species, often seen as dead shells on the banks of the lake, is the tidewater mucket (*Leptodea ochracea*) (Figure 23-8). The shell is much thinner and somewhat shiny, round in outline, and covered with fine green lines.

Although these animals are not cute or cuddly, they play an important role in our ecosystems and are vital and essential to the food web. Mussels are the longest-lived invertebrates. Some have been reported to live over 200 years! More commonly they

Figure 23-7.
The common Carolina slabsell (*Elliptio congaraea*), from Lake Waccamaw. Photo by Art Bogan.

Figure 23-8.
The common tidewater mucket (*Leptodea ochracea*), from Lake Waccamaw. Photo by Art Bogan.

live from 10 to 50 years, depending on the species. It may seem tricky at first, but with a little practice anyone can become good at finding and identifying freshwater mussels. The next time you find yourself walking along the riverbank or lakeshore, look for the shells of these amazing creatures.

Before You Go

The best spot on the lake to get a great view of freshwater mussels is on the southeast shore within Lake Waccamaw State Park. This state park is located about 11 miles (~18 kilometers) southeast of Whiteville and 38 miles (61 kilometers) west of Wilmington (see Map 5). Here you can walk out to the end of the dock into shallow water. If you bring a mask and snorkel, you can spend some time checking out these creatures, and you may even be able to see them siphoning. When you spot a mussel, try hovering at the water's surface, being as still as possible to see if you can follow the water flow into or out of the apertures. You can pick them up gently to observe their shells, but they will probably close the two valves quickly when disturbed.

Consider sketching the different types of shells that you find or photographing them for a digital album of your favorite natural finds.

References and Resources

"River Mussels (Family Unionidae)." *iNaturalist*, https://www.inaturalist.org/taxa/51903-Unionidae. Accessed November 8, 2018.

Website: https://www.ncparks.gov/lake-waccamaw-state-park
Contact: phone: (910) 646-4748; email: lake.waccamaw@ncparks.gov
Address: 1866 State Park Drive, Lake Waccamaw, N.C. 28450
GPS Coordinates: N 35°15.24, W 78°30.54

CHAPTER 24

Carolina Beach State Park and Green Swamp

The Venus Flytrap

LIZ BAIRD

SCIENTIFIC FIELDS OF STUDY: *Forest Ecology, Plant Physiology*

Imagine being a fly buzzing through the steamy pine savanna in eastern North Carolina. The longleaf pines are tall, and bright sunlight filters through the **canopy** to the grasses and shrubs below. The ground is a spongy mixture of sand and **peat**, perfect for holding water and keeping the air humid. You swoop in lazy circles until something bright catches your multilensed eye. You decide to investigate and land on a small, red, clamshell-shaped leaf with an eyelash-like fringe along the edges. Finding a tasty fluid, you step and brush against two small hairs. Suddenly this leaf snaps shut, the teeth interlocking over your body, and as you struggle, the edges of the leaf seal shut. You are doomed. You have been caught by a Venus flytrap.

The Venus flytrap (*Dionaea muscipula* J. Ellis [1768]) is a remarkable carnivorous plant, naturally found only in southeastern North Carolina, near Wilmington. At about 4 inches (10 centimeters), it is small in size but big in legend, having been described by Charles Darwin as "one of the most wonderful plants in the world." This intriguing plant still inspires the imagination, and like other **carnivorous plants**, it consumes animals, primarily insects. Venus flytraps are one of a very few carnivorous plants that actually use an active trapping method. Most of the 450 or so species of carnivorous plants found around the world use a passive trapping method, either by secreting a sticky substance and engulfing their prey in a gooey slime or by having a tube-shaped leaf filled with a special liquid to drown and dissolve their prey into a soup. The soup, containing the bodies of insects, provides the plants with nutrients. Carnivorous plants primarily still use photosynthesis for making food, like other green plants, so consuming an insect is a little like a human taking a vitamin.

Figure 24-1. The multilensed eyes of a black-head horsefly. Photo by Mike Dunn.

These plants tend to live in places with nutrient-poor soils, so they need the extra nutrients found in their prey to thrive.

While Native Americans certainly knew about Venus flytraps, Colonial governor Arthur Dobbs wrote the first known description of them in 1760. He wrote, "Upon anything touching the leaves, or falling between them, they instantly close like a spring trap, and confine any insect or anything that falls between; it bears a white flower; to this surprising plant I have given the name 'flytrap sensitive.'" In 1769, John Ellis, a member of the East India Company, was working in North Carolina and was responsible for shipping plants back to England for the company. He wrote a letter to the famous Swedish botanist Carl Linnaeus about the plant, giving it the name *Dionaea muscipula*. In Latin, *Dionaea* refers to "the daughter of Diana," or Aphrodite, who was the Greek goddess of beauty, love, and enticement. The Roman equivalent of Aphrodite is Venus, which was taken as the common name for the plant. The term *muscipula* in Latin means "mousetrap," referring to the plant's ability to catch its own food. Botanists exploring the region, like John Ellis, did collect samples of Venus flytraps to take back to Europe by boat. But after the plants spent months inside a ship's hold, it is easy to imagine that people did not understand how the brown and wilted specimens could possibly be insect-eating plants, and they likely did not inspire much enthusiasm from the public or from scientists.

To understand the amazing abilities of the Venus flytrap, you have to look at a live one. Look closely and you'll see each trap is actually a specialized leaf. The first 3 inches of the leaf look like any typical narrow green leaf, but at the end it broadens to form two halves of the clamshell-like trap. The inside is generally red, although it can be green. There are 14 to 21 soft teeth around the edge that look a bit like eyelashes, and 3 small trigger hairs on the inside.

When an insect lands on or crawls into the trap, the prey must brush against the trigger hairs twice to get the trap to close. It is a little strange to think about a plant moving at all, much less fast enough to trap an insect; however, the Venus flytrap can do it. While plants do not have a nervous system like animals do, they can carry electrochemical impulses along the cells of their leaves. When an insect bumps up against one of the trigger hairs, a burst of electricity is sent along the cells. There must be two of these electrical bursts within twenty seconds in order for the Flytrap to close. This has made some people say that the Venus flytrap is "a plant

Figure 24-2. Venus flytrap (*Dionaea muscipula*). Photo by Melissa Dowland.

that can count." Needing two touches of the trigger hairs in a short time keeps the traps from closing when they do not need to, such as when a bit of leaf blows in. The flytrap closes because of rapid expansion and contraction, possibly due to water movement into and out of the cells. While the actual mechanism of trap movement is still debated, scientists have shown that electrical impulses stimulate the rapid expansion on the outside of the leaf while causing cell shrinkage on the inside of the leaf. This turns the leaf from convex (curved out) to concave (curved in), which leads to an interlocking of the teeth.

Closing the trap on the insect is just the beginning. Obviously, the plant cannot chew, so it uses chemicals, called enzymes, to dissolve the prey, much like human saliva begins to break down food before it is chewed. Once again, the trigger hairs come into play. As the insect struggles in the trap, it touches the trigger hairs again and again. The trap then closes more tightly, forming a "Ziploc baggie" pouch that will keep all the digestive juices inside, much like our stomachs. The more the prey struggles, the more digestive juices are produced. Once the softer parts of the insect are dissolved into nutritious liquid, the same cells that made the digestive juices start absorbing the nutrients. In humans, the absorption of nutrients mainly takes place in our small intestine. So it is as if this plant has its mouth, stomach, and intestines all combined into one tiny trap!

In the 1930s, B. W. Wells, a famous North Carolina botanist, wrote, "This marvelous plant is in no danger of extinction." However, by 1960 they were beginning to disappear from the wild. Three main activities were impacting the plants. One was overcollection. Venus flytraps have short root systems and are fairly easy to dig up. The plants could be sold for study or curiosity. Some plants were collected legally, but poachers stole thousands of others. Initial laws set a fixed fine as punishment for illegal removal of the plants, but in 2014 North Carolina put new laws into place that make the illegal collection of Venus flytraps a felony, with no limits on the fine

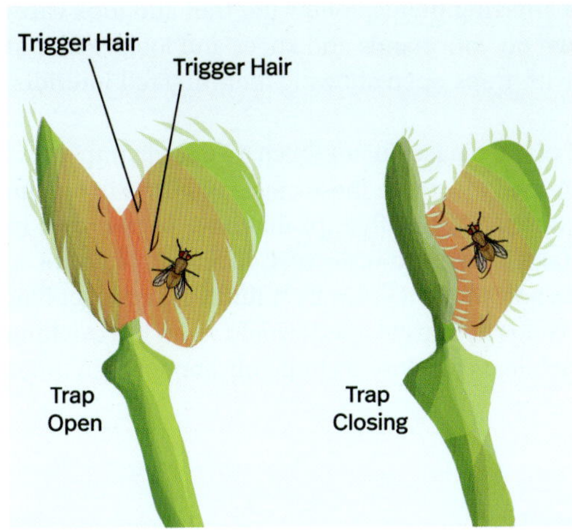

Figure 24-3. Venus flytrap mechanism for catching prey. Drawing by Ashleigh M. Smith.

and up to twenty-five months in prison. Hopefully this law will keep people from stealing plants. Additionally, cloning and growing of plants without the need to harvest them from the wild may reduce the demand for illegally harvested plants. Another cause for the loss of Venus flytraps was the national effort to suppress forest fires. The Venus flytrap needs fire to survive. An annual fire clears out underbrush, allowing bright sunlight to reach the plants on the forest floor. Regular fires might burn through quickly, searing the plant but allowing the parts of the plant below ground to survive. As discussed in Chapters 13 through 16 and 20 in this book, the importance of regular fires for the health of ecosystems cannot be overstated. Without regular fire, shrubs and trees grow up, blocking the light. When a fire does break out, the extra-thick trees and shrubs burn at a much hotter temperature and can actually burn the plant beneath the surface. A loss of habitat has also impacted Venus flytraps. Developments such as houses and shopping areas have taken out large tracts of land that were once a home to Venus flytraps.

Before You Go

There are two easily accessible places to find Venus flytraps in North Carolina. One is at Carolina Beach State Park, located south of Wilmington just off Highway 421. Walk along the 0.5-mile (0.8-kilometer) Flytrap Trail and look for these small plants alongside the boardwalk. Another place to visit is the Green Swamp Preserve on land protected by the Nature Conservancy. Located off Highway 211, about 5 miles (8 kilometers) from the intersection with Highway 17 near Supply, North Carolina, you'll find a small parking area and a trail marked with red diamond markers. This 1.5-mile (2.4-kilometer) trail takes you into an area where you are likely to find many species of carnivorous plants in addition to Venus flytraps. These include pitcher plants, sundews, butterworts, and bladderworts. For the most up-to-date information, check both the Carolina Beach State Park and the Nature Conservancy websites, listed below, before setting out. Also note that part of the Green Swamp's land is open to hunting. Check with the North Carolina Wildlife Resources Commission's Game Land Program for hunting information.

Wherever you go to see these amazing plants, follow the trail and look carefully. When you find one, get down on your hands and knees and look closely at these small bright green plants, with traps open showing their tiny red interiors, and imagine being a fly.

Note: Because it is a protected plant, please do not touch a Venus flytrap growing in the wild; however, if you are curious to see these amazing plants in action, some nurseries and hardware stores sell Venus flytraps that have been grown in greenhouses. Purchase one and take it home to observe. Collect rainwater for it, keep it in partial sun in your home, and watch it grow. By stimulating a trigger hair with a paper clip, you can see the Venus flytrap close as it would when it is catching a meal; however, be aware that each leaf can close its trap only about seven times during its lifetime.

References and Resources

Darwin, C. *Insectivorous plants*. 2nd ed. London: John Murray, 1888.

"Dionaea muscipula—The Venus Flytrap." *Botanical Society of America*, http://botany.org/Carnivorous_Plants/venus_flytrap.php. Accessed November 8, 2018.

WEBSITES:

Carolina Beach State Park (CBSP): https://www.ncparks.gov/carolina-beach-state-park

Green Swap Preserve (GSP): https://www.nature.org/en-us/get-involved/how-to-help/places-we-protect/green-swamp-preserve/

CONTACTS:

CBSP: phone: (910) 458-8206; email: carolina.beach@ncparks.gov

GSP: phone: (910) 395-5000

ADDRESSES:

CBSP: 1010 State Park Road, Carolina Beach, N.C. 28428

GSP: There is no street address for the Green Swamp Preserve, but directions are given above and on the website provided. GPS coordinates are below.

GPS COORDINATES:

CBSP: N 34°2.88, W 77°54.78

GSP: N 34°5.58, W 78°17.94

CHAPTER 25

Jockey's Ridge State Park

Moving Mountains at the Beach

JENNIFER COX

SCIENTIFIC FIELDS OF STUDY: *Coastal Geology, Coastal Ecology*

There are some days in Jockey's Ridge State Park where you can walk past one of the giant sand dunes and see a small portion of what appears to be a miniature castle poking out. When you see it, you'll have to stop and look again, because it will be entirely unexpected. This is a unique place where numerous visitors every year come to see the desertlike terrain, and yet the remnants of a Renaissance-themed miniature golf course from the late 1970s are hiding somewhere underneath all of that sand. Here you find evidence of the eternal sand movement that occurs at Jockey's Ridge. There are other treasures to find here occasionally, as evidence of the attempt of humans to cohabitate with the dunes: a pile of old oyster shells, a clay pipe, a wooden-handled wrench. The bulk of the park is open dune habitat, and when you are on the tallest dunes looking down, you can have the impression of being in a large arena. Legend has it that Jockey's Ridge got its name from the islanders racing their horses through the dunes while observers watched from the surrounding natural arena. Jockey's Ridge was designated as a state park in 1975 after the local island people petitioned for it to be preserved for all to enjoy.

The 426 acres of large, rolling sand dunes, some 90 feet (27.4 meters) high, can stir the imagination because you actually feel like you might be in another time. A short fifteen-minute walk from the parking lot gives way to expansive views from atop various peaks between sandy valleys that make you feel like you are on a different planet. These views help to provide a true perspective of how thin the Outer Banks **barrier islands** are. From the top of the large sand hills you can look out over the Atlantic Ocean toward the east or over Roanoke **Sound** to the west. Facing Roanoke Sound, you can see Roanoke Island, which is 3.0 miles (4.8 kilometers) away as the crow flies, or about 10 miles (16 kilometers) by car. Looking north on a clear night, you can sometimes see the rotating light that sits atop the Wright Brothers Monument. Looking south, you can see the patterned light of the Bodie Island Lighthouse

Figure 25-1. Fulgurites collected from Jockey's Ridge show how lightning transforms sand into hollow glassy tubes. Photo by Jennifer Cox.

blink for 2 seconds on, 2 seconds off, 2 seconds on, then, finally, 22 seconds off, over and over again. This distinct pattern informs passing boats of their location relative to this particular lighthouse.

It is not uncommon, if you look off into the distance, to see a thunderhead cloud forming. As the storm approaches, park staff will sound a siren to warn visitors of possible lightning strikes in the park. Because the dunes are the highest point in the area, they are a magnet for lightning. When lightning does touch down on the dunes, it is so hot, 27,000°F (15,000°C), that it actually melts the sand at the contact point. The sand at Jockey's Ridge is approximately 90 percent quartz, so heating that sand to this extreme temperature melts the quartz, leaving a tube of sand with a glassy sheen on the inside, called a fulgurite. Fulgurites can sometimes be found sticking out of the sand on windy days as the sand is blown around on the dunes. Fulgurites formed from the light sand of the dunes can be very fragile in comparison with the rocklike fulgurites found on the beach, where the sand would have a different **mineral** composition.

Most of the animals in the park are nocturnal, which means that they are most active at night. The combination of many visitors and an extreme environment keeps them sheltered in the vegetation during the day, emerging primarily at night to forage for food. After a good evening rain, the sand is wiped clean of the signs of human visitors, but in the morning, there are abundant signs of wildlife that trekked around the park by moonlight. On any given morning, you can find tracks left from red and gray foxes, deer, coyotes, frogs, toads, raccoons, opossums, and cotton-tailed rabbits. Occasionally the s-curving track of a snake, such as the eastern hognose (*Heterodon platirhinos*), is visible across the dunes. It is also not uncommon to see the small tracks of the six-lined racerunner (*Aspidoscelis sexlineata*) lizard's tail crisscrossing the trails. This lizard is named for the six yellow lines that run down its back and for its ability to run at almost 20 miles (32 kilometers) per hour.

You can also look for nonbiological patterns in the sand, such as sand-ripple marks (see Figure 25-4 for an example). Sand ripples typically form at a perpendicular angle to the wind direction. "Wind shadows" can also help determine wind direction. An area protected from wind, like a small rock or even a post set in the ground, provides a wind barrier where sand drops and accumulates. It is for this reason that sand fences are often put up on beaches, encouraging the deposition of sand and creating new sand dunes.

Jockey's Ridge has three primary ecosystems for you to explore:

1. Open dune area
2. Maritime shrub thicket
3. Estuarine environment.

The open dune area is comprised of soft sands due to the high percentage of quartz where the average grain size is smaller than the local beach sand, thus providing a soft feel. Most of it has been transported to the park by the wind, also known as aeolian transport. The wind's movement affects the sorting of sand grains by size and density in a process called saltation, where heavier particles are dropped more quickly and lighter particles are carried farther away, thereby creating the areas of large deposits in the park. Wind also moves the large dunes to different locations. They migrate constantly through the park, influenced by the direction of the blowing wind on any given day. During hurricanes or large storms called nor'easters, the dunes change dramatically in size and location. The largest dunes tend to move around the middle of the park, while smaller ones appear and disappear around the edges. Hiking in between large dunes gives you the feeling that you are exploring a new world. You can walk through the park without seeing another person, and every turn presents a new berm, a new dune, or a new blowout area.

Hot summer days can be especially brutal on the animals that inhabit the dunes. The sand absorbs the sun's heat, leading to temperatures approximately 30°F (~17°C) hotter than the actual air temperature. This means that a 90°F (32°C) day can easily turn into 120°F (49°C) on the dunes. Heat index and humidity can lead to even more extreme conditions. For this reason, most of the animals wait until nightfall to forage for food, and people generally choose morning and sunset hours in the summer for enjoying the park. One thing you can always count on at Jockey's Ridge is a good ocean breeze. This is one of the main reasons the Wright Brothers decided in 1903 to make their historic first flight on this part of the Outer Banks. The soft sands also provided for an easier landing. Although the brothers actually made their flight a few miles north on Big Kill Devil Hill, Jockey's Ridge is a great example of the back-barrier dune system similar to the one on which they flew. At one time the dune system ran all the way from Nags Head north along the back side of the barrier island to False Cape in Virginia, approximately 88.0 miles (141 kilometers). Much of this amazing dune system now has been replaced by development with homes and businesses, but some of it has matured into maritime forest like Nags Head Woods Preserve.

Maritime shrub thicket area is scattered throughout the park, providing shade from the hot summer sun under a beautiful **canopy** of trees like live oaks (*Quercus virginiana*), wax myrtles, bayberries, and various types of pine trees. In between these trees grow different coastal grasses and wildflowers. Live oaks are the most

Figure 25-2. Deer and other animals reside in the maritime shrub thicket but venture onto the sand dunes at night. Evidence of roaming critters is often present in the morning as tracks in the sand. Photo by Jason Brown.

easily recognizable of coastal trees. They have long limbs spreading out from the base, twisting and turning in different directions. The limbs are often covered by the shifting sands, so that they disappear under the ground, only to reemerge several feet away. The constant ocean breezes and salt spray sculpt these trees into nature's works of art. Live oak trees are evergreens, meaning that they do not lose all their leaves in the fall like deciduous trees, and are found along the Coastal Plain in North Carolina but are most plentiful south of Cape Hatteras. The leaves have a thick cuticle protecting them from harsh sun and salt spray. Many animals living in the shrub thicket under live oak trees find shelter and protection there from the hot coastal sun.

There are dark patches of sandy soil found throughout the park that you may spot as you are walking along and wonder why they are different. Because the shrub thicket is scattered throughout the park, you can easily find areas where the windblown sand dunes have started to cover a patch of trees. As you are crossing dunes, you may feel the sand give way easily, or you may notice the top of a mature tree emerging from the sand. Nearby, you will generally find a slope that indicates which way the sand is being blown. If the wind continues to blow sand in that direction, the covered trees and vegetation may not resurface for many years. After some time, they will begin to decompose within the warm sand, forming a layer of darker sandy soil underneath. It is common to find these layers all over the park, especially after a steady wind blows away the top layers of dry, loose sand grains, exposing wetter sand below.

The west side of Jockey's Ridge State Park is bordered by Roanoke Sound, a highly **productive** estuarine environment that is part of the Albemarle-Pamlico sound system. **Estuaries** form when freshwater rivers meet the salt water of the ocean, resulting in **brackish** water. Brackish water occurs when the salt content of the water varies somewhere between fresh and salt water, depending on the tidal movements. Fresh water is defined as having a salt content less than 0.5 parts per thousand (ppt), while seawater has a salt content of 35 ppt. The sounds of North Carolina, all together called the Albemarle-Pamlico sound system, form the second largest estuarine environment in the United States; the largest is the Chesapeake Bay, just to the north in Virginia. Tides on Earth are affected by both the sun and the moon, but

Figure 25-3. This hiking trail takes you along the Roanoke Sound side of Jockey's Ridge, where you can explore the estuary and marshes. Photo by Jason Brown.

because the moon is closer, it has a much greater effect on our oceans' movements, so these tides are called lunar tides. Wind is often responsible for pushing water higher or lower during the tidal phases. Wave action is minimal on the sound side of the island, and winds affect water levels here more than the lunar tides. Because the estuaries are shallow, less than 30 feet (9.0 meters) deep, sunlight reaches the bottom, allowing plants to grow. The rivers deposit nutrient-rich sediment into the estuaries as well, so the combination of these factors provides a unique habitat that is the perfect nursery for the growth and development of juvenile fish and shellfish. For more detailed information about estuaries, see the ModMon program in Chapter 29, "Pamlico Sound/Neuse River Estuary."

In both Chapter 27, "Bear Island, Hammocks Beach State Park," and Chapter 29, "Pamlico Sound/Neuse River Estuary," we discuss the importance of estuaries and coastal wetland habitats. All of this information holds true for the estuarine environment at Jockey's Ridge as well. Wet sediment harbors microalgae, bacteria, and **detritus** that form the base of the coastal food web, feeding literally hundreds of species of organisms from simple marine worms to large migrating birds, like the magnificent osprey. The osprey is one of many types of birds that find food in estuaries along coastal North Carolina when en route via the Atlantic flyway. See Chapter 22, "Mattamuskeet and Pocosin Lakes National Wildlife Refuges," for more information on the Atlantic flyway for migrating birds. Jockey's Ridge State Park is one of the stops on this flyway where birds can rest and forage for food before continuing their journey south.

Jockey's Ridge State Park is not very big in relation to other North Carolina parks, but exploring each of its habitats and unique features gives you plenty of options for activities while you are there. Kite-flying on the open sand dunes is by far the most popular activity. Bring your own or rent a kite at a nearby kite shop. Depending on how adventurous you are feeling, you can either watch or participate in hang-

Figure 25-4. Flying kites on the dunes is a favorite pastime for all ages. Photo by Jason Brown.

gliding, or parasailing, off a steep dune on windy days. The maritime shrub thicket and smaller dunes scattered throughout the park provide a fantastic opportunity to hike around looking for tracks and other evidence of the animals that were there before you. There are two marked trails that are easy to follow, but you are not restricted to the trails; you can practice your orienteering skills while exploring almost anywhere you want throughout the park. Explorations on your own could help you discover a fulgurite to take home or find a spot that looks like a scene out of a Star Wars movie. The sunsets that splash color over the entire viewing area draw a crowd almost every night to watch.

The west side of the park that is bordered by the Roanoke Sound has an access where you can easily get to the water for all sorts of activities. It is a great place to launch a kayak or harness the wind for kite-boarding or wind-surfing. You can relax and sunbathe on the small sandy beach or float in the water to cool off after a hot walk across the sand. You can even throw a fishing line into the water to catch dinner for the night. The water near this access is fairly shallow due to the sand blowing off the dunes, so you can walk out for quite a distance to fish from the water or just view the dunes from a different perspective.

Before You Go

The rangers at Jockey's Ridge State Park offer a variety of programs throughout the year that you can find listed on the website (see url below). The popular Kayak the Roanoke Sound program allows you to use its kayaks, or you can bring your own.

Figure 25-5. Ranger Barnes gives a presentation to crowds as they join to watch a beautiful sunset at Jockey's Ridge. Photo by Neal Ward.

Call the park office number below to inquire about programs and activities, available rentals, and park hours. Most programs are open to anyone who wants to attend at the designated times and places, but a few require reservations.

Please note that this park is an extreme environment because of the heat in the summer months. To enjoy the park in the most enjoyable and safest way, make sure you wear sufficient sunscreen and bring plenty of water to stay hydrated.

References and Resources

Dame, Richard, Merryl Alber, Dennis Allen, Michael Mallin, Clay Montague, Alan Lewitus, Alice Chalmers, Robert Gardner, Craig Gilman, Bjorn Kjerfve, Jay Pinckney, and Ned Smith. "Estuaries of the South Atlantic Coast of North America: Their Geographical Signatures." *Estuaries* 23, no. 6 (December 2000): 793–819.

Stewart, K. G., and M. R. Roberson. *Exploring the Geology of the Carolinas: A Field Guide to Favorite Places from Chimney Rock to Charleston*. Chapel Hill: University of North Carolina Press, 2007.

Website: https://www.ncparks.gov/jockeys-ridge-state-park/events-and-programs
Contact: phone: (252) 441-7132; email: jockeys.ridge@ncparks.gov
Address: 300 W. Carolista Drive, Nags Head, N.C. 27959
GPS Coordinates: N 35°57.9, W 75°37.98

CHAPTER 26

Fort Fisher and the North Carolina Aquarium

PEGGY SLOAN

SCIENTIFIC FIELDS OF STUDY: *Marine Science, Coastal Ecology*

Do you ever wonder, standing at the edge of the sea, what mysteries lie beneath the waves? The oceans, covering 75 percent of the planet, play a critical role on Earth. More than half of the oxygen that we breathe on Earth comes from plants growing in the oceans. The oceans also control weather, as well as provide food, commerce, and employment for millions of people. Yet despite the oceans' influence, humans know more about the surface of the moon than the ocean floor. Eighty percent of the world's oceans remains unexplored! What we do know about the oceans and marine life, we have learned from marine researchers. Many of these scientists work with universities, government agencies, and other organizations interested in understanding the oceans, and some also share their knowledge with aquariums. A visit to Fort Fisher State Recreation Area presents an excellent opportunity to see, learn about, and explore our ocean both above and below the waves.

One way to "see" beneath the ocean's surface is to visit the North Carolina Aquarium at Fort Fisher, where you can come face-to-face with sea turtles, sharks, jellyfish, and seahorses. The aquarium hosts over 4,000 animals representing 300 different species. These animals primarily live in North Carolina freshwater and saltwater habitats. Twice a day a SCUBA diver answers questions from inside the 235,000-gallon (889,572-liter) Cape Fear Shoals exhibit. The dive show and surrounding exhibits provide guests with a better understanding of and a greater curios-

Figure 26-1. Jellyfish tank inside the North Carolina Aquarium. Start your day at Fort Fisher learning about all that North Carolina's coast has to offer. Photo by Bob Griffin, courtesy of North Carolina Aquarium at Fort Fisher.

ity about the ocean, and guests can experience up-close interactions with horseshoe crabs, stingrays, and other coastal species.

The aquarium also offers guided trips for guests to the **salt marsh** or a rocky outcrop for surf fishing and canoeing to encourage exploration of the surrounding natural habitats. Fort Fisher Aquarium is uniquely situated among some of southeastern North Carolina's most interesting places to explore. The salt marsh surrounding Fort Fisher serves as a nursery for many juvenile, or young, animals, including some that spend their adult lives in the open ocean but whose mothers come to the salt marsh to give their young better protection from **predators**. When you explore this amazing ecosystem with an aquarium expert, you can net and identify samples from the marsh. Your releasable catch might include blue crabs, juvenile fish, shrimp, and other marsh creatures, like the *Uca* fiddler crabs.

Figure 26-2. Explore the mud flats and marshes at Fort Fisher. Catching crabs is fun and is a great way to learn about the organisms living in North Carolina's coastal environments. Photo by Bob Griffin, courtesy of North Carolina Aquarium at Fort Fisher.

To reach the marsh requires a twenty-minute walk through a maritime forest and behind sand dunes. These areas combined—the forest, dunes, and marsh—make up a balanced coastal ecosystem. When traveling to and from the marsh, keep an eye out for resident alligators, ibises, herons, pelicans, and native snakes. To see more elusive coastal fishes, you can try your luck at surf fishing. Learn to cast a rod into the waves in hopes of catching North Carolina's state fish, the red drum (*Sciaenops ocellatus*), or other coastal fishes. Please expect to release any fish caught during your exploration class.

The only natural rocky outcrop on a North Carolina beach protrudes from Kure Beach (pronounced Ker'-ee), 2.0 miles (3.2 kilometers) north of the aquarium. At low tide, stranded sea creatures inhabit tide pools, and **invertebrates** cling to rocks waiting for the water to return. You might discover sea stars, crabs, and even some fishes in the outcrop. You can choose to explore the outcrop on your own or with an aquarium expert who is used to negotiating the slick rock surfaces and can help you identify marine life. You might plan to take along a handy field guide to get more information on coastal marine life. If traveling on your own, check the tides before you go. If you would like to participate in a program through the aquarium, you will need to call well ahead for a reservation and a guide.

Between the outcrop and the aquarium, Fort Fisher State Recreation Area offers easy beach access and a 1.0-mile-long (1.6 kilometers) trail where you can explore the marsh. In addition to providing essential habitat for marine life, the marsh performs important ecological functions. Marsh plants and sediments help filter water from the land before it reaches the ocean. Runoff after rain events carries residue from streets and parking lots, fertilizers from fields and gardens, and other waste products to the ocean. This is often referred to as **nonpoint source pollution**.

Figure 26-3. Take a guided canoe or kayak trip to see the tides and currents in action. Photo by Bob Griffin, courtesy of North Carolina Aquarium at Fort Fisher.

Please see Chapter 19, "Eno River State Park," for more discussion on the topic. When this runoff water passes through the marsh, much of the pollution is filtered out, sending cleaner water on to the ocean. For this reason, marshes and other wetland areas have been called "nature's kidneys" because they help filter out impurities. In coastal North Carolina, salt marshes also offer great protection from the threat of general storms and hurricanes. A combination of too much rain and a rise in sea level due to storm activities can cause serious flooding, often putting many coastal homes and businesses in danger. When a marsh system is healthy, one of its critical jobs is to absorb much of that excess water. Marshes act like sponges, capturing as much extra water as possible when there is too much and storing it to release later.

Exploring the beach on a trip to the coast is a must. Aside from offering an exceptional natural playground in the sand and surf, beaches are essential habitat for some important coastal wildlife. Shorebirds such as plovers, oystercatchers, and black skimmers nest on North Carolina beaches from April through June. From May through October, sea turtles nest on North Carolina beaches. Five species of sea turtles, all threatened with extinction, spend time in North Carolina waters. The loggerhead sea turtle (*Caretta caretta*) is most abundant on our shores, and occasionally green sea turtles (*Chelonia mydas*) or rare leatherback sea turtles (*Dermochelys coriacea*) might choose a North Carolina beach on which to nest. It is hard to predict when you may see a turtle nesting or hatching—it is always at night. However, nests are protected and marked by state scientists, and you might see one of the fenced-off areas indicating a sea turtle nest. You can read more about shorebirds and sea turtles and **barrier island** ecology in Chapter 27, "Bear Island, Hammocks Beach State Park."

Not far from the aquarium and recreation area, the Fort Fisher State Historic Site provides an opportunity to visit one of the most significant sites of the Civil War. In 1865, when Fort Fisher was defeated, the Confederate supply line was closed, essentially sealing the defeat of the Confederacy. You can tour the fort starting at the visitor center. The museum includes a beautiful trail through ancient oak trees and along the Cape Fear River. You also can explore the North Carolina Underwater Archaeology headquarters in Kure Beach, where you can learn about how archaeology researchers have searched the ocean bottom and in North Carolina rivers to better understand our history. You can even learn about the efforts to recover the Queen Anne's Revenge, the ship sailed by Blackbeard the pirate in the early 1700s.

Before You Go

For a comprehensive look at North Carolina's coastal environments, from the river to the sea, it is hard to beat a trip to Fort Fisher. The aquarium, state recreation area, and Fort Fisher State Historic Site reside within a peninsula of protected habitat. Beautiful scenery and wildlife encounters are guaranteed on a visit to the area, and because of the healthy surrounding habitat, many visitors enjoy bonus views of native wildlife such as deer, fox, osprey, pelicans, and more.

Admission to the North Carolina Aquarium at Fort Fisher is free for all preregistered public school groups. Costs for general admission tickets can be found online at the url below. Find out about field trip options and chaperone costs here: http://www.ncaquariums.com/fort-fisher-field-trips.

Admission to the Fort Fisher State Recreation Area and Civil War Museum is also free. See the urls below.

References and Resources

"Carolina Beach to Fort Fisher," https://sites.google.com/site/carolinabeachtofortfisher/home/fort-fisher. Accessed November 9, 2018.

"Fort Fisher State Recreation Area." North Carolina State Parks, https://www.ncparks.gov/fort-fisher-state-recreation-area. Accessed November 9, 2018.

"Ft. Fisher—Civil War National Historic Landmark." North Carolina Historic Sites, http://www.nchistoricsites.org/fisher/. Accessed November 9, 2018.

"Underwater Archaeology Branch." North Carolina Office of State Archaeology, https://archaeology.ncdcr.gov/underwater-archaeology-branch. Accessed November 9, 2018.

Website: http://www.ncaquariums.com/fort-fisher
Contact: phone: (910) 772-0500
Address: 900 Loggerhead Road, Kure Beach, N.C. 28449
GPS Coordinates: N 33°57.72, W 77°55.56

CHAPTER 27

Bear Island, Hammocks Beach State Park

Barrier Island Ecology

SAM BLAND

SCIENTIFIC FIELDS OF STUDY: *Coastal Ecology, Marine Science, Barrier Island Dynamics*

As the warm, sticky breezes of a soft summer night drift over the island sand dunes, the katydids hum their mesmerizing sound to attract a mate. Below the dune, at the edge of the Atlantic Ocean, a giant female loggerhead sea turtle (*Caretta caretta*) swims out of the ocean and then drags her heavy body onto the white sandy beach of Bear Island at Hammocks Beach State Park. Here, during the late spring and summer months, these ancient reptiles will dig a pit with their rear flippers where the female will deposit 100 to 120 ping-pong-ball-sized eggs. She will then cover the nest and return to the ocean not knowing what will become of her eggs. Under the heat of the summer sun, the eggs will incubate for about sixty days as the hatchlings develop in their warm underground nest. The miniature sea turtles, about the size of the face of a large watch, will bust out of the soft egg casings and dig their way out of the cramped sandy nest. Under the cover of darkness, the whole group will scurry across the beach and escape into the ocean, leaving only wispy tracks in the sand.

Bear Island, located near Swansboro, North Carolina, has hosted the magnificent nesting ritual of sea turtles for thousands of years. This alluring island provides a great example of an undisturbed natural **barrier island**. Barrier islands have been referred to as "ribbons of sand" that run parallel to and just offshore of the mainland, with a water body, called a **sound**, separating the two. These long, thin islands are comprised of large amounts of loose sand that is constantly being moved about by waves and wind.

Figure 27-1. Loggerhead sea turtle hatchling up close. Photo by Sam Bland.

Figure 27-2 Loggerhead sea turtle hatchlings moving toward the sea. Photo by Sam Bland.

The formation of barrier islands is not completely understood; however, one theory is that these islands were formed many thousands of years ago when sea levels began to rise due to the melting of glaciers. Eroded and weathered rock from the Appalachian and Piedmont Provinces were carried to the ocean by river systems, forming extensive sand dune ridges at the edge of the mainland. As sea level rose, the ancient dune ridges were breached, or broken, by ocean water during storms. The storm waters cut into the dune ridges, creating inlets that allowed water to flow behind the dune ridge, creating an island. These barrier islands protect the mainland by soaking up wave energy from the ocean during hurricanes and strong winds. More importantly, they provide several distinct ecological habitats

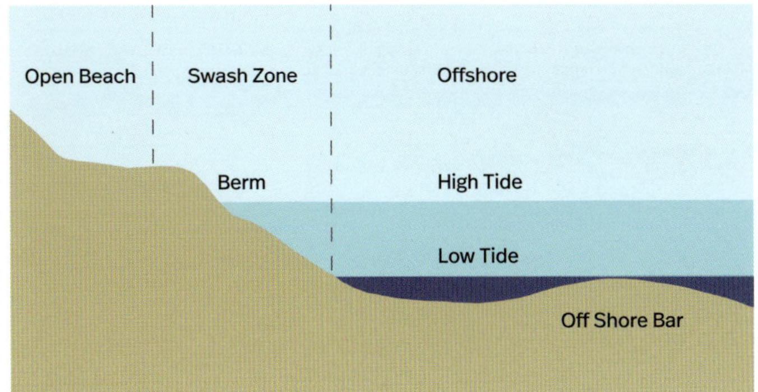

Figure 27-3. Diagram showing the typical structure of a beach. Drawing by Ashleigh M. Smith.

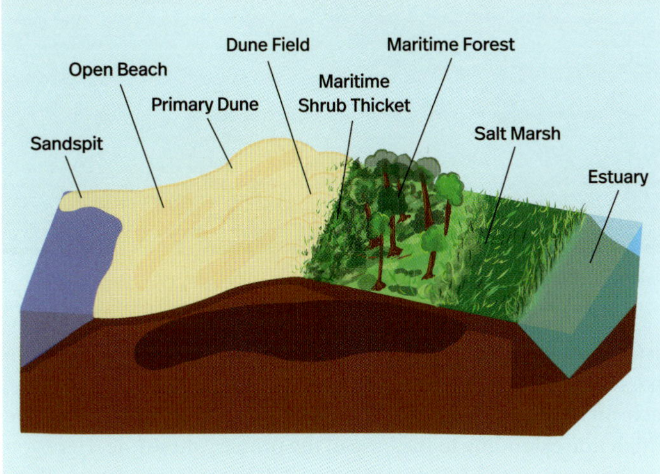

Figure 27-4. Diagram showing the typical structure of a barrier island with mature maritime forest. Drawing by Ashleigh M. Smith.

that support a wide diversity of wildlife and plants. Now let's learn about each of Bear Island's habitats—the swash zone, open beach, sandspits, primary dune, dune fields, maritime shrub thickets, maritime forest, **salt marsh**, and estuary—so you can start exploring on your own.

The swash zone is an area of high energy where the constantly crashing waves spill onto the shore, allowing only the hardiest of creatures to survive and thrive. Tiny 1.0-inch (2.5-centimeter) clams, called coquina clams (*Donax variabilis*), can be seen digging into the wet sand as waves retreat back into to the sea. These multicolored **mollusks** will feed on algae and **detritus**. They will, in turn, be fed on by crabs, fish, and birds. They also provide a tasty treat for humans and are used in various stews and chowders. Another **invertebrate** creature that shares the turbulence of the swash zone is the Atlantic mole crab (*Emerita talpoida*). Anyone who has waded through the surf zone has seen these fat, torpedo-shaped crustaceans darting about as a thin layer of water spills onto the beach, then they quickly burrow into the sand as the wave retreats. These crabs are 1.0–2.0 inches (2.5–5.0 centimeters) long and are fully adapted for their habitat. Their smooth shell is tapered at both ends to allow for easy digging into the wet sand. Once buried just barely below the surface, they will wait for a wave to wash over them. Then they will extend two feathery antennae to

Figure 27-5. Bear Island's shoreline. Photo by Sam Bland.

extract **plankton** (tiny plants and animals) from the water for food. They only move backward to make sure that their antennae are at the surface of the sand.

The open beach, including the flat, raised berm, is the area of dry sand just above the reach of the high tide extending to the base of the primary dune line. Here you can find the open burrows of the Atlantic ghost crab (*Ocypode quadrata*). Even though they can be spotted during the day, ghost crabs are most active during the night. Due to their pale coloring that provides great camouflage and their ability to run 10 miles per hour, they often disappear like ghosts into the night. They will forage about looking for just about anything to eat, including insects and dead fish. Their eyes are on long stalks allowing them to see 360 degrees as they peer like periscopes out of their burrows. Ghost crabs are notorious for targeting sea turtle hatchlings as they race to the sea in the moonlight. The open beach is also of great importance to a multitude of shorebirds. Sanderlings, willets, ruddy turnstones, red knots, and various plovers can be seen darting into the surf zone to snatch a mole crab or coquina clam as waves recede back into the ocean.

At the ends of Bear Island, wide-open sandspits form along the inlets. Here, many species of shorebirds find safety and will rest and roost for the evening with a clear open view to detect any potential **predators**. These open sand fields are also attractive to a variety of colonial nesting shorebirds. Several species of terns and plovers as well as black skimmers will nest in large groups, called colonies. On Bear Island, least terns (*Sternula antillarum*) are the most abundant colonial nesters, with a few common and royal terns, as well as black skimmers. The large massing of nesting birds in one site provides safety in numbers. With more birds available to conduct surveillance and keep a watchful eye out for danger, there is

Figure 27-6. Piping plover adult with chick. Photo by Sam Bland.

Figure 27-7. Piping plover chick blends into the beach shells. Photo by Sam Bland.

a better chance for survival. When a threat, such as a fox or raccoon, is detected, a large angry flock of the nesters will descend upon the intruder, driving it away with a behavior called mobbing. Humans foolish enough to venture too close to a nesting colony will be rewarded with sharp beaks aiming for their scalps. Other shorebirds such as oystercatchers, willets, piping plovers, and Wilson's plovers also will nest in close proximity to the site to take advantage of the colony protection. Birds nesting in a colony also benefit by watching and following one another to the closest available food hot spot. Abundant food nearby is crucial for adults with newborn chicks, allowing them to conserve energy for more important tasks, such as ensuring the survival of the chicks.

The primary dune system is not only crucial to prevent oceanwater overwash during most storms, but it is also where the first line of vegetation begins to grow. In early July each year, the lumpy dune line of Bear Island is transformed into a fuzzy haze of gold as the seed heads of sea oats (*Uniola paniculate*) sway in the muggy summer breeze. Sea oats along with American sea rocket (*Cakile edentula*) and sea elder (*Iva imbricata*) are the first plants to sink down roots that help stabilize the loose sand, thereby preventing the sand from blowing away with strong winds. Seabeach amaranth (*Amaranthus pumilus*) is **endemic** to the Atlantic coast and was once scattered broadly along the coastline. It is now a threatened species, but it can be seen growing on Bear Island along the base of the primary dune.

Just behind the primary dune line, many species of plants populate the interior dune fields. Like all plants on the barrier islands, their adaptations help them survive the harsh, limiting factors in a desertlike environment. Limiting factors generally refer to environmental conditions that limit growth, abundance, or distribution. These include factors such as (1) frequent high winds that can blow smothering sand and loosen root systems, (2) hot ground temperatures, (3) salt spray, and (4) nutrient-poor soil. Adaptations to these limiting factors may include (1) waxy leaves to block out damaging salt spray, (2) roots and stems designed for storing moisture, (3) extensive root systems that spread out to firmly anchor plants to the ground, (4) and wispy stalks that bend, but do not break, in strong winds. Two of these soil-anchoring plants are also important to butterflies. Each spring a small, rare butterfly called the crystal skipper (*Atrytonopsis quinteri*), found only on Bear Island and the adjacent Bogue Banks, lays its eggs on the leaves of a plant called little bluestem (*Schizachyrium scoparium*). The crystal skipper larvae feed on this host plant (a critical plant for survival), so the butterfly can grow and continue its fragile existence. Each October, the spectacular migration of the monarch butterfly (*Danaus plexippus*) can be witnessed along the coastal barrier islands as well. Flowering plants, such as seaside goldenrod (*Solidago sempervirens*), provide vital energy-boosting nectar that sustains these insects on their long, arduous journey to central Mexico.

Deeper into the island, maritime shrub thickets take hold, forming islands of shrubs among the dune grasses. Plants such as wax myrtle (*Morella cerifera*) and yaupon holly (*Ilex vomitoria*) dominate in dense evergreen chambers. Although these plants are growing farther from the ocean, wind-blown salt causes stunted and pruned growth. Among the tangle of thickets, a number of migratory songbirds seek refuge. In the winter, flocks of yellow-rumped warblers (*Setophaga coronata*) flutter about the wax myrtles, stripping them of their waxy berries. There is little competition for these berries because few other animals are able to digest the waxy coating. In late spring and summer, the arrival of the painted bunting (*Passerina ciris*) decorates the thickets with a splash of rainbow color. Painted buntings are members of the cardinal family that migrate north from Cuba, the Caribbean islands, and southern Florida to nest among the thickets until mid-September. Avid bird-watchers flock to Bear Island for a chance to see the colorful male painted bunting.

Near the back of the island on ancient well-stabilized dunes, shrubs and trees form what is known as the maritime forest. Magnificent live oak, loblolly pine, holly, bay, red cedar, swamp magnolia, and red maple trees create a forest rarely experienced by humans today. Most maritime forests have been lost to coastal development; these habitats are now rare on the North Carolina coast, with the remaining examples primarily protected in state and national parks. A great diversity of plants

Figure 27-8. The dune field, just behind the primary dune line. Photo by Sam Bland.

and animals is found within the maritime forest. Reptiles such glass lizards, rough green snakes, corn snakes, green rat snakes, and the Carolina anole move about the forest floor to find shelter and an abundance of food. In the lowest areas of the forest, rainwater will create freshwater **wetlands** that attract amphibians such as toads and treefrogs. Mammals such as the white-tailed deer, gray fox, marsh rabbit, and raccoon will stop by to quench their thirst at these water holes. For all of these animals, the maritime forest **canopy** provides protection from the sun, wind, and rain.

On the north side of Bear Island lies a vast body of estuarine waters. Here in the estuary, the salty ocean waters swirl and mix with fresh water flowing from mainland streams, creeks, and rivers. A vast patchwork of emerald green vegetation called saltmarsh cordgrass (*Spartina alterniflora*) creates a maze of tidal channels and creeks that lead to open water. Each year these plants will drop older dead leaves into the water, where they decay, creating bits of detritus. This material forms the base for a highly complex food web consisting of numerous estuarine species, thereby creating one of the most productive environments on the planet. The estuary is home for marsh grasses, oyster reefs, and eelgrass beds that provide habitat for hundreds of juvenile species, earning it the nickname "nursery of the sea." Our most important recreational and commercial species, such as crabs, clams, shrimp, oysters, scallops, and numerous fish species, begin and live their lives in the estuary. The abundance of these species in the salt marsh attracts shorebirds, wading birds, and prey birds that will feed on the diverse species. Shorebirds such as dunlins (*Calidris alpine*) and short-billed dowitchers (*Limnodromus griseus*) probe the sand flats exposed at low tide for marine worms, while American oystercatchers (*Haematopus palliates*) jab their long orange bills, prying open unfortunate oysters. Silent sentinels of the marsh, great blue herons (*Ardea herodias*) and great egrets (*Ardea alba*), patiently stalk unsuspecting fish or crabs, snatching them in their sturdy, strong bills. The osprey (*Pandion haliaetus*), on the other hand, plunges from the air, feet first, grasping a fish in its powerful talons. Depending on the time of year, thousands of birds of various species depend on the salt marsh for food, shelter, and nesting. Saltmarsh plants, such as the cordgrass and black needlerush (*Juncus roemericanus*), grow along the shorelines of barrier islands, serving as important filters that trap pollutants and sediments flowing from the land during rainstorms. These marsh plants cushion the blow of storm surges, which are rising waters associated with storms. Their root systems also help to stabilize the fragile shoreline.

Shaped by the wind and waves, barrier islands are mobile and dynamic, always on the move and constantly changing, if ever so slightly. Their habitat zones create a complex ecosystem that demonstrates the magic and power of nature that educates, entertains, and inspires.

Before You Go

Before heading out to Bear Island, it is advisable to check the website for updates regarding the ferry service and bathhouse schedule. Indoor showers, occasional lifeguards on duty, and a concession stand are open for campers during the summer months.

References and Resources

Cornell Lab of Ornithology. *All about Birds: Bird Guide*, https://www.allaboutbirds.org/guide/search/. Accessed November 9, 2018.

Frankenberg, Dirk. *The Nature of North Carolina's Southern Coast: Barrier Islands, Coastal Waters, and Wetlands*. 2nd ed. Chapel Hill: University of North Carolina Press, 2012.

Painted Bunting Observer Team, https://www.paintedbuntings.org. Accessed November 10, 2018.

Wells, John T., and Charles H. Peterson. *Restless Ribbons of Sand: Atlantic and Gulf Coastal Barriers*. Baton Rouge: Louisiana State University, Louisiana Sea Grant Program, 1986.

Website: https://www.ncparks.gov/hammocks-beach-state-park/park-news/bear-island-current-information

Contact: phone: (919) 326-4881; email: hammocks.beach@ncparks.gov

Address: 1573 Hammocks Beach Road, Swansboro, N.C. 28584; then take ferry to Bear Island.

GPS Coordinates: N 34°38.4, W 77°8.52

CHAPTER 28

The Lower Roanoke River

Exploring the Secrets of Bottomland Swamps

MELISSA DOWLAND

SCIENTIFIC FIELDS OF STUDY: *Wetlands Ecology, Ornithology, Herpetology, Fish Hatchery Management*

The swamps of eastern North Carolina have a lot of history. They have been the scenes of Revolutionary and Civil War battles, as well as hideouts for escaped slaves. For some people, the term "swamp" might evoke images of creepy darkness, strange animals, and whining mosquitoes. European settlers called them "dismals" because attempts to travel west from the coast through swamp habitats often seemed dangerous or physically impossible. In contrast, many early inhabitants of eastern North Carolina, such as Native Americans and African Americans, relied on swamps to provide food, water, and shelter. Today, many of these important ecosystems have been compromised by drainage, clearing, and farming. Swamps are often poorly understood by those who have never visited, but if you spend a little time paddling a canoe or kayak along the Roanoke River in eastern North Carolina, one of the east coast's largest remaining swamps, you just might find that a swamp is much more than you expected.

The Roanoke River is one of the largest rivers in North Carolina, flowing from the Blue Ridge Mountains in North Carolina and Virginia all the way to the Albemarle **Sound** at the coast. In some places in the flatlands of eastern North Carolina, the river's **floodplain** is more than 5 miles (8 kilometers) wide. It is because of the river's potential for catastrophic flooding that it was once known as the "river of death" to Native Americans and early settlers. Even up to the mid-1900s, flooding remained a huge problem for landowners. In 1940, 10–15 inches (25–38 centimeters) of rain fell in two days and inundated towns, homes, and farmland in eastern North Carolina. The river rose 42 feet (~13 meters)—that's about the height of a four-story building. The flood spurred the Army Corps of Engineers to construct a dam on the Roanoke River that was completed in 1953, creating Kerr Lake. The lower Roanoke **River Basin** is not quite the "river of death" that it once was, but it is still a wild place, and much of it has been preserved to provide habitat for a variety of interesting species.

Figure 28-1. The beautiful Roanoke River in eastern North Carolina. Photo by Melissa Dowland.

Figure 28-2. A barred owl is a swamp resident that lives here. Photo by Melissa Dowland.

Wildlife

The Roanoke River is a great place to study the amazing diversity of birds that call North Carolina home. Two species of interest here are barred owls (*Strix varia*) that are year-round swamp residents and prothonotary warblers (*Protonotaria citria*), migrants that spend winters in tropical climates.

Most owls are nocturnal and can be difficult to find, but barred owls can often be seen and heard as they hunt and call during the day. The term "barred" refers to their striped feather pattern that helps them blend into their surroundings. Their call is very distinctive and follows the rhythm of the phrase "Who cooks for you, who cooks for you all." Try to mimic their call with your voice, and if you are very good, one might come to check you out. Spotting a barred owl in the swamp is challenging, but the best place to look is between 15 and 40 feet off the ground, where they often perch on tree limbs while searching for a meal. A favorite meal for barred owls is crayfish, but they also enjoy frogs, toads, and snakes, as well as small mammals. Sometimes, especially at night, pairs of owls can get quite rowdy. When they do, most people think they sound more like a troop of monkeys than a pair of birds.

Prothonotary warblers typically arrive from their Central and South American wintering grounds in mid-April to begin setting up nesting territories. Warblers are a group of small songbirds, many of which have bright yellow in their plumage, or feathers. Often called "swamp canaries," both male and female prothonotaries

Figure 28-3. Prothonotory warbler male sitting in a tree cavity. Photo by Melissa Dowland.

have bright golden yellow on their heads (males are brighter), necks, and bellies, with olive to gray coloration on their backs and wings. They are one of only a few warblers that nest in tree cavities. Males spend time defending their territory by singing a loud "sweet, sweet, sweet, sweet, sweet, sweet" from low perches and chasing one another around. Insects are a favorite food of prothonotaries, and you may even have the opportunity to watch one snacking on a newly emerged dragonfly. Dragonflies spend their younger years as aquatic nymphs, which are juveniles, living in the water. When they are ready to transform into an adult dragonfly in the process called metamorphosis, they crawl up on the bases of trees and grasses, split open along their back, and emerge from their nymph **exoskeleton**. Their wings are damp when they first emerge, so they wait for them to dry and harden before they can fly. During this time, they are vulnerable to hungry prothonotary warblers that snag them in their beaks and beat them around to knock off their still-damp wings before gulping them down. Sometimes a prothonotary will carry a dragonfly snack back to a tree cavity, most likely to feed a female warbler sitting on eggs or a group of 3 to 7 hungry babies.

Other creatures that you are likely to encounter in warmer months along the Roanoke River are reptiles. Because they are exothermic, or cold-blooded, meaning they do not possess a cooling or heating system like mammals, they need to sit in the sun on logs and in bushes along the river to warm their bodies. The most common species of snakes are the brown watersnake (*Nerodia taxispilota*), the red-bellied watersnake (*Nerodia erythrogaster*), and the banded watersnake (*Nerodia fasciata*). There are also venomous cottonmouth snakes (*Agkistrodon piscivorus*) in the area, so it is best to observe them with binoculars from a safe distance. When swimming, cottonmouths tend to ride high in the water, exposing much of their bodies above the surface. Other water snakes swim with more of their bodies below the water line. One of the most common turtle species you will see is the well-named yellow-bellied slider (*Trachemys scripta scripta*). As you paddle up to them, they slide right off their log into the water. Painted turtles (*Chrysemys picta*) are also common and are more likely to let you get a closer look. Turtles have specialized scales called "scutes" on their shells; a painted turtle has cream-colored lines between its scutes and red markings along the edge of its shell.

Anadromous Fish

The Roanoke River is home to several species of anadromous fish. "Anadromous" means that they spend most of their lives in salt water but swim up into freshwater rivers to spawn, or lay eggs. In the 1800s, millions of herring, shad, and striped bass migrated from as far away as the Bay of Fundy in Canada and swam up the Roanoke River to spawn in the fast-flowing upstream waters. Unfortunately, a combination of factors has led to the decline of anadromous fishes in the Roanoke and other eastern rivers: overfishing in the rivers and sounds, water pollution, and the construction of dams that prevent fish from reaching some of their upstream spawning grounds.

Dams also changed the rate of water flowing through the river. Before the dams were constructed, the river would flow high and fast after storms, particularly in the early spring when anadromous fish arrived for spawning. As the river flooded its banks, nutrient-rich soils were deposited on the floodplain. During dryer periods the river would recede, allowing vegetation to grow in the fertile soils left behind. While the construction of dams benefited humans by limiting flooding and providing hydroelectric power, it negatively impacted habitat for some plants and animals by changing normal flow patterns and preventing rivers from naturally replenishing the land. Fortunately, scientists and resource managers are working with dam officials to release more water in the spring when fish are spawning, to more closely mimic natural conditions. Look for water marks or rings of debris on tree trunks and low-hanging branches, as well as bunches of twigs and leaves stuck in low tree branches, as evidence of higher water levels and changes in water levels over time.

Biologists and resource managers have also created programs to help fish like American shad (*Alosa sapidissima*) more directly. In the spring, fisheries biologists transfer broodstock from the Roanoke River to the National Fish Hatchery in Edenton, North Carolina. Broodstock are adult fish that are ready to breed. The hatchery is well worth a visit to learn more about North Carolina's fish. At the hatchery, the fish are placed in large tanks. At night, with the right water temperatures, the female fish disperse their eggs into the water, while the male fish broadcast milt, or sperm, to fertilize the eggs. The fertilized eggs are collected and transferred to egg-hatching jars, where the eggs are bubbled with air hoses for oxygen—an environment similar to what they would encounter at the bottom of a river. When they hatch, the tiny juvenile fish, also called fry, are cared for until they are 0.4–0.8 inches (1.0–2.0 centimeters) in length. Then the biologists load them into a tank on a truck and take them to the Roanoke River near Weldon, North Carolina, for release. From there, the fry begin their harrowing journey to the sea, eating tiny **plankton** along the way and trying to avoid predation by larger fish. American shad will make their way as far north as the Bay of Fundy in Canada before returning to the Roanoke River after about five years to lay eggs of their own. If you want to see some of these fish for yourself, get a fishing license and take a fishing rod with you on your paddle, or ask local fishermen. They are usually happy to show interested spectators what they are catching.

Bottomland Hardwood Forest

The incredible diversity of wildlife along the Roanoke River is mostly due to the extensive bottomland forest habitat. Smaller creeks along the river are some of the best places to see the two dominant tree species in these swamps: water tupelo (*Nyssa aquatica*) and bald cypress (*Taxodium distichum*).

As mentioned in Chapter 21, "Merchant's Millpond," water tupelos have swollen bases and large leaves and produce a 1.0-inch (2.5-centimeter) purple fruit called a drupe. But many water tupelos also have strange shapes and swellings due to the growth of mistletoe. Mistletoe is the common name for a number of different semiparasitic plants in the order Santalales. A parasite is an organism that lives off of another organism, known as the host; the parasite benefits while the host is harmed. Mistletoe is considered semiparasitic because it does provide some food for itself through photosynthesis, like other plants; but it also requires help from its host tree, which is harmed over time. Mistletoe tends to rob its host tree of both water and nutrients. Because it is evergreen, mistletoe is easiest to see in the winter when the trees have lost their leaves. Mistletoe produces white berries that appear to be a crucial food source for birds. Mistletoe also depends on birds to spread its seeds: the sticky pulp of the berries allows them to hang on to the beaks and feathers of birds and can even remain intact after passing through a bird's digestive tract, which transfers the seeds to new sites for germination, when the seeds sprout.

There are fewer bald cypress trees along the lower Roanoke than there once were. Many of them have been logged for their high-quality, pest-resistant wood, but there are still some large cypress trees standing along creeks. You know you are in an area with bald cypress trees when you look out and see knobby wooden "knees" rising from the water. Bald cypress trees are also a common host for bagworms (*Thyridopteryx ephemeraeformis*), which are moth caterpillars that form a bag out of needles and twigs to provide shelter for both the caterpillar and pupa stages. Their bags are oblong and often attached to twigs with silk. For more information about bald cypress trees, refer again to Chapter 21, "Merchant's Millpond."

Many cypress and other trees along the river are hung with gray, stringy Spanish moss (*Tillandsia usneoides*). Spanish moss is an epiphyte, which means that it grows harmlessly on another plant or surface above the ground. Surprisingly, Spanish moss is more closely related to pineapples than to moss. Although Spanish moss is usually gray-colored, if you get it wet, the scales along the tendrils will pull away to reveal the green photosynthetic tissue underneath. Spanish moss has been used by humans for woven skirts, braided rope, floral arrangements, and even bed-stuffing;

Figure 28-4. A nesting northern parula. Photo by Melissa Dowland.

however, it is also quite useful to wildlife. Many birds, like the prothonotary warbler, will use it in their nests. In fact, one tiny warbler, the northern parula (*Setophaga americana*), makes its nest in clumps of Spanish moss. Keep your eyes open on a springtime paddle. If you see a small bird with a buzzy call and a yellow breast fly into a thick clump of Spanish moss, it is likely a nesting northern parula.

Before You Go

Note that for the Roanoke River this section is much more detailed than in other chapters because planning this adventure will require more resources. Please plan carefully and use the contacts listed for any questions you may have.

Visiting the Roanoke River

The best way to see the bottomland swamps along the Roanoke River is by canoe or kayak. And if you are looking for a little adventure, you can spend the night on a camping platform managed by Roanoke River Partners. Below are a few suggestions for paddle trips.

Figure 28-5. A camping platform for paddlers along the river. Platforms are managed by Roanoke River Partners. Photo by Melissa Dowland.

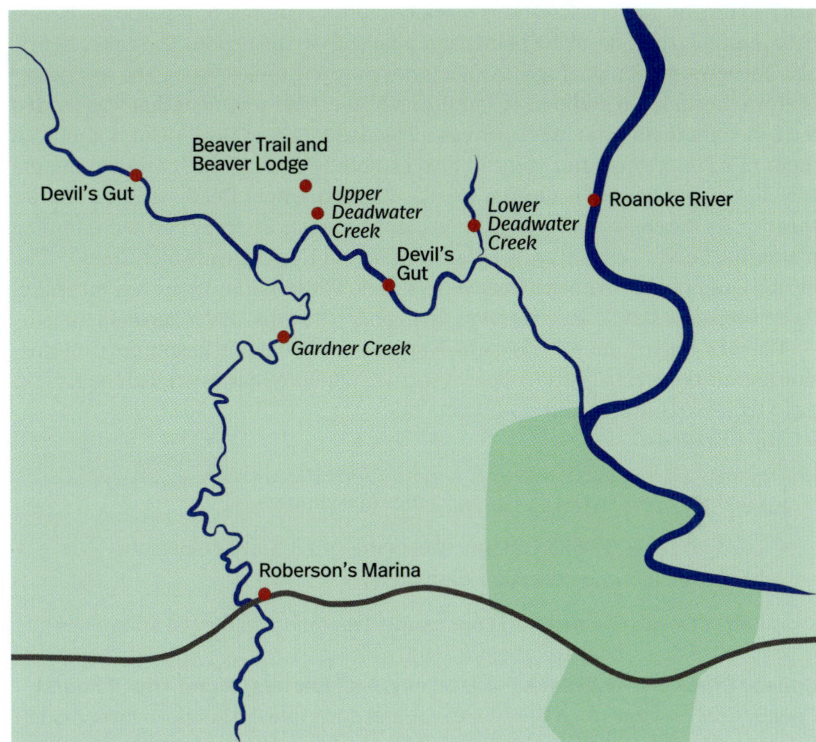

Map 6. Mapped locations along the Roanoke River for your explorations.
Map by Ashleigh M. Smith.

Resources for Planning Your Trip

Roanoke River Partners, www.roanokeriverpartners.org, can provide paddling information, maps of the river, reservations for camping platforms, and urls to additional resources.

Use Map 6 to get a visual for your trips. Take a look on Google Maps for more details.

Gardner Creek to Jamesville (~9.0 miles [14.5 kilometers]; 4.5 hours)

Paddle out-and-back along Gardner Creek, or all the way through to Jamesville with a shuttle back to your starting point. The put-in is the Gardner Creek Access at 24245 US-64 W near Jamesville. There are no facilities available, but you can park your car while you paddle. Because it is adjacent to a private residence, please be courteous, and check with Roanoke River Partners, www.roanokeriverpartners.org or (252) 792-3790, before you go to make sure it is still open to access.

The beginning of the paddle is about 4.0 miles (6.4 kilometers) along beautiful blackwater Gardner Creek. If that's enough for you, you can turn around and head back the way you came—the flow in the creek isn't very strong, and it's easy to paddle upstream. If you want to continue on from Gardner Creek, turn right (downstream) at mile 3.7 (kilometer 5.6) when you reach Devil's Gut, a channel that cuts off a large meander of the Roanoke River. You will notice a change in the color of the water from black to brown. The creek water is black because of tannins, or organic acids, that have leached out of decaying plants and **peat** soils in the region. The water here is also not very turbid, meaning the water is not churning up sediment. The river water is brown because, in addition to tannins, it also carries sediment that was eroded from the mountains and hills upstream. The paddle along Devil's Gut is about 3.0 miles (4.8 kilometers), but you can also explore two additional creeks along the way: Upper and Lower Deadwater Creeks. The first, Upper Deadwater, is a shorter side trip. As the creeks narrow upstream, look for Roanoke River Partners camping platforms: Beaver Tail and Lodge platforms are on Upper Deadwater Creek, while Barred Owl Roost is on Lower Deadwater Creek. These platforms are a great option for an overnight stay. You can reserve them on the Roanoke River Partners website.

The take-out in Jamesville is at the North Carolina Wildlife Resources Commission Astoria boat ramp (http://ncpaws.org/wrcmapbook/baa.aspx). This boat ramp has a large parking area and a pit toilet.

Trip distances:

- Gardner Creek to Devil's Gut: 3.7 miles (5.8 kilometers)
- Gardner Creek/Devil's Gut juncture to the end of Devil's Gut at the Roanoke River: 3.0 miles (4.8 kilometers)
- End of Devil's Gut to Astoria boat ramp: less than 1.0 mile (1.6 kilometers)

Conaby Creek Out-and-Back (~8.0 miles [13 kilometers] round-trip; 4 hours)

Conaby Creek is larger than Gardner Creek and flows into the Roanoke River near its mouth at the Albemarle Sound. The put-in and take-out for this paddle are the North Carolina Wildlife Resources Commission Conaby Creek boat ramp (http://ncpaws.org/wrcmapbook/baa.aspx). You can paddle a short distance and turn around or go all the way to the Royal Fern platform (about 4.0 miles [6.4 kilometers]). Conaby Creek starts fairly narrow but widens downstream. Royal Fern platform is about 1.0 mile (1.6 kilometers) up a small creek that leaves from the right side of Conaby Creek after about 3.0 miles (4.8 kilometers). Royal Fern is a great place for an overnight camping trip. You can reserve it on Roanoke River Partners website as well.

Outfitters and Guides

If you do not have your own boat, these outfitters can provide everything you need to help you plan your trip:

- Roanoke Outdoor Adventures, www.roanokeoutdooradventures.com: Heber Coltrain was born and raised in the area and knows it very well. He provides canoe and kayak rentals, guide services, and shuttles.
- Frog Hollow Outdoors, www.froghollowoutdoors.com: Based in Durham, Frog Hollow offers guided camping trips to the platforms along the Roanoke River.

When to Go

The best time of year to visit the swamps along the lower Roanoke River is between late fall (after mid-October) and early spring (before mid-May). Spring is best for migrating songbirds like the prothonotary warbler. Mosquitoes tend to be more numerous in the late spring and summer months.

What to Bring

For a day paddle, you should have

- Food and plenty of drinking water
- Sturdy sandals or water shoes, quick-dry clothing, hat
- Sunscreen and insect repellent
- Binoculars and camera in a dry bag or Ziploc
- Personal floatation device (provided if you rent a boat).

For an overnight trip, you'll also need

- Tent with a rainfly
- Sleeping bag and pad
- Portable toilet (some outfitters will provide this; there are no facilities on the camping platforms)
- Flashlight or headlamp
- Camp stove, if you plan to cook (you cannot have a campfire on the platforms)
- Lots of drinking water
- Pots, dishes, biodegradable soap if you plan to do dishes
- Long sleeves and long pants for cool nights and insect protection.

Land-Based Options

If you're not a paddler, there are a few locations where you can take a short walk to explore the bottomland swamp habitat:

- The town of Windsor, North Carolina (http://www.windsorbertiechamber.com/16.html), has a wetland boardwalk trail through a bottomland swamp and out to the Cashie (kuh-SHY) River, a blackwater river that enters the Albemarle Sound adjacent to the Roanoke. It's a great place to observe some of the common swamp tree species, including bald cypress and water tupelo, and maybe even see a barred owl. Just down the road, the Partnerships for the Sounds (http://www.partnershipforthesounds.net) manages the Roanoke-Cashie River Center with exhibits about the river, inexpensive kayak and canoe rentals, and regularly scheduled free pontoon boat tours.

- The North Carolina Wildlife Resources Commission boat ramp in Williamston, North Carolina (http://ncpaws.org/wrcmapbook/baa.aspx) has a short boardwalk along the Roanoke River.
- The Edenton National Fish Hatchery (https://www.fws.gov/edenton) raises striped bass, blueback herring, and American shad to help their **populations** recover in the Roanoke River. It has a small aquarium where you can see many of the common fish species in North Carolina. You can see the ponds where fish are raised and take a walk on a short boardwalk to Pembroke Creek. While not part of the Roanoke River system, Pembroke Creek is a great location to explore a blackwater swamp.

References and Resources

Powell, William S. *Encyclopedia of North Carolina*. Chapel Hill: University of North Carolina Press, 2006.

Wilson, Anthony. *Shadow or Shelter: The Swamp in Southern Culture*. Jackson: University Press of Mississippi, 2006.

Website: See urls above.
Contact: See contacts above for your specific needs.
Address: Addresses are provided above (or information to acquire addresses), depending on the location to be explored.

GPS COORDINATES:
Paddling put-in at Gardner Creek: N 35°48.72, W 76°55.98
Paddling put-in at Conaby Creek: N 35°53.6, W 76°42.25
Windsor's Cashie River boardwalk: N 35°59.58, W 75°56.58
Edenton's National Fish Hatchery Aquarium: N 35°3.48, W 75°38.34

CHAPTER 29

Pamlico Sound/Neuse River Estuary

Water Quality Monitoring

HANS W. PAERL, ALAN R. JOYNER, BENJAMIN L. PEIERLS, & KAREN L. ROSSIGNOL

SCIENTIFIC FIELDS OF STUDY: *Water Quality Management, Estuarine Ecology*

Just north of Durham, the Eno River and the Flat River join to form the Neuse River, one of the oldest rivers in the country at approximately 2 million years old. It runs rapidly for about 150 miles before slowing to a crawl and spreading out to form the brackish, tea-colored Neuse River **Estuary**, which then empties into the Pamlico **Sound**. Archaeologists have shown that human settlements have existed around the river and estuary for the past 14,000 years. The name "Neuse" means "peace" and was taken from the Neusiok tribe with whom early European explorers connected in the sixteenth century.

This chapter discusses the importance of this estuarine system to the state of North Carolina, but it also introduces a valuable research effort called **Citizen Science**. Citizen Science encourages citizens, young and old, to become involved in the collection and analysis of data from the natural world, forming collaborations with scientists and furthering our knowledge of various scientific endeavors. It also makes great strides toward increasing the public understanding and awareness of scientific undertakings in local communities while highlighting the importance of science-based decision making and science-based management practices. In this chapter, we are introducing you to the ModMon and FerryMon programs, which monitor water quality trends throughout the Neuse River Estuary and Pamlico Sound, and you can be involved. You can also apply your newly found water quality knowledge to assess any body of water that you believe may need monitoring for the health and safety of the environment. See the "Before You Go" section at the end of this chapter to learn how you can be involved in measuring water quality in this important estuary and how being a citizen scientist can aid researchers in their efforts to monitor the health of our coastal waters over time.

What's So Important about This Estuary?

Throughout the Coastal Plain section of this book, we describe an estuary as a semi-enclosed, transitional body of water where fresh water from a river mixes with salt water derived from the ocean. See Chapter 25, "Jockey's Ridge State Park," and Chapter 27, "Bear Island, Hammocks Beach State Park," for more discussion of estuaries and the waters within. Estuaries are impacted by tides but are often shielded from powerful ocean waves by **barrier islands** or reefs that border them. They are critical zones of environmental importance. Estuaries are highly **productive** and beneficial habitats for many types of finfish and shellfish. In the United States, approximately 90 percent of recreationally caught fish and 75 percent of commercially caught fish spend part of their lives in estuaries.

The Neuse River Estuary is a major tributary of the second largest estuarine complex in the United States, the Pamlico Sound in North Carolina. This is a very important fisheries nursery, meaning that, for marine organisms living here, the estuary provides a safe habitat and protection for their young while they mature. "Fisheries" refers to businesses or activities that deal with fish and shellfish, including harvesting, buying, and selling the fish and shellfish that you like to eat. In North Carolina, these activities contribute about $1.7 billion per year to the state's economy. There are currently about 3.9 million people living within the Albemarle-Pamlico Sound Watershed area. In addition to the human **population**, this region also contains 16,000 farms and 4.8 million acres of farmland, including swine and poultry operations. With a large number of people building homes and businesses and managing farms here, it is very important that this estuarine system be closely monitored to ensure it is productive, healthy, and safe for future generations.

Ongoing Water Quality Monitoring Efforts

Researchers at the University of North Carolina's Institute of Marine Sciences (UNC-IMS) continuously sample and evaluate the water in order to monitor the health of these important estuarine ecosystems using several methods of water quality monitoring: (1) the Neuse River Estuary Modeling and Monitoring Program, called ModMon (http://paerllab.web.unc.edu/projects/modmon/); (2) a ferry-based water quality monitoring program, called FerryMon (http://paerllab.web.unc.edu/projects/ferrymon/); (3) several autonomous vertical profilers (AVPs, see figures below); and (4) a set of monitoring stations on the Pamlico Sound.

The ModMon program provides researchers with continuous information about the health of the estuary. ModMon has 11 sampling stations for assessing water quality that are located down the main channel of the Neuse River, from upstream above New Bern to the mouth, where it discharges into the Pamlico Sound. This is shown by the green dots on Map 7. Twice a month, researchers visit each station

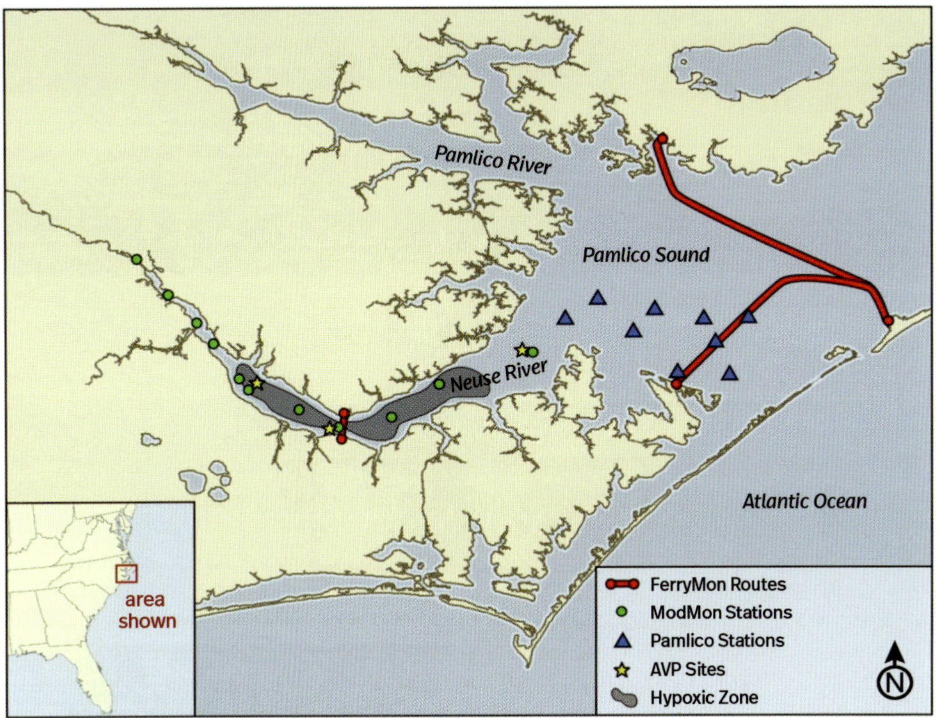

Map 7. Locations of UNC-IMS monitoring stations and routes in the Neuse River and Pamlico Sound. Map by Alan Joyner.

by boat. Water quality conditions are first measured using a multisensor probe, or "sonde," that is lowered down through the water column (see specifics below). Water samples are then collected near the surface and near the bottom from each station and brought back to the lab. The ModMon program also uses AVPs to monitor at strategic locations in the Neuse River. While the ModMon stations require a boat-based crew to perform the sampling, these buoy-based profilers are floating platforms that are continually on the water, automatically taking measurements of different parameters. Details of these parameters are described below. Data, or the information collected, are sent wirelessly from the AVPs to UNC-IMS in Morehead City, North Carolina.

Along with the ModMon program, FerryMon also operates on the Neuse River and Pamlico Sound, enabling researchers to continually collect surface water quality data along the routes that the ferries travel. Data are linked to a GPS location, logged to an onboard computer, and sent via wireless connection to computer servers at UNC-IMS.

ModMon, FerryMon, and the AVPs all use sondes for measuring water quality. These sondes have sensors to measure water depth, light (irradiance), temperature, dissolved oxygen, salinity, turbidity, chlorophyll fluorescence (algal biomass), and pH. Water samples are also collected from Pamlico and ModMon stations and checked for parameters, as described below.

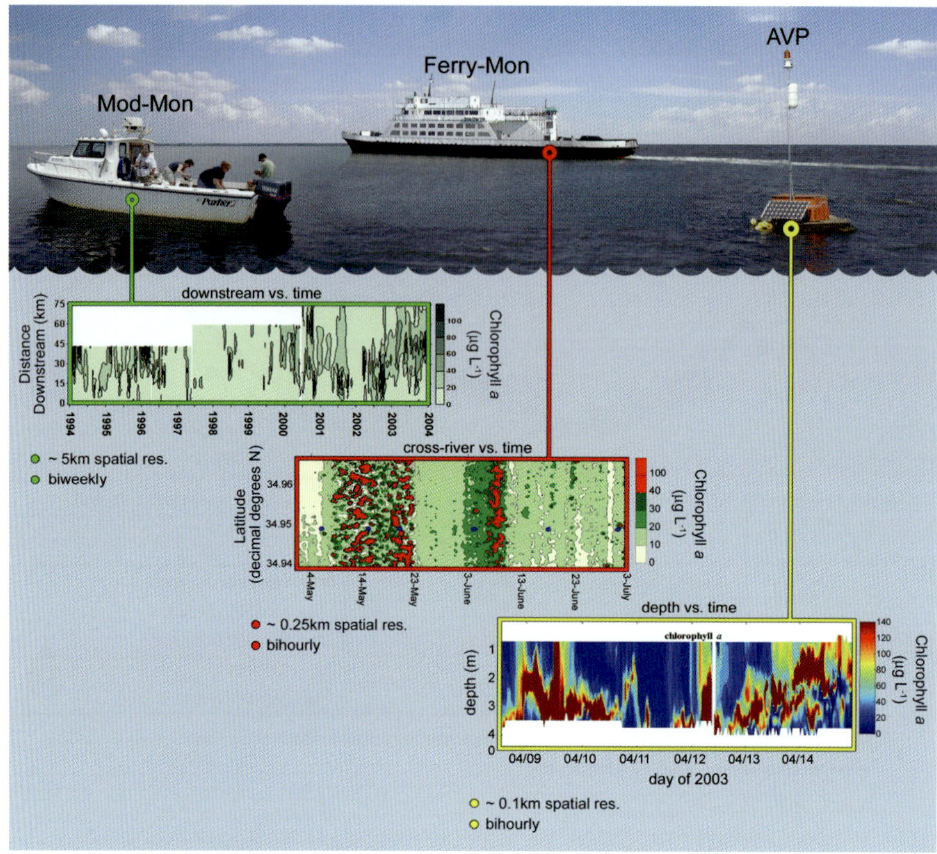

Figure 29-1. Examples showing how monitoring data collected from ModMon stations, FerryMon routes, and AVP sites can be plotted to visually assess trends in water quality parameters over time. Figure by Alan Joyner.

How Are Data Being Used?

After the data are collected and processed, we can visualize the results by converting the collected numbers into graphs and tables. We then share our new knowledge with many different organizations, including state and federal governments, environmental and fisheries agencies, schools and universities, and other public/private groups. This information can be evaluated to determine the health of our estuarine water today and to evaluate changes in water quality over time, going back to the early 1990s.

ModMon's data are used to evaluate the response to the Total (allowable) Maximum Daily (nitrogen) Load, or TMDL, which is a U.S. Environmental Protection Agency and N.C. Department of Environmental Quality mandated reduction in the amount of nitrogen being put into the water. The TMDL is needed to help control **eutrophication**, harmful algal blooms, and excessive oxygen consumption (known as hypoxia) resulting from too much nitrogen being discharged from the watershed. These data are used to evaluate alternatives for reducing nitrogen loading as specified by the North Carolina legislature. ModMon's data are used to calibrate and validate several predictive water quality models that then help test the effectiveness of the TMDL in our local waters. In addition, ModMon and FerryMon chlorophyll *a*, temperature, and turbidity data are used to calibrate various satellite- and aircraft-based remote sensing systems, enabling us to "scale up" views of water quality conditions across the entire Albemarle-Pamlico Sound system.

The data collected by ModMon and FerryMon also allow us to observe the effects of storms, hurricanes, and nutrient and pollution discharge on the environment, and to create a way to monitor water quality over a longer period of time. Most importantly, data collected from this network of monitoring programs are used to help scientists learn what affects water quality on the coast of North Carolina. These are essential ingredients for long-term environmental management and protection of the Albemarle-Pamlico Sound's precious resources.

Parameters: What We Monitor and Why It Is Important

"Parameters" is the term used to indicate a long list of physical, chemical, and biological factors that must be accounted for before scientists can determine the water quality in a body of water. The following parameters are important factors with which you should be familiar if you're interested in measuring and analyzing water quality yourself.

Nutrients

Nutrients found in the water, like nitrogen (N) and phosphorus (P), are essential for supporting the growth of **phytoplankton**, the floating microscopic algae that form the base of estuarine and coastal food chains. We can measure nutrient concentrations either directly with sensors or through laboratory chemical techniques. It is important to monitor the levels of nutrients because high concentrations can at times cause uncontrolled growth of algae, or eutrophication, seen as distinct greening of the water column. These algae "blooms" sometimes even become toxic to many organisms, including fish and humans. When blooms sink and die, the water at the bottom of the estuary starts to run out of oxygen, which severely stresses and kills shellfish and finfish trapped in those zones. How does the water get high nutrient concentrations? Human activities provide nearby sources that either discharge directly or wash into the estuary when it rains. Fertilizer runoff from farmland; waste from animal operations; discharge from septic systems; urban stormwater runoff; sediment loss from exposed, eroded soils; and discharge from industries and wastewater treatment plants all contribute to excessive algae growth.

Chlorophyll

Chlorophyll is the green pigment found in plants, including algae. Plants use this pigment to trap the energy from the sun and convert it to chemical energy for growth in the process of photosynthesis. Chlorophyll is measured by fluorescence, using sensors in the water or after extracting the pigments from samples. Chlorophyll tells us how much algae is in the water. Too much algae can cause problems, as discussed above. As algae blooms die, bacteria decompose the dead cells, using up oxygen in the process. Also, some species of algae are poisonous to fish, shellfish, and even humans.

Temperature and Dissolved Oxygen

All plants, animals, bacteria, and algae prefer specific temperature ranges, and most grow faster in warmer waters. The temperatures in the Neuse River and Pamlico Sound usually range from about 43°F to 86°F (6.0°C to 30°C). Warm water holds less oxygen than cold water, so waters are more likely to have dangerously low levels of oxygen during the summer months. Dissolved oxygen, or the amount of oxygen in the water, is measured in percent saturation or absolute concentration (milligrams per liter). If oxygen concentrations get too low, some of the animals and plants in the water can die.

pH

Parts hydrogen, or pH, is a measure of how **acidic** or **basic** the water is. See Chapter 3 and Figure 3-1 (p. 32) for an explanation of pH. On a scale of 0 to 14, the majority of aquatic animals need a range of 6.5 to 8.5 to survive. Low pH can make toxic compounds in the water, like heavy metals, more available to marine organisms, creating harmful conditions for aquatic life. Some **mollusks** have trouble making their shells under acidic conditions. pH can be affected by pollutants entering the water from acid rainfall, runoff, and surface and groundwater discharge. Also, increasing atmospheric levels of the greenhouse gas carbon dioxide (CO_2) can lead to more CO_2 being absorbed in fresh and marine waters, which then lowers pH in the waters. This is called acidification. Climate change is also caused by rising CO_2 emissions into the atmosphere due to increases in the burning of fossil fuels. By encouraging companies to stop burning fossil fuels, we can do our part to change ocean acidification and slow down rates of global warming.

Salinity

Salinity is a measure of the salt content of water. Salinity can be measured in parts per thousand (ppt). Parts per thousand is how many grams of salt are dissolved per liter of water. Plants, animals, bacteria, and algae have certain salinity ranges where they can grow and survive best. Sudden changes in salinity can kill an organism. The salinity in the Neuse River and Pamlico Sound can range from 0 ppt to 30 ppt. Fresh water is less dense than salty sea water, so when a surge of fresh water from the Neuse River enters the saltier Pamlico Sound, the lighter fresh water sits on the surface, while the denser, heavier salt water stays on the bottom.

Turbidity

Turbidity is a measure of how transparent the water is. **Organic** and **inorganic** solid matter can become suspended in the water, causing the water to look cloudy. This can prevent sunlight from reaching aquatic plants underwater that need light for growth. In the Neuse River, high turbidity is often caused by high wind, high flow rate, stormwater runoff that has floating sediment, and algal blooms. Colored dissolved organic matter—like when fallen leaves from trees turn river water brown—may also block sunlight by absorbing the light energy.

Before You Go

Getting Involved as a Citizen Scientist

You can participate in water quality monitoring for the Neuse River Estuary/Pamlico Sound (suggested locations below). To begin, go to this website to order a test kit: http://www.monitorwater.org/Order_Kits.aspx.

Kit instructions and video tutorials can be found at http://www.monitorwater.org/Event_Resources.aspx. With this kit, you will be able to collect temperature, dissolved oxygen, pH, and turbidity data at your sampling site. All of these parameters are described above if you need a reminder for why they are important. If possible, return to your site(s) periodically to sample and monitor how the water quality at your location changes over time. Use your test kit to sample a series of shore-based sites along the Neuse River complementing our ModMon sampling sites, which can be found at http://paerllab.web.unc.edu/projects/modmon/. We would love to include your data to help monitor the health of the estuary!

Also consider monitoring other bodies of water for which you have an interest or concern. Once you have collected data from your site(s), log on to www.monitorwater.org to upload your recorded data.

Here is a list of public access locations along the Neuse River, starting upstream in New Bern and ending downstream in Oriental:

- Boat Ramp dock at Glenburnie Park, New Bern, N.C. (N 35°8.383, W 77°3.592)
- Boat Ramp dock at Union Point Park, New Bern, N.C. (N 35°6.292, W 77°2.084)
- Neuse River/Flanners Beach Recreation Area (N 34°59.065, W 76°56.931)
- Pine Cliff Recreation Area, Havelock, N.C. (N 34°56.361, W 76°49.322). When exiting Pine Cliff Recreation Area, take a left onto Ferry Road. Drive to the end of the road to take the ferry across the Neuse River to Minnesott Beach to continue to the next sampling location.
- Janiero Rd., Arapahoe, N.C. (N 34°59.572, W 76°45.403)
- South Ave., Oriental, N.C. (N 35°1.479, W 76°41.509).

As a reward for your hard work, be sure to sample some ice cream at The Bean in Oriental (http://www.thebeanorientalnc.com/) before you return home.

Did you see a change in indicators you measured as you traveled downstream? You can compare your data to ModMon data at http://paerllab.web.unc.edu/projects/modmon/.

References and Resources

Burgess, Carla, ed. *Neuse River Basin*. Raleigh: North Carolina Department of Environment and Natural Resources, 2013.

Powell, Chris. *Neuse: The Fight for the River of Peace*. Wildlife in North Carolina. Raleigh: North Carolina Wildlife Resources Commission, 1999.

Website: http://paerllab.web.unc.edu/

Contact: Hans W. Paerl, Kenan Professor of Marine and Environmental Sciences, UNC-CH Institute of Marine Sciences, phone: (252) 726-6841, ext. 133; email: hans_paerl@unc.edu

Address: See suggested sampling sites above.

GPS Coordinates: See above listing.

CHAPTER 30

Cape Hatteras

Coastal Processes and Conflicts on North Carolina's Outer Banks

STANLEY RIGGS & DOROTHEA AMES

SCIENTIFIC FIELDS OF STUDY: *Coastal Resources Management, Coastal Ecology, Barrier Island Dynamics*

North Carolina's Outer Banks beckon visitors from all over the world to the sandy beaches, expansive **sounds**, and a wealth of natural attractions found within the coastal system. Ironically, these natural resources are being threatened by man-made changes in an attempt to support larger numbers of both residents and visitors. It is inevitable that natural coastal processes, like currents, tides, and winds, trigger continuous change that is not in sync with human plans. When storms move sand from one place to another, people generally want to replace it or move it back. When a road is washed out by high tides, we want to rebuild it. Human structures are vulnerable to these forces, but we must also recognize that human-built structures can disrupt a coastal system's natural ability to rebuild and renew itself.

In this chapter, we will explore the need for creating solutions that provide long-term success for both society and coastal ecosystems. It is our goal to introduce you, the explorer, to ideas that will best utilize valuable resources in harmony with the energy and processes of the natural system. Although there are many interesting sites within North Carolina's coastal system, the focus here is on one site as a representative example to illustrate the changing landscape: the Cape Hatteras Lighthouse.

History of the Lighthouse

The placement of buildings and roads should take into account the certainty of change in **barrier island** shorelines. This is illustrated quite dramatically by the history of the Cape Hatteras lighthouse. The light and lens of the original Cape Hatteras lighthouse, built in 1802, were destroyed in 1862 during the Civil War. The remaining base sat abandoned for nearly 100 years until it finally washed into the sea in 1973 as storm energy on a rising sea level eroded the shoreline. In 1870, during the Reconstruction period, a new lighthouse (and the present Cape Hatteras

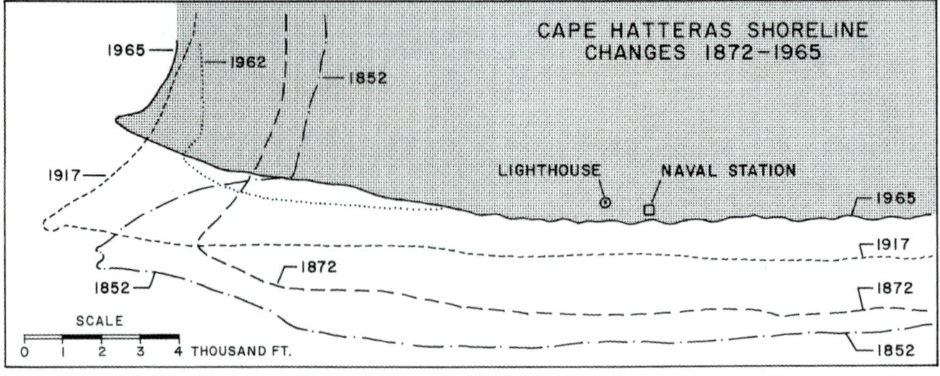

Figure 30-1. Map of historic shorelines showing a constant rate of shoreline recession from 1852 to 1965. The map is oriented south to north (*left to right*). Figure is from Fisher, "Development Pattern of Relict Beach Ridges," and modified and reproduced in Riggs and Ames, *Drowning the North Carolina Coast*, as Figure 6-3-1, p. 64.

lighthouse) was constructed. At the time, it was approximately 2,500 feet inland of the ocean shoreline, as indicated in Figure 30-1. This map of historic shorelines reflects a fairly constant rate of shoreline recession, where sea-level rise leads to decreased shoreline on the east-facing shoreline between 1852 to 1965, a period of 113 years, for the area from Buxton to Cape Hatteras.

Builders of the current lighthouse anticipated a long lifespan for the structure. However, as the shoreline began to erode and wave action moved closer and closer to the lighthouse, an extensive series of shoreline hardening structures was built, including steel groins, rock revetments, and sandbag walls. This, in combination with a series of beach nourishment projects where sand was added to the shoreline, showed the desperate efforts that were being taken to "hold the shoreline" and protect the lighthouse between the 1960s and the 1990s.

Several decades of heated debate occurred in the 1980s and 1990s about the future of the Cape Hatteras lighthouse as loss of the shoreline continued to threaten the structure. Many citizens wanted to preserve the lighthouse in its original location at all costs, some wanted to move it farther inland, while others wanted to allow natural forces to destroy the lighthouse. The latter choice might have provided a lesson about the constant change of barrier islands and the vulnerability of man-made structures on the barrier islands. The loss of this great lighthouse to the sea most certainly would have led to more careful construction policies on barrier islands. However, in 1999, the decision was made by the U.S. National Park Service and Cape Hatteras National Seashore to move the lighthouse 2,900 feet (884 meters) inland of its original location. Figure 30-3 shows the lighthouse in preparation for the move to its new location farther inland.

Climb to the top of the Cape Hatteras lighthouse, where you can see the original location of the lighthouse and its proximity to the shoreline, as well as the path taken to move the lighthouse to its current location. This view also gives you the incredible perspective of exactly how narrow the barrier islands are and, therefore, how vulnerable they are to storms and sea-level rise, which we discuss below.

Figure 30-2. These photos show a steel bulkhead, a steel groin, several rock revetments, and many layers of sandbags that have been used over decades in desperate attempts to protect the lighthouse from shoreline erosion. Photos by S. Riggs.

Figure 30-3. Preparing to move the Cape Hatteras Lighthouse inland 2,900 feet (884 m) to its present location. Photo by Mike Booher, National Park Service.

Storms and Rising Sea Level

So now let's talk about the two biggest natural factors that have fueled this debate for the Outer Banks: storm energy and sea-level rise. Both separately and together they have tremendous effects on any coastline. But on the North Carolina coastline, where a thin ribbon of sand literally can move overnight, these two factors are taken seriously.

Storms input energy to a coastal system, eroding shorelines, transporting sediment, and building beaches. Storm energy causes shorelines to change and evolve through time. When waves hit the beach, the sand has to absorb that physical energy occurring where the sea meets the land. Little happens to a beach on calm summer days, but when a storm blows through, storm energy resulting from wind, waves, and currents results in tremendous changes to the shoreline. Figure 30-4 shows the same location before and after a hurricane to illustrate the significant impact of wind and water from a 10-foot (3.0-meter) storm surge in front of a 100 mile-per-hour (161 kilometer-per-hour) wind. Storm surge refers to the increase in seawater levels due to atmospheric pressure and winds associated with a storm.

The second factor that we need to address for North Carolina's shoreline is sea-level rise due to ongoing climate change. Most scientists agree that sea-level rise

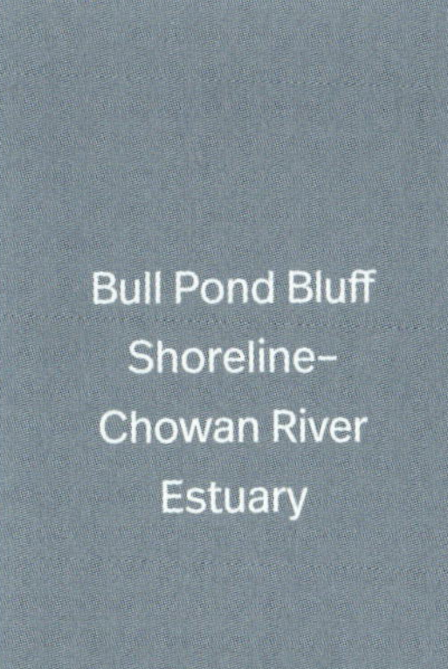

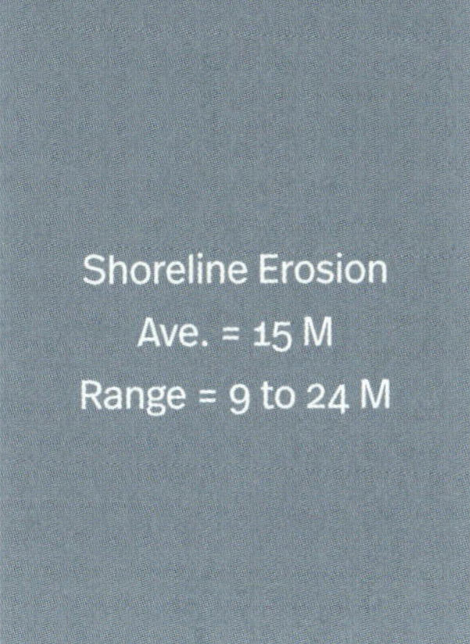

Figure 30-4. Two photographs of an eroding estuarine sediment-bank shoreline along the western side of the Chowan River. This massive change occurred during the few hours when hurricane Isabel struck the North Carolina coast in 2003. The red dashed line in panel B shows shoreline location of panel A before the hurricane. Figures are the front and back cover of Riggs and Ames, *Drowning the North Carolina Coast*.

has been accelerated by human activities, like burning fossil fuels and cutting down tropical forests. These activities rapidly release heat-trapping gases like carbon dioxide into the atmosphere, causing the planet to warm. Warmer atmospheric temperatures on Earth increase rates of melting ice in the polar regions, and that water flows directly into the oceans, causing the sea level to rise globally. The scientific community understands the connections between global warming and sea-level rise. Scientists also project the sea level to rise in North Carolina between 1.0 and 3.3 feet (0.3 and 1.0 meters) by the year 2100. The Earth has continually experienced climate change throughout its history, but evidence suggests that the current high rate of sea-level rise is a direct response to human activities.

Current Issues

Decision makers in North Carolina have used many methods to deal with the problems of a dynamic coastal system. In some cases they built hard structures, like those used around the Cape Hatteras lighthouse, that were once considered permanent solutions to coastal erosion (see Figure 30-2). However, by the mid-1980s, North Carolina no longer allowed hard structures on the beach because they increased the erosion and loss of beaches. That may seem counterintuitive to most people. It would seem reasonable to think that by protecting the shoreline with hard structures, we could prevent sand from washing away; but in reality, adding hard structures like rock revetments, bulkheads, and sandbags cuts off the internal supply of sand, and beach sands begin to disappear. Adding hard structures to one property along a shoreline generally increases the erosion rates for the properties next door. As those properties lose their beaches and owners begin adding hard structures, thinking they are stabilizing the sands, further adjacent properties lose their shorelines as well. As this continues, we begin to see a domino effect, rapidly accelerating the rate of beach loss. Ultimately, hardened shorelines lose their sandy beach completely. While the dynamics of an estuarine system on the landward side of a barrier island are different from those of the seaward coastline, the results are the same. The delivery of sediment to the shoreline is cut off, and there is no land "growth" to keep up with the rising sea level. There are currently no existing rules regarding the hardening of estuarine coastlines. This has resulted in the extensive use of hardened structures associated with most estuarine shoreline developments.

Other Observation Spots

The very road on which you will drive to reach the Cape Hatteras Lighthouse, Highway 12, is good example of why current methods are not working. An understanding of the science behind natural barrier island renewal can clarify the problem. NC 12 runs from Ocracoke, south of Cape Hatteras, north to Corolla. Please note that Ocracoke is a separate island, so if you are traveling along this route, you will have to take a ferry between Ocracoke and Hatteras. This road provides a critical transportation link for all the Outer Banks villages, as well as an evacuation route during hurricanes. Take a look at NC 12 on Google Maps in satellite view. You'll see the long, skinny strip of land with a small road running north and southwest of Cape Hatteras. Major sections of this road are vulnerable to storm overwash and flooding. When this happens, there are often new inlets created that cut through the islands, completely destroying the road. The current method being used to "protect" Highway 12 is to build and maintain barrier-dune dikes along the narrow sections of the barrier islands, such as the Avon-Buxton area just north of the Cape Hatteras Lighthouse.

As you drive along Highway 12 toward Buxton, take notice of these barrier-dune dikes. Get out and explore the area around the dikes. The intended purpose of the dune dikes is to hold back rising water to prevent storm overwash from occurring and opening new inlets through the islands. Can you image water rising in a storm to break through these dikes? Before any buildings or roads were placed here, water cutting new inlets through the islands naturally provided new sand to the top and back sides of the island, helping it grow longer and wider through time. Preventing

Figure 30-5. Hardened structures along the shorelines within the estuarine system were built in an effort to stabilize the rapidly eroding shoreline. Notice that there are no sand beaches in front of these stabilized estuarine shorelines. Photos by S. Riggs.

Photo 30-6. A dune dike built in an effort to protect Highway 12 from an approaching storm. Photo by S. Riggs.

Photo 30-7. The dike was completely washed away by the storm, and Highway 12 received extensive damage. Photo by S. Riggs.

these processes prohibits the barrier island from keeping up with the ongoing rise of sea level. Consequently, the island is becoming more and more narrow because of (1) ongoing erosion on both sides of the barrier and (2) the island's lack of ability to increase elevation and width over time. Without periodic sand renewal along the backside of the barrier island, there is increased loss of back-barrier estuarine **wetlands** and marshes. As you make observations on this part of the island, think about how the island might look today if these natural processes had not been restricted.

While few people live on a narrow barrier island subject to hurricane forces, every community must consider the natural processes at work locally in their region and consider the consequences, both for the environment and for people. Those who do not live near the ocean probably have a river or stream near their school or home. The energy of moving flood waters is incredible and can have effects on inland areas that are just as destructive as storms on the Outer Banks.

The Solution

Society must learn to work and live with nature's dynamics instead of ignoring them. Understanding the natural processes that occur along the Outer Banks is important in making wise decisions about the use of this unique island environment. It is absolutely certain that humans cannot control the work of storms and sea-level rise, but we can adjust our activities to accommodate the changes that we know are inevitable. Although the effects of storms and sea-level rise are particularly dramatic on the Outer Banks, natural processes produce changes in all environments. Knowledge about the natural processes of any ecosystem allows for better decisions that are made in harmony with the natural dynamics of the environment. Poor decisions only lead to an increase in loss of land and species that depend on a specific ecosystem. Wise decisions are essential for minimizing economic and human disasters.

Before You Go

The National Park Service encourages visitors to the Cape Hatteras National Seashore. It is located along NC 12 on the Outer Banks of North Carolina. Take US 64, 264, or 158 to Nag Heads, North Carolina, and then turn onto NC 12 to Cape Hatteras National Seashore. Another option is to pay for a N.C. Department of Transportation car ferry from either Swan Quarter or Cedar Island to Ocracoke Village on Ocracoke Island. Then go north on NC 12 to the free N.C. Department of Transportation car ferry from Ocracoke Island to Hatteras Village and proceed north on Highway 12 to Buxton and Cape Hatteras. Basic information for visiting Cape Hatteras is found on the National Park Service website, listed below.

The Cape Hatteras Lighthouse is generally open for visitors from April through October. The climb to the top is long but provides awesome views from the tallest brick lighthouse in North America. This experience provides a great view of the cape from above, as well as a better understanding of the barrier island structure and its narrow strip of land. Check the website for entrance fees and up-to-date information before visiting.

If you're looking for an interesting barrier island hike that's not along the beach, consider checking out Buxton Woods Coastal Reserve, a mature maritime forest located south of Highway 12 between Buxton and Frisco.

References and Resources

Fisher, J. J. "Development Pattern of Relict Beach Ridges, Outer Banks Barrier Chain, North Carolina." Ph.D. diss., Department of Geology, University of North Carolina, Chapel Hill, 1967.

Riggs, S. R., and D. V. Ames. *Drowning the North Carolina Coast: Sea-Level Rise and Estuarine Dynamics*. Publication no. UNC-SG-03-04. Raleigh: North Carolina Sea Grant College Program, 2003.

Riggs, S. R., D. V. Ames, and K. Dawkins. *Coastal Processes and Conflicts: North Carolina's Outer Banks. A Curriculum for Middle and High School Students.* Publication no. UNC-SG-08-02. Raleigh: Sea Grant College Program, 2008.

Riggs, S. R., D. V. Ames, S. J. Culver, and D. J. Mallinson. *The Battle for North Carolina's Coast: Evolutionary History, Present Crisis, and Vision for the Future*. Chapel Hill: University of North Carolina Press, 2011.

WEBSITES:

Cape Hatteras: https://www.nps.gov/caha/planyourvisit/basicinfo.htm

Cape Hatteras Lighthouse: https://www.nps.gov/caha/planyourvisit/lighthouseclimbs.htm

Contact: phone: (252) 473-2111

Address: 46379 Lighthouse Road, Buxton, N.C. 27920

GPS Coordinates: Cape Hatteras Lighthouse: N 35°15.12, W 75°31.74

Glossary

acidic: A solution with a greater concentration of hydrogen ions than hydroxide ions. Measured from 0 to 14, a pH of 0 to 6 indicates an acidic pH, while 7 is neutral, meaning that the concentrations of hydrogen and hydroxide ions are equal. See also **basic**.

Acidic Cove Forest: See **Cove Hardwood Forest**.

adiabatic lapse rate: A ratio that describes the decrease in air temperature by 3° to 5°F (~5° to 9°C) for every 1,000 feet (305 meters) in elevation gain.

amphibolite: A coarse-grained metamorphic rock that is composed mainly of amphibole minerals and plagioclase feldspar. As this rock weathers, it helps to create a soil with a slightly basic pH.

Ashe Metamorphic Suite: A geologic formation comprising the Craggy Mountain range and the Black Mountain range that was named after Ashe County, North Carolina.

balsam woolly adelgid: A small wingless invasive insect that infests and kills fir trees (especially balsam firs and Fraser firs); introduced from Europe around 1900.

barrier island: Often referred to as "ribbons of sand," these islands run parallel to and just offshore of the mainland with a water body, called a **sound**, in between.

basalt: A black igneous rock that forms much of the crust of the seafloor.

basic: A solution with a greater concentration of hydroxide ions than hydrogen ions. On the pH scale that measures hydrogen ion concentration from 0 to 14, a pH of 8 to 14 indicates a basic pH, while 7 is neutral, meaning that there are equal concentrations of hydrogen and hydroxide ions. See also **acidic**.

Beech Gap Forest: a very rare forest subtype community of Northern Hardwood Forest. Beech Gap Forests are generally small, exist at high elevation (typically greater than 5,000 feet [1,524 meters]), and are often found as small intact islands within a spruce-fir forest. It is estimated that less than 10,000 acres of this type of forest are remaining.

biodiversity: "Bio" means life; "diversity" means different. Biodiversity indicates the different kinds of plants and animals that are present in an environment.

Boulderfield Forest: Open forests and woodlands containing relatively unweathered fields of boulders.

brackish: More salty than fresh water, but less salty than sea water; usually this is a mixture of sea water and river water and is often found in estuaries where rivers meet the sea.

canopy: The top layer of forest composed of the tallest tree tops.

carnivorous plants: Plants that trap insects, actively or passively, and consume their nutrients to supplement the plants' growth in nutrient-poor soils. (e.g., Venus flytrap or pitcher plant).

Citizen Science: Various research programs conducted through collaborations between scientific researchers and volunteers from the community, where data can be collected by citizens and submitted to scientists. This collaboration expands researchers' capabilities for acquiring larger data sets on specific topics and involves the community in local environmental concerns.

community composition (ecology): The percentage of different species within a community.

composition (geology): The kinds of minerals from which a rock is made.

correlation: A connection between two things. Often used to determine relationships in nature.

Cove Hardwood Forest: Moist, shady, dense forests below 4,500 feet (1,372 meters) elevation with tall tree canopies. There are two variations: **Acidic Cove Forests** have a thick midstory of rhododendron plants preventing light from reaching soils. A large accumulation of organic matter leads to increased acidity in soils. **Rich Cove Forests** have a rich, low-growing understory of plants that thrive in moist soils. High calcium and magnesium concentrations derive from the bedrock, giving the soils a slightly more basic, or alkaline, pH.

Crevice Community: A subcommunity of rocky outcrops, where plants, and even trees, grow in the cracks of exposed rock. This is considered an extreme environment because there may be a lack of water for long periods.

detritus: Decaying organic matter that serves as a source of nutrients for many organisms.

Dry-Mesic Forest: These forests are well-drained so that there is no standing or pooling water. Dry-mesic forests in the South are fire-dependent, oak or oak-hickory forests.

Dry Ridge Forest: A dry forest found on mountain ridges, generally containing oak trees.

ecological succession: Gradual change occurring in the structure of a community over time.

endemic species: A species that exists in only one geographic region.

erosion: Weathering of a substance by wind, water, or other natural agents.

estuary: A semi-enclosed, transitional body of water, where fresh water from a river mixes with salt water from ocean inlets.

eutrophication: An uncontrolled growth of algae in an aquatic system due to high concentrations of nutrients entering the system.

evolution: Changes in heritable traits, those that are passed down to offspring, over successive generations. **Evolutionary** refers to the gradual change or development of those traits over time.

exoskeleton: A rigid covering on the outside of the body for protection (e.g., insects and crustaceans have exoskeletons).

extinction: The global disappearance of a living organism.

felsic: Used to describe rocks containing feldspar.

floodplain: Low-lying flat land next to a river that is often flooded when the river becomes too full.

fractures: Natural joints, or breaking points, in rocks.

gneiss: A metamorphic rock with distinct bands of alternating light and dark minerals. Formed by the metamorphosis of granite or sedimentary rock. Has more quartz and feldspar than mica.

granite: Coarse crystalline rock with felsic minerals.
Grassy Bald: See Mountain Bald Community.
Heath Bald: See Mountain Bald Community.
hemlock woolly adelgid: A small, wingless, invasive insect from Asia that has infested and killed many hemlock populations in our country.
herbaceous: Plants that grow close to the ground.
High-Elevation Rocky Summit Community: Vertical outcrops of fractured rock, generally above 4,000 feet. They have sparse vegetation with patches of shrub cover.
hydrology: The natural flow of water.
igneous: Rocks that are formed when magma or lava cools. This can occur at the Earth's surface due to volcanoes, or it can occur deep inside the Earth.
indicator species: Organisms living in a certain habitat that usually are either sensitive to or tolerant of certain types of pollution. Their presence or absence helps scientists determine if the environment is polluted or clean.
indigenous: Native or occurring naturally.
inorganic matter: Materials that did not derive from living organisms.
invasive: Tending to spread rapidly and harmfully, often uncontrolled.
invertebrates: Animals without backbones. Approximately 95 percent of all animals on Earth are invertebrates.
island biogeography: The study of species richness and community composition within a small, isolated ecosystem, like an island or mountaintop, with a goal of trying to establish causal relationships between groups of organisms.
lichens: Lichens appear to be a single organism growing on rocks or trees, but they are actually a symbiotic relationship between three organisms: a fungus, an alga, and a special type of yeast.
limestone: A sedimentary rock formed by the accumulation of calcium carbonate shells from many ocean organisms that died and settled over time.
magma: Melted rock within the Earth.
Mesic Mixed Hardwood Forest: Indicates that the forest is moist, and the trees that grow there are mostly hardwoods of varying types.
metaconglomerate: A metamorphosed conglomerate rock. Formed when particles of rock or sand collected in sediment beds of streams, rivers, or oceans and hardened over time, and then were exposed to heat and pressure.
metagraywacke: A metamorphosed sedimentary rock (a coarse-grained sandstone) with poorly sorted grains of quartz, feldspar, and small rocks in a fine clay matrix.
metamorphic: Rocks that are formed when a preexisting rock "morphs," or changes, into something new with heat or pressure. This generally occurs deep inside the earth.
mica schist: A metamorphic rock that contains quartz and mica. Resembles slate.
mineral: An inorganic (nonliving) chemical compound that forms crystals.
mollusk: A soft-bodied animal that often has a shell for protection (e.g., clams, mussels, snails).
monadnock: An isolated hill or mountain that is resistant to erosion because its rock is harder than the rock surrounding it.
Montane Woodland Seep: Rare mountain wetland where soils are saturated and low-growing herbaceous plants adapt to the soggy, waterlogged habitat.
Mountain Bald Community: Located at higher elevations, balds are open spaces on Appalachian mountain summits where forest typically would be expected. Instead,

low-growing shrubs and thick native grasses dominate. There are two types of Mountain Balds: **Heath Balds** are characterized by shrubs, such as Catawba rhododendron and mountain laurel. **Grassy Balds** are composed of several grass species, sedges, mosses, and flowers.

nonnative: Not originating locally.

nonpoint source pollution: Pollution that does not have an obvious source. Usually considered primarily as runoff when rain drains into waterways, it collects and carries man-made pollutants with it.

Northern Hardwood Forest: Mixed hardwood forests occurring at high elevations between 3,500 and 5,400 feet (1,067 and 1,646 meters) in North Carolina.

Oak-Hickory Forest: Forests that are more prevalent in drier areas below 3,500 feet (1,067 meters), with 60 percent being oak and hickory species, and often including pine and maple.

organic matter: Matter containing carbon compounds that are derived from previously living organisms.

orographic effect: "Oro" means mountain; "graphic" means topography. Occurs when air is forced up over a mountain range, where it cools and the moisture within condenses, causing rain or snow. Typically on the windward slope of the mountain.

Pangea: The supercontinent formed approximately 300 million years ago when all the known land masses on Earth collided to form the Appalachian Mountains.

peat: Partially decomposed organic matter that appears brown and spongy in nature. Peat resists decomposition because of the wet, acidic bog environments in which it is found. It is very flammable and can be harvested for fuel.

Piedmont Alluvial Forest: Situated in a floodplain where nutrient-rich river sediments provide favorable growing conditions.

Piedmont/Coastal Plain Heath Bluff: Generally located on north-facing bluffs in a cooler microclimate within the Piedmont or Coastal Plain regions. Vegetation is dominated by a dense shrub layer.

Piedmont Monadnock Forest: A dry pine-oak forest that is common in the Piedmont region, but not the Coastal Plain. A dominance of chestnut oak is the characteristic that distinguishes this forest from other dry pine-oak forests in the Piedmont.

pioneer species: The primary organisms to establish growth on rocks, trees, or other surfaces exposed to the elements. Lichens are often a pioneer species.

plankton: Microscopic plants and animals that live, drifting or floating, in fresh water or sea water. They are the primary source of food for many aquatic animals of varying sizes, ranging from small fish to large whales. **Phytoplankton** are the plants within this group of organisms, while **zooplankton** are the small animals and larval forms of larger animals.

pocosin: An upland swamp of the Coastal Plain in the southeastern United States. Usually covered in thick shrubs, pocosins have saturated soils that do not fully decay and accumulate as peat over time.

point source pollution: Pollution with a single, identifiable source (e.g., a discharge pipe).

population: A group of organisms living together that are all the same species.

predator: An animal that hunts, kills, and eats other animals.

productive: Producing a large amount of something. In ecology, this refers to the rate of generation of biomass in an ecosystem, or the increase in living organisms.

protolith: When an older rock has been pushed deep into the earth and baked by intense heat and pressure into a new kind of rock, the original rock, or "parent rock," is called the protolith.

quartzite: Metamorphosed sand.

Rich Cove Forest: See Cove Hardwood Forest.

river basin: An area of land that is drained by a river and all its tributaries.

Rocky Outcrop Community: A sparse community of lichens that grow on rocks and plants that grows in the crevices of a visible exposure of bedrock.

salt marsh: Coastal wetlands inhabiting salt tolerant plants that are regularly flooded and drained by salt water or brackish water from ocean/estuarine tides.

saturated: Filled with water.

schist: A rock formed from the metamorphosis of fine-grained sediments, like silts and clays. In schist, there is a higher degree of crystallization of mica minerals, which generally results in larger crystal formation than what is seen in slate rocks.

sedimentary: Rocks that are formed by a buildup of sediment over time, as in the bottom of a streambed.

shrub layer: Bushes that grow under the understory in a forest.

sound: A stretch of water forming an inlet between two bodies of land.

species richness: The number of different species within a community.

Spruce-Fir Forests: Forests containing primarily spruce and fir trees that grow on high mountaintops in western North Carolina, usually at an altitude above 4,500 feet (1,372 meters).

sustainable: Existing in a manner that does not deplete natural resources.

tectonics: Processes that control the movement and structure of the Earth's crust and its change through time.

texture (geologic): The size and arrangement of mineral crystals or other particles in the rock (e.g., think rough or smooth).

thermal inversion: When cooler, denser, and therefore heavier air flows downslope of a mountain at night, collecting in the valleys and drainages below. Because the air temperature is cool, the water vapor in the air condenses to form fog, resulting in low clouds surrounding the bottom of the mountain while the peak is visible above.

thrust fault: A break in the Earth's crust where older rock is pushed over younger rock.

understory: Refers to the trees growing at mid-level in a forest.

uplift: (geology) When rocks are raised to or near the surface of the Earth, where they experience erosion.

vernal pools: Temporary pools that form after a wet period, usually during the spring, but are dry most of the year. These pools cannot support fish or other predatory aquatic animals, so they are used by salamanders as a safe spot to lay their eggs.

weathering: The breaking down of rock into smaller parts due to wind or water. **Physical weathering** occurs due to the mechanical forces from water, wind, or ice. **Chemical weathering** is the result of chemical reactions that occur when rainwater and the minerals dissolved in it work to break down a hard surface.

wetlands: Transitional zone between aquatic (water) habitats and terrestrial (land) habitats, where the natural water level sits roughly at the surface of the land, such that sediments remain waterlogged most of the time.

white-nose syndrome: A fungal disease that infects various kinds of bats, causing them to wake during hibernation, after which they starve to death because their metabolism is too high and the food supply is too low.

Acknowledgments

From start to finish, this book has consumed four years of my life, and none of it would have made it to paper without my incredibly patient, loving, thoughtful, brilliant, and awe-inspiring husband, Steve. You are my star, every second of every day, and I love you.

My children constantly help remind me of what is important in this world. Thank you to Ashleigh, Jacob, and Amelia for teaching me about what it means to be a mom and for showing me how much fun life can be.

My Dad is one of those dads who will always be proud, no matter what I've done. Daddy, I'm so thankful to always have your support and encouragement.

Scientists are not always aware that their lingo can impede others from learning. Excellent educators can help overcome that barrier. Sarah Carrier provided superior educational editing throughout this book to ensure that it is suitable for all readers. Sarah, it has been a pleasure working with you, and I appreciate your commitment to this book.

Thank you to Kristen Nightingale for long talks about nonprofit work, kids and families, exploring the world, and many other things. Your thoughtful and encouraging words truly helped me put this project into perspective. And to Elizabeth Gilleland for serving on the In Situ Explorers board with Kristen and myself, thank you for so much insightful educational advice in the early phases of this project. Both of you amazing women helped make this project possible.

Only occasionally in a lifetime does an advisor come along who forever will be considered a friend, a mentor, and the possessor of perpetually good advice. Thank you, Kevin Carman, for sharing your wisdom with me. Twice throughout this project you have set me on a better path–I am forever grateful.

In the early phases of this project, recruiting contributors was quite challenging. The contributors who appear in this book are scientists, researchers, and naturalists who shared my vision for encouraging the citizens of North Carolina, particularly young people, to get outside, explore, and learn about their state in a new way. I am thankful for their eager participation and for the donations of their very valuable time to see this project through. In particular, I would like to thank Andy Heckert, Mike Dunn, Brad Daniel, and Randy Bechtel for encouraging others to join in the effort, for help with edits and reviews when I most needed it, for always having exactly the right photo, or for selflessly agreeing to do just a little more.

Marty Wiggins and Lisa Tolley are powerhouses of information and goodwill who have kept me moving forward almost from day one. When I didn't know who to call next, you two always had the answer. Many of the contributors in this book came to the project because of you. I can't thank you enough for all of this amazing support, as well as for your input on the manuscript. It is better all the way around because of you.

Liz Baird had a brilliant idea to send her chapter to several elementary and middle school classes to get input on the style of writing and information included. I was so impressed with the outcome that I decided to steal her idea, and I sent a number of other chapters out to other North Carolina schools. Thank you to the following young reviewers—your comments have been most valuable: Hilburn Academy, Newport Middle School, Cary Academy, Francine Delany New School for Children, Poplar Springs Elementary, and Irwin Intermediate School, as well as Katie Pike, Josie Green, and Thomson Meyre.

At the eleventh hour, Kevin Stewart willingly jumped in for a quick geology review and provided some very valuable thoughts on this project. Thank you, Kevin, for helping me find the missing piece and pull it all together.

Lanie Gross and Sarah Davis of Linville Caverns were incredibly helpful with the Linville Caverns chapter. Thank you for ensuring the accuracy of the historic details and for allowing access to the caverns for photos during a very busy time.

Chris Moore and Chris Swezey set me straight on the Carolina bay issue. Thank you both for your knowledge, your emails and phone conversation, and your willingness to make sure I got it right.

Brandy Belville, Tom and Vicki Randolph, Joy Greenwood and Jane Wyche, and Debbie Crane were all instrumental in helping with the chapters for Elk Knob, Mount Jefferson, Merchant's Millpond, and Bluff Mountain Preserve, respectively. Your commitments to education and the conservation of natural resources is admirable and noteworthy in all respects.

Skip Stoddard was incredibly helpful with a super quick geology review for one of the chapters under a tight deadline. Thank you, Skip, for your careful eye and thoughtful suggestions.

I greatly appreciate two very thorough reviews by two anonymous readers. Your input on this manuscript made it 200 percent better.

And finally, thank you to my wonderful editor, Elaine Maisner, and all the staff at UNC Press who believed in this project and helped me make it a reality.

Contributors

Ms. Dorothea Ames, research instructor, geology, East Carolina University.

Mr. Jesse A. Anderson, park ranger, Pilot Mountain State Park.

Ms. Liz Baird, director, North Carolina Aquarium at Pine Knoll Shores.

Mr. Randy Bechtel, interpretation and education specialist, North Carolina State Parks.

Mr. Sam Bland, retired coastal specialist for the North Carolina Coastal Federation. Sam is also a former superintendent at Hammocks Beach State Park.

Dr. Arthur E. Bogan, research curator, mollusks, North Carolina Museum of Natural Sciences.

Ms. Misty Buchanan, director, Natural Heritage Program, North Carolina Department of Natural and Cultural Resources.

Ms. Cindy Carpenter, retired education/interpretation program manager, U.S. Forest Service, Cradle of Forestry in America Historic Site/Forest Discovery Center.

Mrs. Jennifer Cox, park ranger, Jockey's Ridge State Park.

Dr. Richard Bradley Daniel, executive director of 2nd Nature TREC (Training, Research, Education, Consulting).

Ms. Melissa Dowland, coordinator of teacher education, North Carolina Museum of Natural Sciences.

Mr. Mike Dunn, natural science educator, North Carolina Botanical Garden; "Road's End Naturalist" nature guide and photographer.

Ms. Christine L. Goforth, head of Citizen Science, North Carolina Museum of Natural Sciences.

Dr. Steven J. Hageman, professor of invertebrate paleontology and paleoecology, Department of Geological and Environmental Sciences, Appalachian State University.

Dr. Andrew B. Heckert, professor of vertebrate paleontology and director of the McKinney Geology Teaching Museum, Department of Geological and Environmental Sciences, Appalachian State University.

Ms. Kim Hyre, retired park ranger, Weymouth Woods-Sandhills Nature Preserve.

Mr. Joel Jakubowski, former superintendent, Medoc Mountain State Park.

Mr. Andrew Jenkins, lecturer, Department of Biology; curator of the I. W. Carpenter Jr. Herbarium, Appalachian State University.

Mr. Mark Johns, operations and program supervisor—environmental, Hemlock Bluffs Nature Preserve.

Mr. Alan R. Joyner, illustrator and current art teacher at the Tiller School in Carteret County, North Carolina.

Dr. Hans W. Paerl, Kenan Professor of Marine and Environmental Sciences, UNC-Chapel Hill Institute of Marine Sciences, Morehead City.

Dr. Benjamin L. Peierls, previously at UNC-Chapel Hill Institute of Marine Sciences, Morehead City. Ben is the current research director at Lakes Environmental Association in Bridgton, Maine.

Mr. Jesse Pope, president and executive director, Grandfather Mountain Stewardship Foundation. Jesse is the former director of education and natural resources for Grandfather Mountain.

Dr. Stanley Riggs, Distinguished Research Professor and Harriot College Distinguished Professor of Geology, East Carolina University.

Ms. Karen L. Rossignol, research technician, UNC-Chapel Hill Institute of Marine Sciences, Morehead City.

Ms. Peggy Sloan, former director, North Carolina Aquarium at Fort Fisher. Peggy is the current chief animal operations officer at the Shedd Aquarium, Chicago, Illinois.

Dr. April C. Smith, president, In Situ Explorers, a nonprofit organization that provides opportunities for fun and interesting science education. April is also a science writer and editor.

Ms. Jamie M. Smith, collections manager, mollusks, North Carolina Museum of Natural Sciences.

Ms. Liz Stabenow, middle school science teacher, The Expedition School. Liz is the former education director for the Eno River Association.

Dr. Kathryn Stevenson, assistant professor, Parks, Recreation & Tourism Management, North Carolina State University.

Ms. Elisha Taylor, youth and family education manager, North Carolina Botanical Garden.

Ms. Laura K. White, Friends of Hemlock Bluffs. Laura is the former Hemlock Bluffs program supervisor.

Ms. Crystal Wilson, senior lecturer (2006–18), Department of Geological and Environmental Sciences, Appalachian State University.

Index

About the Author

April C. Smith, president of In Situ Explorers, is a former environmental researcher who has spent countless hours up to her waist in pluff mud. When she and her family had the opportunity to travel globally for two years, living in seventeen different countries, she learned that teaching science to her own kids is the best job in the world. Together they have cruised with basking sharks in the North Sea, hiked to see fairy penguins in Tasmania, explored the geology of the southern coast of England, floated through cypress swamps in the American Southeast, and climbed mountainous colored sand dunes in the Southwest.

April and her husband, Steve, live in the Research Triangle with their three children and an overly aggressive angelfish. They all enjoy taking off at every single opportunity to find new adventures together. The fish usually stays home. Some of their favorite explorations in the entire world have occurred between Banner Elk and the Outer Banks, right here in the phenomenally beautiful state of North Carolina.